AF477725

Governance and civil society in the European Union, volume 2

Manchester University Press

Governance and civil society in the European Union, volume 2

Exploring policy issues

Edited by Vincent Della Sala and Carlo Ruzza

Manchester University Press

Manchester and New York

distributed exclusively in the USA
by Palgrave

Published by Manchester University Press
Oxford Road, Manchester M13 9NR, UK
and Room 400, 175 Fifth Avenue, New York, NY 10010, USA
www.manchesteruniversitypress.co.uk

Distributed exclusively in the USA by
Palgrave, 175 Fifth Avenue, New York,
NY 10010, USA

Distributed exclusively in Canada by
UBC Press, University of British Columbia, 2029 West Mall,
Vancouver, BC, Canada V6T 1Z2

British Library Cataloguing-in-Publication Data
A catalogue record for this book is available from the British Library

Library of Congress Cataloging-in-Publication Data applied for

ISBN   978 0 7190 7495 0   *hardback*

First published 2007

16 15 14 13 12 11 10 09 08 07   10 9 8 7 6 5 4 3 2 1

Typeset by R. J. Footring Ltd, Derby
Printed in Great Britain
by Cromwell Press Ltd, Trowbridge, Wiltshire

Contents

Contributors

Emanuela Bozzini received her PhD in political sociology from Florence University in 2005. She has been a Research Officer at the University of Essex, UK, and she is currently research officer at Trento University, Italy. Her research focuses on new forms of participation in the context of multi-level governance, with specific attention to the local level, and on social movements. She has been involved in the project 'Organised Civil Society and European Governance' (CIVGOV), funded by the European Union, which deals with methodological issues and empirical research in the fields of antiracism and environmentalism. Her publications include studies on the inclusion of pro-migrant organisations in policy processes in Italy and the UK, on antidiscrimination policy at the European level and on the peace movement.

Vincent Della Sala is Associate Professor of Political Science at the University of Trento, Italy. He has held positions at the University of Durham, UK, and Carleton University, Canada. His research and publications have concentrated on the changing role of the state and new forms of governing in industrialised societies. He has examined these questions with respect to a range of issues, from the European Union to the legalisation of gambling.

Klaus Eder took his doctorate at the University of Konstanz, Germany; he was Research Fellow from 1971 to 1983 at the Max-Planck-Institut für Sozialwissenschaften at Starnberg/Munich and from 1983 to 1989 was Research Director at the Münchner Projektgruppe für Sozialforschung e.V. The 'Habilitation' at the University of Düsseldorf followed in 1985.

From 1989 until 1994 he was Professor of Sociology at the European University Institute in Florence, Italy. Since 1994 he has been Professor of Sociology at the Humboldt-Universität zu Berlin, Germany, where he teaches comparative macro-sociology, with particular emphasis on the sociology of culture and communication, as well as political sociology.

Justin Greenwood is Professor of European Public Policy at Robert Gordon University, Aberdeen, UK, and a Visiting Professor at the College of Europe. He is the author of *Interest Representation in the European Union* (Palgrave Macmillan, second edition 2007).

Fortunata Piselli is Professor of Sociology at the Faculty of Sociology of the University Federico II of Naples, Italy. She has written on female occupation in underdeveloped and advanced urban-industrial areas and on underdevelopment in southern Italy. Specific themes of research have been analyses of social capital, patronage and social networks. Currently she is working on theories and methods of network analysis and on their application to the study of social and political change. Her publications include *Parentela ed emigrazione. Mutamenti e continuità in una comunità calabrese* (Einaudi, 1981) and *Caminhos silenciosos da mudança* (Gulbenkian, 1996). On social capital and networks she has edited works such as *Reti: L'analisi di network nelle scienze sociali* (Donzelli, 2001) and published articles in *Stato e Mercato* and *Rassegna Italiana di Sociologia*.

Carlo Ruzza is Associate Professor of Sociology at the University of Trento, Italy. He has written in the fields of civil society organisations, policy analysis, social movements and European studies. His publications include a volume on the role of civil society at the European level (*Europe and Civil Society*, Manchester University Press, 2004) and numerous book chapters and articles in journals on European Union (EU) environmental policy and antidiscrimination policy. He has recently completed the scientific coordination of an EU-funded ten-country, three-year project entitled 'Organised Civil Society and European Governance' (CIVGOV).

Anthony R. Zito has been Reader in Politics at the University of Newcastle, UK, since 2005. His broad research interests focus on the European Union's decision-making process and how it makes policy. He is a 2007 Leverhulme Fellow, conducting a comparative analysis of environmental agencies in the European Union and United States. In 2000–3, he was co-investigator (with his co-researchers Drs Wurzel and Jordan) on a project (within the Economic and Social Research Council's Future Governance Programme) that examined the use of new environmental policy instruments in Austria, Germany, the Netherlands, the UK and the European Union, and was rated as 'Outstanding' by the Economic and Social Research Council. He has authored *Creating Environmental Policy in the European Union* (Palgrave, 2000) and articles in *Political Studies, Public Administration* and other journals, focusing on the European Union policy process and environmental actors and policy-making.

Introduction: governance, public policy and the Europeanisation of civil society

Vincent Della Sala and Carlo Ruzza

Much has been laid at the doorstep of civil society in the last decade. It has been seen as the fount of the movements that toppled communist regimes in Europe as well as the basis for new forms of delivery of social programmes. It is thought to be the source for renewed forms of democracy as well as the answer to growing doubts about the nature of representation in liberal democracies. It would seem that much is being asked of civil society as a source of both input and output legitimacy for both established and fledgling polities. Civil society not only is the great hope for providing democratic legitimacy to decision-making but is also supposed to be the source of more effective policy-making through the participation of experts and those more closely associated with specific policy spheres. Given such high expectations, it is not surprising that scholars have attempted to trace the boundaries of new forms of governing in such a way as to include a prominent role for civil society, despite the difficulty in providing a clear demarcation for it.

The expectations of a central role for civil society in enhancing the quality of democracy and the output of its institutions have led to a corresponding challenge of how to understand this development. This is especially the case in the European Union (EU). Like all evolving institutional structures, the EU has generated a range of responses from observers and policy-makers. It is seen as both an opportunity and a constraint for the generation of sources of input and output legitimacy. It is both a foil to and a promoter of forms of economic globalisation that seem inherently to conflict with postwar European social models. What is common to each of these positions is the view that something called 'Europeanisation' is taking place, that this represents a shift to a form of governing that is widely known as 'governance' and that this includes an emphasis on the role of civil society in making policy. Trying to understand the nature and role of civil society in the making of policy in the EU is increasingly the focus of research into the rapidly changing political landscape.

A good place at which to start to understand these changes is with this notion of Europeanisation, as the contributors to this volume do. At the risk of simplification, if not conceptual stretching, Europeanisation has a dual character (Radaelli 2000). On the one hand, it refers to the ways in which the European level has become an important policy-making arena, with its own dynamics, norms and structures. This top-down approach emphasises how Europe 'hits home' with policies that are made at the European level. This implies that civil society needs to be organised and to act at the European level, interacting with and through European institutions. The contributions to this volume by Justin Greenwood, Carlo Ruzza, Anthony Zito and Emanuela Bozzini tend to focus on the making of European policy at the transnational level, which raises its own set of issues and problems. The same questions that appear in domestic politics about defining exactly what is 'organised civil society' and how it can resolve issues concerning representation in contemporary democracies are present at the European level.

On the other hand, a different view of Europeanisation focuses less on the role of civil society at the European level and more on the ways in which civil society at the national and local level seeks to define itself within the parameters of a much more complex policy-making process. The discussion here is not simply about the ways in which what comes down from Brussels shapes civil society at other levels but also about the ways in which the EU interacts with parts of civil society at the local and national levels. This is equally important in policy issues that have broad, universal implications, such as antiracism, as well as in more local issues, such as strategic urban planning. This view of Europeanisation also looks at the resources that civil society can call upon in shaping public policy. As the chapter by Fortunata Piselli reminds us, it is not just the financial and organisational resources that matter but also the social capital. Klaus Eder, in his chapter, focuses on the importance of the emergence of a European public.

Civil society, then, is at the crossroads of a number of recent conceptual developments, such as the emphasis on governance, the exploration of sources of malaise within liberal democracy, the assertion that the state's monopoly on governing and political authority is being eroded and the discussion of social capital. In many ways, it is a rearticulation of a long-standing debate about pluralism, except that it is now taking place beyond the confines of national borders.

Some clear normative implications for the nature of democracy are generated by this debate. These have been explored in depth in volume 1. As was the case in the earlier explorations of pluralism (e.g. Dahl 1969), understanding the role of civil society in governing is enhanced by exploring areas of public policy. The chapters in this volume address this question by looking at organised civil society in the EU. They provide an insight into how civil society is a prism through which a number of recent developments in governing are refracted and reshaped. But before going on to these discussions, a short look at definitions is in order.

Governance and civil society: definitions

Given the conceptual ambiguity of the concepts of governance and of civil society, it is useful to point out at the start the converging definitions that are, implicitly or explicitly, used by the contributors to this volume. Different authors have emphasised different aspects of a coherent vision of governance and of civil society.

In referring to a decentralised decision-making system, one which includes shifting actors networked across state boundaries, across levels of government and across institutional roles, all authors emphasise the contributions of *civil society* actors, both organised and non-organised, to decision-making beyond the state. All the contributors stress that the involvement of interrelated networks of decision-makers, and often previously marginal types of actors, does not imply direction-less processes, but rather the need to identify the new forces steering policy-making.

Anthony Zito (with reference to Peters 1997; and Kooiman 1993) examines the role of social movement actors – in particular environmentalists – and conceptualises 'governance' as the capacity of authorities with public responsibilities to steer their economy and society in a goal-oriented way that differs from what the spontaneous cooperation of actors in the markets and society would achieve on its own. He points out that in a period of 'small state' ideologies and of economic processes hollowing out states, these steering processes increasingly rely on contributions from civil society, but he notes that the power of organised business far outweighs that of other civil society actors.

Both 'governance' and 'civil society' have come to carry many and sometimes conflicting meanings. For the purposes of this volume, and similarly to other recent works, economic and non-economic groups are treated separately within civil society (Cohen and Arato 1992). Contributors emphasise the multiple organised and unorganised forms that civil society can take, and its multiple roles of service delivery and as a channel both for advocacy and for alternative forms of representation. In differentiating economic interests from other kind of organisations, they avail themselves of the possibility of exploring the consequences of vast differences in resources and political influence.

Justin Greenwood, with reference to the EU's Economic and Social Committee (ESC), emphasises the intermediating role of civil society between public authorities and citizens. He cites the ESC, which conceptualises civil society as 'organisational structures whose members serve the public interest through discussion and function as mediators between the public authorities and the citizens' (Economic and Social Committee 2000a: 107). Anthony Zito, citing Linz and Stepan (1996), emphasises its internal diversity, solidarity and relative autonomy. He quotes their definition of civil society as 'that arena of the polity where self-organizing groups, movements and individuals, relatively autonomous from the state, attempt to articulate values, create associations and solidarities, and advance their interests'.

Civil society and governance in the EU

This collection of essays was written to investigate relations between organised civil society and governance in Europe. The authors approach this issue with particular reference to the implications for policy-making across territorial boundaries. The EU system of governance has, over the years, produced complex interrelations between the institutions of electoral representation at different levels of governance. These issues have been examined in detail in their operations at each level of governance and across levels, often with particular attention to the impact of the process of European construction. However, besides a growing integration of levels of government, a new phenomenon is emerging: the expansion of civil society organisations. Indeed, these organisations are taking over some of the tasks of states, such as delivering services and providing information; they also have a growing role in relation to decision-making institutions and their number is growing in most member states as well as at EU level. If government institutions are strengthening their interrelations under the umbrella of the process of EU construction, they are doing so with a growing contribution from organised civil society. This volume acknowledges the increasing importance of civil society and explores the manifold ways in which relations between EU governance and civil society are being shaped.

The frequently posited theme of a transition from government to governance has attracted the attention of a range of disciplines, and so has the issue of an expansion of the roles, economic importance and numbers of civil society organisations. Although clearly connected, the two topics have not been addressed jointly, certainly not from a policy analysis perspective. As Anthony Zito points out in his chapter, the literature has so far not looked at the interlocking challenges of governance and civil society. In beginning to build a coherent picture of this interaction, the contributors to this volume have utilised various bodies of literature and begun to enrich them with an awareness of the connection between governance and civil society. Focusing exclusively on the EU level, the chapters by Justin Greenwood and Carlo Ruzza provide an overview of the policy roles and ideological positions of EU and civil society actors. Greeenwood frames the granting of a policy-making role to civil society groups as a response to generalised perceptions of weak input legitimacy. He provides a general overview of the role of interest groups at the EU level, and of the connection between interest group politics and the strategies of the Commission, as well as of the latter's approach to interest groups. He also examines groups' access, strategies and resources. Ruzza reports on a textual analysis of EU documents on civil society and on the uses of the concept of civil society in three policy sectors; he documents the several ways in which 'civil society' has come to constitute a contested ideology utilised for different purposes by different actors. He proposes a typology of the normative uses of civil society within EU institutions.

Ruzza's contribution is followed by two chapters that provide an in-depth examination of the role of advocacy groups in specific policy sectors: Anthony Zito examines environmental policy, while Emanuela Bozzini shifts the analysis from a Brussels-centred concept of Europeanisation to a broader one. She looks at the process of consultation that accompanied the redefinition of the European Monitoring Centre on Racism and Xenophobia as the European Fundamental Rights Agency. This consultation exercise solicited a broad input from civil society – not only in its organised form but also as individual citizens acting in the public sphere. Citizens from all over Europe had a chance to express their views on the transformation. Bozzini examines the multiple filters that accompanied the consultation exercise and directed its outcome. Antiracism policy is therefore studied with reference to the distinctive impact of individual-level civil society, showing the inevitable distortions of the process of aggregating opinions and representing them to policy-making institutions.

The last substantive chapter shifts the focus of the analysis to a broader perspective. Fortunata Piselli looks at the impact of civil society on governance beyond the EU level and considers the interactions between different levels of government. She concentrates on the impact of civil society on policies of local development. The chapter departs from the usual assumptions that the EU has created a set of programmes that encourage and even require the participation of civil society actors, and that these programmes have an impact at local levels of governance (and might even affect individuals' attitudes, thus improving institutional effectiveness and engendering the conditions for good governance). Piselli examines issues of governance and civil society with reference to classic contributions to the literature on social capital, such as those from Putnam and Coleman. With Piselli's chapter, the volume's enquiry into the impact of the processes of Europeanisation on the role of civil society focuses away from Brussels, to show the long-distance impact of what the (unratified) 2004 Treaty Establishing a Constitution for Europe called a 'participatory democracy'. Both EU-sponsored programmes of local development and experiments with transnational policy coordination outside the EU framework are considered. The role of civil society is studied in depth by examining its value for policies of urban regeneration and 'territorial pacts' for local development. Aspects rarely identified at other levels of governance are examined at the level of local development policies – for instance, Piselli shows the positive role that civil society can have in creating a barrier to social formations such as mafias and other forms of solidarity against the state, as well as in developing social capital. Civil society bridges levels of government and in so doing provides a functional equivalent to institutions of representative government networking with other actors in activities of vertical governance.

Perhaps talking about civil society is not enough. We need, as Klaus Eder argues in the opening chapter, to explore the ways in which there is a 'public' emerging in Europe that is capable of having political agency. This public is the counterpart of the flatter, more horizontal form of governing that is governance. These complementary processes taking place beyond the boundaries of the nation state are creating new modes of social and cultural integration without the 'glue' that previously held societies together. Such new forms of participation are both the source and the consequence of governing that no longer has the state as its reference point. This forces us to rethink forms of participation that are not strictly limited to the formal institutional or even the political sphere. It also calls into question the ways in which the normative basis of this public and its counterpart in terms of political authority is communicated. As Eder points out, the normative basis of the 'public' is that it is a counter to political power. This is, perhaps, a good place to begin an exploration of the relationship between civil society, governance and public policy in the EU.

Chapter 1

The construction of a transnational public: prerequisites for democratic governance in a transnationalising society

Klaus Eder

Introduction

Global governance is self-governance of a world society, that is, governance without a state. The state is replaced by a series of collective actors that act together based on some shared understanding of the global situation. If we define globalisation as the emergence of increasingly integrated markets over ever larger territories, the European market appears to be a particular version of this process, that is, 'regional' economic integration, unified around specific rules, a range of novel political and economic institutions, and an extraordinarily high degree of both regional economic interdependence and trade between member states. Thus, Europe represents a case of organising structures of transnational governance within a territorially bounded space, in a territorially defined region of global politics.

Such transformations require new modes of social and cultural integration. The old solution to the problem of such integration, developed in the last 200 years, has been the nation as the cultural basis of the modern state, that is, the nation state. A functionally equivalent solution is necessary for integrating the new political form emerging in Europe, which necessarily must be a transnational community, beyond the nation. The model of a 'united nations' in Europe is insufficient to deal with the effects that the new coordination of nation states is producing in its evolution. Above all, such a model would not allow the generation of a collective will capable of acting on the governance structures developing at the European level. It would even impede the making of 'a public' in Europe and thus the development of modes of controlling those in power at the supranational level by those subject to this power. The public exists – to paraphrase Marx when he talked about the small tenants in his *The Eighteenth Brumaire of Louis Bonaparte* (1852) – as a sack of national peoples, but not as a collective actor.

The representation of nations in intergovernmental modes of governance produces an artefact: it binds people together who do not have any politically sensitive social and cultural relation to each other. Even the flavour of indirect democracy produced by the fact that those acting at the supranational level are representatives of nations, and thus of national democratically elected governments, no longer produces the political identification which hitherto had made the national representation of the people in a national government work.[1] The chain of representation is getting too long and too indirect.

The analytical concept of 'a public' is a useful starting point from which to clarify emerging links between supranational governance and the people subject to it. This concept takes into account the institutional pattern, which is crucial for shaping political systems in Europe. Here, three analytical notions come in the form of: a public as the carrier of a type of political action that is concerned with the public good, as opposed to private goods; a communicative space in which such action over public goods takes place; and, finally, a public sphere, separated from political decision-making and oriented to the idea of instituting collective action for the public good. A public sphere is analytically conceived as a sphere of deliberation and argumentation, which contrasts with the sphere of decision-making and political control.

Such analytical clarification is necessary to make sense of the intuitive idea of a public sphere as normatively relevant to the nation state. We know of such a public sphere as participants in it and we take it more or less for granted. Yet problems start when we try to pin down this phenomenon, beyond normative descriptions which refer to a shared narrative of democratic participation and deliberation – the democratic narrative. This is the self-evident institutional culture within which a public sphere makes sense for us and therefore produces events of political agency in social reality, that is, behaviours and/or actions carried out by a range of actors, from persons to organisations.

Thus, the idea of a public sphere is a normative one, embedded in an institutional culture and based on the democratic narrative which produces – under certain conditions – an important phenomenon: a public capable of political agency directed, at times, against those in power. This public varies in time and space. In this sense, when we speak of a public space, we should speak of a public in the making, not as something that exists but as something that has its particular temporalities.

Yet a public sphere beyond the nation state has yet to exist as something in which we, as participants, can act intuitively. It might be accessible to the sensible observer who can see the spaces and the temporalities of the public, yet the public does not conceive itself in that way. Therefore, good analytical tools are needed to make adequate sense of the co-evolving phenomena of a transnational public and supranational governance.

Defining a public sphere – some analytical clarifications

The public sphere: enabling and reproducing public communication

The public sphere[2] has been conceived within the national ontology tradition as a space between state and society. It is neither a political organisation nor a social structure, but an instance from which political and social institutions are observed and in which their meaning (especially their legitimacy) is communicated, in either an affirmative or a critical way. The public sphere has thus been described as a third sphere, between that of the state and the sphere defined as society (Somers 1993, 1995a, 1995b, 2001). In this third sphere, some speakers attempt to address a public and the media generally allow these speakers to be heard. The mass media provide a space for such communication and guarantee that communication can address any issues that may be raised (Ferree et al. 2002). This idea contains two analytically separate elements: actions of a specific type (namely, addressing the public); and a space where communication between actors is possible. These two elements provide the key for understanding the empirical variation of a public sphere.

The theories that try to make sense of action in the public sphere vary according to action-theoretical assumptions. Theories of rational action suggest the system results from the coordination of individual opinions in an equilibrium (a temporary consensus), which provides the starting point for other opinions to intervene again in such 'consensus'. Opinions are coordinated in a way analogous to the market mechanism.[3] What we call public opinion is the result of a mechanism transforming private opinions into a (more or less stable) public opinion. Theories of dramaturgical action emphasise the function of staging, or the use of the public stage as a means to create collectivities that share an interpretation of the world, that is, that share a text that allows them to utter a (prefabricated) opinion.[4] The theory of communicative action, finally, makes the strongest assumption: that the public sphere offers a mechanism for generating a rational collective opinion, as collective will, through public debate (Habermas 1962). The public appears (under certain conditions) as the carrier of 'public reason'. This does not imply that public debate automatically creates a rational order which is in the interest of all. But it is a necessary condition for arriving at such an order.

Thus, a public sphere is a mode of coordinating social action that takes place in the public realm. It is linked to some kind of consensus that emerges in the course of the interactions emerging from such coordination. The theories differ only with respect to the mechanism which generates the coordination. Whether it is the choice among options that the actions of others open for an actor, whether it is a script that we follow, or whether it is the force of the better argument that forces us to cooperate, is open to debate on making sense of the dynamics and evolution of the public sphere.

All these theories have to assume an institutional context within which these actions take place. This is, first of all, a system of rights to free speech. This institutional condition has to exist as a shared cultural presupposition and it is secondary whether it receives political or legal support.[5] Furthermore, these action-theoretical approaches have to assume a group of actors capable of communicating with each other. To assume that everybody can speak with everybody else in public overlooks the many requirements that have to be fulfilled to guarantee that one public communication can be linked meaningfully to a successive one. The minimal condition for such linkages is the sharing of a 'language game', that is, speaking a language that the other is capable of understanding.[6] A public sphere is thus a social form contingent on highly demanding institutional and cultural preconditions.

The space of public communication

Public communication (whether understood as a mode of rational, dramaturgical or communicative action) takes place in a space. The basic measure here is, first of all, the size of the space. It can vary from being the sum of all interaction-based spaces, where people meet as persons, to the sum of all organised spaces, such as party congresses, which differentiate between speakers and a public which is restricted in its mode of communication (for example simply to clapping). The most extended form of a public space is the one created by the mass media, where people 'meet' (such as by reading the newspaper every morning during breakfast) who do not (normally) interact as persons at all.[7] With the increasing functional differentiation of modern societies, the dominant space of the public sphere will be the mass media, which maximises the non-presence of actors, thus offering not only the feasibility of a nationwide public sphere but also the possibility of transnational public spheres.

These spaces provide opportunities for public communication, which we take as signs of the existence of a public sphere in the normative sense. Put differently, a public sphere is based upon a spatially bounded capacity for action of a public that develops over time. As such, it corresponds to the institutionalised normative premises of political action and interaction in present-day societies.

A public sphere does not evolve only in the field of politics but also in scientific, religious and other cultural realms. In all of these, a public sphere is considered to be the institutional pattern on which to base legitimate cultural or scientific action: any such action has to be exposed to a public who scrutinise the claims of actors in these fields. It is in the public sphere in the political realm that the claims of those subject to power as well as the claims of those in power are scrutinised. To the extent that such scrutiny is effective, we have a powerful public, full of agency, and we have legitimate power.

The type of action that the public sphere generates is either political support or political contention.[8] This public sphere serves as the medium through which individual actors are transformed into a people, either by supporting or by challenging those in power. In either case, we need action events to produce political agency. Such events transform a language community into a nation, into a carrier of a collective political will. Yet the nation is by no means the natural end of such a spatial and temporal formation of a public. The nation is a highly contingent type of public sphere, which requires the systematic reduction of communication to the belief that only people of my language community can be true and competent members of a public. Such a nationalist theory implies that people are the victims of the language they have learned as children. It certainly underestimates the possibility of transgressing the boundaries of one's life world and reifies the limits imposed by institutions on what a people is capable of doing.

The public sphere also varies according to the degree of functional differentiation of a society. Thus, a public sphere manifests itself as a scientific public sphere, as an intellectual public sphere, as an entertainment public sphere or as a political public sphere, the last bringing together people as participants in the process of collective will formation. A public sphere is, therefore, from an analytical point of view, a phenomenon which varies substantively (from political to non-political topics), spatially (small or large) and in time (a self-enforcing process of increasing communication in public).

Its basic role is voicing. When people remain silent, we have to assume that the institutional framework defining democratic societies is heading into 'crisis'. Silence means that power can no longer draw upon its source of legitimacy and the public does not have a sense of collective agency. The crisis of legitimacy consists of withdrawing the loyal mass support that democratic political systems require.

The 'public' as a collective actor

Still, the performative (or 'agency') capacity of a public remains to be clarified. How is 'a public' constituted in public communication or in its participation in a 'public discourse'? It is unclear what emerges structurally from the coordination of public communicative acts. We simply assume that, in a public sphere, 'a public' emerges, in the sense of a collective actor that can act against other collective actors, such as governments, churches or business organisations. We assume that it has an opinion and intervenes in a particular public discourse. Such an 'actor' has a special power to act, which is 'communicative power'. This actor is then called, within a temporally and spatially specific context, a 'people' or a 'nation'. The notion of a public, having a public opinion or being involved in a public discourse, is more than a metaphorical one. It assumes that, in modern societies, such an actor, acting on and interacting with other political actors, in fact exists. This leaves open the question of how things such as a public opinion and a public discourse or even a collective actor called 'the public' come about. When they are present, such phenomena can be described as 'things'; they are instances of processes kept in motion by specific mechanisms and following a developmental path, or maybe even a developmental logic, towards the permanent making of such an actor.[9]

The current debate on the theory of and research into public opinion and public discourse stops short of these obvious problems. It reduces the idea of 'a public' to its being either 'news-makers' or an 'audience'. Both ideas separate the unity of the public as an actor into two halves, each with its own associated lines of conceptualisation and research. The first line is the tradition of research into news-making. It starts with what is communicated and how it is communicated 'in public'. It analyses the discourse, that is, the statements that represent – in a more or less distorted fashion – reality. The combination of European cultural criticism and US empiricism in recent years has made this type of analysis a dynamic field of research, where notions of ideology and power play a prominent role.[10]

The second strand in theory and research relates to the people as 'the audience' of public communication. It has developed into what has been called 'cultivation research' or 'reception research'. Combined with the methods of survey research, this tradition has further developed that of public opinion research. Public opinion is the sum of individual attitudes that assimilate information from the outside world.[11]

The theoretical strategy of linking these two lines of research in the communicator–receiver model, which assumes that there was a causal link from the communicator via what was communicated to the receiver, has proven to be not only inadequate but also misleading and false. This has further contributed to the decoupling of the two sides of the model – the public as a speaker and as a listener.[12] The theoretical problem is, then, to recouple the two sides and to conceive of the public as a collective actor which is capable of speaking and listening at the same time. This actor develops such agency of speaking and listening within public discourse. The notion of discourse, in fact, forces an emphasis on the relationship that links the speaker and the listener in a permanent process of switching between the two roles.

The public sphere is the institutional locus of a public acting in both directions. Thus, we have a collective actor, the public, which is the outcome of a public discourse, that is, a process chaining one interaction with the next, producing events in the public sphere which institutionalise and stabilise this particular collective actor called the 'public'. To avoid the pitfalls of the old model of mass media research, we have to reconceptualise the audience not only as an active factor but also as one side of the coin, as a moment in ongoing 'discursive' inter-actions. Then, we have to think about the possible interfaces between public discourse and the agency of this public. There are two concepts that offer such a link: *agenda setting* and *public opinion*. Both concepts look at the interface, which is the 'public' from two complementary analytical perspectives. The public 'answers' with a public opinion and it sets the public agenda by producing claims that are to be answered.

This question brings us back to the problem of who is able to understand the other in a public sphere. Any public produces rules that define who is competent in public communication. A scientist will have a clear idea about who will be competent in a public debate on scientific matters and will try to exclude those who are regarded as incompetent. The same will happen in political discourses. Here, boundaries of those included are drawn by political parties (a conservative will have a hard time communicating publicly with a communist and they will accuse each other of not being able to take part in a rational debate). The boundaries of a public sphere are thus created and constituted within public discourse itself. They may refer to different criteria that rationalise the exclusion of 'the other' from discourse. Such strategies work as long as they are reinforced by stable institutional boundaries. When such boundaries change, 'the public' has to reinvent itself in the medium of public discourse. 'The public' is made in a process of defining the boundaries of public discourse. We therefore arrive at a dynamic notion of a public sphere: a self-producing collective actor situated in time and space and embedded in a democratic institutional culture.

The role of the public in democratic governance

Best cases for researching the public emerging in the public sphere

The emergence of a European public space presents a case for identifying the boundaries of the public beyond the national scale. The institutional presuppositions continue to exist: the idea of a public sphere also holds for the political organisation of society beyond the nation state. A Europe without a public sphere is culturally excluded. The question is, how can a public be constructed as a collective actor beyond the nation? We need a dynamic perspective to grasp the shifting boundaries of this public, on the path towards a transnational 'public'.

This dynamic perspective is also required when taking into account the type of organisational environment a European 'public' is confronted with: a system of political decision-making bodies arranged as a network of actors. A network, not a government, provides the other of the 'public'. It is a network held together by on-going processes of renegotiating what had been negotiated the day before. This organisational environment is no longer the world of a formal, rational form of government, but the world of governance. This world of governance turns out to be an ambivalent 'other': friend and foe at the same time. Governance provides an environment in which 'a public' will probably follow different mechanisms of its making than those where the public is confronted with a clear-cut 'state'.

Two differences seem to be decisive. Firstly, the governance system as the 'other' (or alter) is a moving target for the public. Therefore, the relations that emerge in the interaction between a system of governance and a transnational public are much more differentiated than those underlying the interaction between the public and the state within national boundaries. Secondly, assumptions about the homogeneity of the public (i.e. the idea of the public as a nationally conceived 'demos') become inadequate. The public is rather to be described as a having a 'multiple self' or a 'hybrid identity'.[13] It is obvious that the making of such a collective actor is not only more difficult but also riskier than the collective identity or self of a national, relatively homogeneous, public.

The institutional role attributed to the public sphere as a normative framework of modern political cultures is not discontinued in the process of transnationalisation and Europeanisation. Yet it requires new forms of constituting the public as the collective actor. To understand how the public sphere functions as an institution, the national public sphere still can serve as a best case, since it allows some simplifying assumptions to be made about the processes and mechanisms producing and reproducing the public in the modern public sphere.

Governance organisations facing the public sphere

The basis of modern government is reference to the people. In theory it has been argued that the people make a contract among each other to give to government the power and the right to govern in their name.

Locke in his *Two Treatises of Government* (1680–90) gave a more liberal answer to this theory by saying that the contract is something to be renewed permanently. Such ideas lead to the development of principles of how the procedures should look through which people are linked to government. In practice this has been parliamentary representation and voting. This form was followed by types of direct democracy and finally types of advocacy democracy. In the last case, the public is the ideal advocate of the people: it acts upon governments, and thus participates in political decision-making.

This idea of advocacy has been institutionalised in modern political organisations, from parliaments and parties to local organisations of political life. It also exerts its power on more encompassing levels of the political organisation of power. This institutional logic will also affect the transfer of political power from the nation state to the European Union (EU). To adapt the transnational situation to these institutional imperatives, the form of organising political power shifts, as argued above, from government to governance. This concept tells us that the type of political actor is changing and registers it by giving it a different name (namely governance). Political organisations acting beyond the national confines act with the capacity of governance, of governing in ways other than those of governments within the confines of the nation state.[14]

Governance – as government – assumes the presence of an actor who is legislating within the institutional prescriptions of a culture that requires that 'the people' participate. The idea of a public sphere holds for legislators in systems of governance as it did, and does, in systems of government. These institutional prescriptions generate problems for the capacity of agency of the legislators. To keep that capacity, they have to avoid becoming accountable for what cannot be rationally calculated. Yet such incalculability increases for these actors. Therefore, they turn from hierarchical governing (government) to horizontal governing (governance). In order to survive, these legislators redefine what they do, with whom they do it and why they do it:

- Legislators no longer regulate outputs but inputs; they no longer decide what would be a good outcome but instead what is a good strategy to produce legitimate outcomes.
- Legislators prepare decisions with experts, in which process they place accountability on networks of collective actors, instead of presenting themselves as being accountable; accountability is thus held to be shared by many.
- Legislators define procedural rules as the principles to be followed in decision-making while leaving substantive decision-making to deliberative political bodies.

This strategy resolves two problems: it allows decision-making even in situations of insecurity due to the complexity of the issues at stake; and it further gives legitimacy even to potentially wrong decisions because they can be attributed to the deliberative action of representative actors. In the national situation, governments are accountable to the people for decisions. The more networks replace the institutional design of a government, however, the more the diversity of interests in society becomes accountable for the decisions taken. 'Governance' is the term that tries to grasp this phenomenon.

The ideal case for this emerging network agency named governance is the EU. It works (more than less) and the question provoked by this case is, why does it work? The old narrative of legitimacy through democratic participation does not lose its grip on such systems of governance. It strengthens the institutional belief that a public sphere is unavoidable and that it cannot be bypassed (except under exceptional conditions). This is not different to the classic case of representative democracy. Interesting questions arise. What is the complement to the agency capacity formed in systems of governance on the part of the governors? What kind of 'other' to the governance legislator emerges as required by the normative idea of legislation being bound to the collective will of the people governed?[15] This other is the 'transnational public' that emerges in the making of political Europe.

What follows below are some arguments which might explain the particularities of this emerging public as the 'other' of governance actors and which defend the thesis that the evolution of this 'public' is reinforced to the extent that governance actors stabilise their capacity of agency.

Some empirical observations for the theoretical claim

The observation of policy-makers and policy-making in Brussels by diverse publics is increasing. This observation is necessarily selective, since some issues are more prone to public attention than others. The link between observers and observed in this case has to be clarified. The model of the nation state which has shaped our perception of this link is already complex. It can be described as a two-step observation: people observe their representatives, who observe those who act in the name of the state. This second step does not entail a clear-cut difference, but in principle this was the idea. There is still another observer, independent from the people and the representatives: the judicial system. This amounts to saying that the mode of observing political decision-making is already a complex one on the nation state level. Democratic control as public control at least could be imagined through the first type of observation: people observe their representatives.

We have to expect that such institutionalised patterns of observation become even more complex on the supranational level. Who observes whom, and how? And how will the agency capacity of the public observing the legislators be constructed? We assume that the link and interaction between legislators and a public is still normatively required, but then how does the public emerge in the evolution of this link in the political making of transnational societies?[16]

These questions will be addressed in the following section: firstly, by looking into the relationship between public observation and political decision-making in *stateless societies*; secondly, by looking into the emergent phenomenon of transnational *volatile publics*, which, thirdly, develops new *soft linkages* between supranational policy-makers and transnational publics. This is the idea of the co-evolution of agency in the mode of governance and of agency of the public in the course of Europeanisation. The answers presented will target: the role of public debate for European governance in sensitive issue areas; the kind of publics which emerge in the course of Europeanisation in these issue areas; and the strategies that policy-makers follow in order to gain (relative) control over the public sphere and the counter-strategies the public is developing within this dynamic process.

In the following section, we will look into the role the public develops in transnational contexts. We will look into the problem of making a public in transnational contexts, and argue: firstly, that transnational actors are necessary to construct a collective voice; secondly, that they are dependent on transnational resonance in the public; and thirdly, that transnational publics are evolving in three discursive modes – as normative communication on ideal orders, as narrative communication on what is shared, and as practical communication on shared interests. A concluding section provides some hypotheses on the link between transnational publics and political decision-making in terms of the dominant normative (institutional) account of Western societies and the consequences for the democratic narrative for a world beyond the nation state.

A volatile demos in a stateless society

The functional specification of legitimacy in modern forms of governance

How can public control emerge in complex governance systems? It could be conceived as the self-control of governance systems by the members of this system, not by its constituencies. In that case the legitimacy of political institutions depends upon the claim to act as the advocate of the public. This would be similar to the economic or the cultural systems. Markets control themselves by a banking system that makes winners and losers identifiable. No outside observer is required. Culture controls itself by a system of reputation that makes the fascinating and the boring identifiable. In this vein, politics makes advocacy an instance of systemic self-control (such as a 'fourth power' of government[17]). The public remains internal to the system; in fact, a series of system-specific publics act in the name of the people and therefore no longer require the agency of the people. They comply with the cultural institution that requires that decision-making and power are bound to the people, that is, the idea of the public sphere as the locus of generating the public weal.

This process can be studied in the European case. Instead of looking at the national forms and the derived models of public space and democratic control,[18] we will examine the emerging transnational forms of a functionally differentiated polity. Our discussion will take up the question of democratic control in transnational settings that are no longer constrained by the traditions of the nation state but follow instead the iron logic of functional differentiation as the central mechanism of social change and reproduction in contemporary societies. If public discourse takes place in a social system of transnational communication, then an interesting question arises: How is it possible to observe legislators in governance systems when the system of observation itself follows its own functionally specific logic of self-organisation?

The people and the governance of complex societies

The effects of public discourse taking place in a social system of transnational communication will be twofold: firstly, the distance between politics and the public will increase; and secondly, there will be greater freedom within the system of social relations constituting the social system of communication – the public space. We should expect on the European level the following process to be more marked than in the traditional context of the nation state: a higher density of communication processes, on the one hand, and a growing capacity to produce legitimate decisions, on the other.

In terms of the problem of legitimacy, we should expect, firstly, a stronger trend towards self-legitimation. Such self-legitimation is realised by claiming regulatory efficiency. Secondly, we should also expect an increase of communication and the making of political claims in the social system. The interaction between the two processes has yet to be adequately analysed. This is not because of a lack of studies on the new forms of self-legitimation through 'deliberative efficiency' (on the contrary, they abound); rather, it is because of a lack of analytical and empirical work on what is occurring on the other side of the border of the political system, namely, in its communicative environment.[19]

The attempt to represent this communicative environment as the agency developed by the European Parliament does not suffice. The aspect of agency is largely restricted in this case. The observation that the European Parliament has not solved but rather has increased the problem of legitimacy (Blondel et al. 1998) supports the hypothesis that the transfer of national forms of democratic participation does not lead to more legitimacy. Public agency is instead moving to other actors. Here the counterintuitive thesis is that the people represented by parliaments in systems of government are themselves such an actor. The people act not via representatives but via a collective voice in the public sphere, that is, as a 'public'.

A series of serious arguments can be raised against this thesis, based on some first-hand observations that might lead us to doubt that the 'public' has the capacity of agency:

- people do not want to participate, and this is a rational choice;
- people increasingly talk with each other, that is, communication in society increases, but this rarely crosses the threshold to become a public voice;
- the public has turned into a series of highly volatile publics that are unaccountable.

The critiques based on such observations produce, in fact, problems on the normative level. Yet they do not do away with the fact that such publics have increased in importance for the process of decision-making precisely because of these properties. This is because of the increased public visibility of decisions, not necessarily on the input side of the decision-making process but especially on its output side (it is of secondary importance whether the output is imagined or real). In particular, a system of governance is vulnerable to such public visibility, since it is dependent on public approval of its efficiency while exposed to an incalculable public which at times intervenes in the chain of decision-making. This limits the capacity of self-legitimation of political institutions by undermining the communication of their positive self-images to the public.

The first lesson to be drawn from such first-hand evidence is that there is an increase in the importance of the public and simultaneously a decrease in participation in the political system. The second lesson is that the public no longer acts as a decision-maker, as the classic democratic narrative conceived it. It avoids being drawn into the decision-making process (as in deliberative co-optation) and acts by producing negative images and by engaging in non-action (such as non-voting or not having an opinion). The voice of the people is often transformed into a negative voice.

Governance systems have to reckon with these effects, which undermine their legitimacy based on efficiency as well as their legitimacy based on deliberative and participatory procedures. This gives to the people, organised as a public having a voice, increasing power. The question then is how to make this work for the collective good, given such systems of governance. A normative theory has to provide new models that describe the parameters of a situation where governance actors meet the public and both are forced to generate the public good.

The issue of links between the people and governance

Since we can no longer expect the classic stable link between the people and their government that has characterised the model of the representation of people in their national governments, we have to reckon with alternative links. The proposal is that instead of *strong links* we should look for *soft links*. The former require a strong conception of the cultural homogeneity of a public. If government is the outcome of the will of the people (however mediated its production might be), then we need a clear conception of the 'we' who are to be represented. As soon as this 'we' speak with one voice, then we have democratic (self-)government. To arrive at such a common voice, that is, a consensus, 'the people' have to go through a series of processes to coordinate their originally diverging views. This, though, is the nation – formed in the course of such consensus-building. The will of the people is the will of a people that emerges within the boundaries of the nation state.

Such a strong link is no longer feasible on the transnational level. The will of a European people can be aggregated only by federalist or functionally equivalent modes of aggregating the plurality of the wills of the people. Centrifugal tendencies in collective will formation are to be expected, and these will weaken the link of 'a people' to decisions to issue-specific links. For example, when agricultural issues are to be decided, concerned farmers are likely to form a collective will in competition with the collective will of consumers or other occupational groups. Thus, a plurality of demoi, and not only a plurality of national demoi but also a plurality of interest-based or morally based demoi, will emerge and be linked to a system of governance.

In the following section we will look into the making of a transnational field of communication where the European people organise their positive and negative voices and create a capacity of agency to which the emerging polity has to react. The European polity will react – this is the hypothesis – in two ways: by strengthening its self-legitimation, that is, by developing its system of deliberative bodies that allow for the sharing of responsibility, which is constitutive for efficient decision-making in complex political systems; and by developing a mode of docking on to the social world outside these institutions, through symbolic staging of itself and increased political campaigning.

The making of a public in transnational contexts

The transnational situation

The making of supranational institutional arrangements and the concomitant process of the transnationalisation of society represent a major break in the evolution of a public sphere. Supranational institutions problematise the national closure of public spheres. The national people and the national public space no longer suffice to control those institutions. Supranational institutions expand the social space but we still find national public spheres and these are only partially networked to each other. National public spheres turn into provinces of supranationally organised political communities. They continue to exist, yet no longer control what is going on beyond their confines. National publics turn into local publics.

The key case is that of the EU. That case has provoked a debate on whether Europe lacks a public space or whether it represents a further step in the process of linking public spaces to changing social and political contexts. That there is a public sphere in Europe seems to be beyond doubt:[20] it is the space in which citizens of the EU can speak freely. There are events that regularly make Europe the object of critical public debate. Politics in Europe is ritualised according to the calendar, which guarantees that we are regularly confronted with events that provoke comment. The real problem is that of the democratic coding of this space. The people within it do not unite 'quasi-naturally' into a coherent body that is conscious of itself as one people. A transnational public sphere – here specifically a 'European demos' capable of constituting a political community – has to be created out of a diversity of people.

Instead of concluding that there cannot be a European demos because there is no European public sphere or of concluding that there is no European public sphere because there is no European demos, the making of such a demos could be conceived as the co-evolution of a European demos and a European public sphere. In this sense, Habermas has emphasised the role of constitutional debates in the public sphere as constituting such a space and constituting a European demos. Thus, the public sphere becomes the key to democracy in the 'post-national constellation'.[21]

Historically, a European people constituting and being constituted by a public sphere has already existed: the traditional European elite and popular groups that made themselves heard as voices in Europe. From the Renaissance to the period of national liberation and unification, a discursive network of elites (academics, philosophers, musicians, literary figures and artists) constituted a public sphere in which a European aesthetic and intellectual tradition was created and reproduced. This elite public existed alongside a bourgeois public in the cities, cross-cutting territorial forms of political domination and creating particular legal and political traditions which corresponded to the idea of a public sphere (Breuilly 1996). This bourgeois public space in the cities was central to the making of middle-class 'citizens', the carriers of an autonomous public sphere.

Alongside these elite and city-bound public spheres in Europe, a popular public sphere made itself heard at times. The concept as such assumes a homogeneity which it rarely had. Such homogeneity emerged only when revolution or revolts called forth a unifying theme of popular resonance, namely of suppression and injustice.[22] The normal state of a popular public sphere is to act locally, bound to the communal space of collective experience. The exceptional state is when the many voices of a 'contentious popular Europe' (Tilly et al. 1975; Tilly 1986) coalesced and produced rebellion and at times even revolutions.

Present-day Europe continues these different modes of existence of a public sphere: an elite public, a middle-class public of mobilised citizens and a popular public. These socially embedded publics are constituted and reconstituted as precarious, temporary and fluid, issue-specific publics. They turn into consumer publics, lorry driver publics, human rights publics and environmentally concerned publics. These issue-specific publics can be conceived as networks, mobilised *ad hoc* through common preoccupations. The model of a society in Europe consisting of a series of demoi constituted in the course of their mobilisation comes close to describing this phenomenon. Such mobilisation has often been contained by invoking national symbols, which have produced conflicting publics: a people against other people, a mechanism of the dynamics of nationally defined public spheres which worked through the nationalist century in Europe.

A transnational public exists in Europe as a cross-cutting of elite publics, citizens' publics and popular publics, related to each other by some supranational institutional environment. Youth, tourist and even new religious cultures mixed with remnants of old elite cultures provide a tradition within which the making of a European public, as a carrier of a European public sphere, produces real events. This turns on a spiral of reciprocal observation of this people and supranational political actors. The consequence is rising protest, the increase in Euroscepticism, a public sphere in which much noise is created, thus continuing the tradition of being 'a contentious continent' (Tilly 1986). This mechanism produces a public sphere that transcends the national public spheres in Europe while instrumentalising the means of public communication offered on the national level.

A parallel process is the emergence (and the making) of a European public opinion, produced by surveys (Eurobarometer) and made public by political institutions (Niedermayer and Sinnott 1998; Reif and Inglehart 1991). The permanent observation of this public opinion is extended by special observatories, such as those that look into the dangers of rising racism and xenophobia in Europe. A mass public in Europe is thus created, to a large extent, from above (Trenz 2004a, 2004b). A people is made not in the direct mode of making a national people, but in the fluid form of a latent public, manifested in an unforeseeable way. This public is mostly silent, while the mass media give it a voice to make sure that what is there is not forgotten, a lesson that is, at times, hard to accept by the dominant political supranational and national actors.

This latent and basically silent public sphere talks indirectly. It is spoken by representatives, media actors (e.g. journalists), non-governmental organisations (e.g. Statewatch) and other self-declared civil society activists. A European public sphere is not a chimera but a thing that turns up at critical times. Thus the European protest in the course of the Iraq war in 2003 was interpreted as a sign of an emerging public sphere in Europe. What counts as an event indicating a European public sphere is the emergence of a conflictual, but open, space of political communication where a public constitutes itself.

The claim is that there is a path dependency in the making of a European public, which explains why, in times of crisis, such a public becomes visible, transcending the national borders of political communication and producing a political voice in Europe. A transnational public is, therefore, one which is no longer tied to a reified body of people such as the nation, but to a latent demos that can be there when it is required. Thus, the public sphere can be conceptualised as a mechanism that allows voices to be raised, whether in Europe or in other transnational settings (Guidry et al. 2001). Whether this voice is strong or weak is an empirical question.

The role of transnational actors in constructing a collective voice

We can speak of a public which neither shares a 'life world' nor a language, but is based on social relations that bind through nothing other than socially constructed ties such as market relations or legal relations.

Additional bonds are expected to emerge, substituting for the lack of cultural commonality and homogeneity. Such additional bonds emerge when actors speak on behalf of other actors while creating particular networks between each other. The phenomenon referred to is the increase in the number of advocates of the people, of advocacy groups. This is the phenomenon of transnational actors, who have multiplied enormously in the last few decades. Calculations have been done by Boli and Thomas (1997, 1999) and Anheier et al. (2001) regarding the sheer number of transnational actors speaking on behalf of actors tied to local, regional or national 'life worlds'. The evidence forces an expansion of the simplifying assumption of a public sphere made up of people communicating on the basis of shared cultural traits in a culturally well defined space. We have individual and collective actors competing to be heard and permanently moving the boundaries of the space of public communication. The question now is when and under what conditions these groups are linked in terms of a European public. They do it at times, and at other times they act in national, local or global public spaces. A European public space is no longer a permanent thing, measurable in terms of the continuous presence of actors, themes and actions in the public space. The public moves through these public spaces and appears at times in local and, what is important here, in the European public space.

The first conclusion would be that, in the public sphere, a European public emerges that has to be identified outside of historically contingent boundaries and institutional opportunities. What we can measure is its gradual appearance in certain spaces, its presence in a European public space at a given time.

The structure of a transnational public – the concept of civil society

A transnational public is a potential public with particular features. It exists in three discursive modes: as the carrier of normative communication on ideal orders; as the carrier of narrative communication on what is shared; and as the carrier of practical communication on shared interests. All three modes have been applied to identify the elements of a public sphere in Europe carried by it. Thus, some have found shared normative ideas, especially those who argued that the shared language of this transnational public is the language of constitutional rights. In this sense, the European public shares an ideal order, one that should be realised in a constitution. Others have looked at the way in which this public shares a tradition, tells to itself a shared story of its past, which is some kind of European story. In this sense references to the Renaissance and to Christianity produce a public who share a language of tradition, who share a narrative bond. Finally, some have argued that the practical experience of acting together in everyday life creates sufficient bonds for forming a public in the European public space. All these claims regarding a European public refer to potentialities, to the potential transformation of an aggregate of people living in Europe (to be more exact, in the EU) into a people sharing some 'non-natural' bonds. Since Europe cannot escape the normative premises of the public sphere as an institutional force in any modern polity, these bonds are turned, in certain situations, into political bonds, into a contentious European people, into a European public. Yet these transformative processes are as yet little understood.

On the conceptual level, the concept of civil society has tried to incorporate these transformative and generative processes. Yet a mere concept does not provide explanations: it only focuses on a problem. It does so not by providing a narrative that resonates with an idea of how to fill emerging governance structures with democratic meaning. As with all ideological work, it cannot be reduced to the mere production of illusions. Illusions have consequences – they shape the discourse of a society. Therefore, the concept is not one that can be affirmed or refuted on empirical grounds, but can be analysed only by its position in the making of a discourse, by its relation to ideas linked to democracy and people and power.

Civil society is a mode of societal self-description. A European civil society provides an ideal self-description of Europe. To what extent it really helps to transform an existing people into a public capable of acting collectively against the emerging system of governance in Europe remains an open question. It has to be answered by research on the social bonds that link particular actors within the European public space. Since we have to expect a multiplicity of such bonds and also cross-cutting between bonds, the research will be much more demanding than research that focuses on the national public, which is much less multiplex.

The concept of civil society helps us to locate the network of bonds that make up the public within the European public space. It also helps us to focus on the 'other' of civil society, namely the system of governance. We already know a lot about their interaction within the system of governance, but we do not yet know enough about how the individuals and groups acting in front of this system of governance are becoming a public. To argue that this 'becoming' is made by the system of governance is an empirical possibility, namely the making of a public from above. In normative terms, this solution is not ideal, since it does not comply adequately with the institutional rules that demand that modern societies be democratic and made from below. To argue that civil society should emerge from below and to argue for civil society as a collective actor capable of acting collectively on and against political power, such as the system of European governance, corresponds ideally with the normative premises. From a non-normative perspective, however, both are empirical possibilities, and only research can determine and explain the mechanisms behind the making of a transnational public in Europe.

Conclusion: rewriting the democratic narrative for a world beyond the nation state

The theory of the public sphere is a central element in the theory of modern society. It points to the reflexive element accompanying the unfolding of modernity in nationally or imperially bounded societies and to the process of further modernisation beyond these boundaries. In these societies, from early modern to late modern ones, the public sphere can be seen as a normative reference overarching their political dynamics. This normative reference implies two basic ideas: the counterfactual idea of the collective will of the people; and the idea of a public sphere made up of equal and free people. These normative ideas are part of an institutional pattern that worked when societies were just beginning to democratise as well as in their further course. This normative reference can be considered the basic mechanism shaping the dynamics of the evolution of the public sphere. The explanation for the effectiveness of this mechanism is found in the particular structure of public communication unveiled by Habermas's theory of the public sphere, that is, the counterfactual construction of a world in which free and equal people enter the inescapable logic of public argument (Habermas 1962). This mechanism can be blocked, undermined or instrumentalised, yet all these practical uses (and misuses) of this mechanism have to reckon with the logic constituting it: the logic of discursive rationality inherent in human beings endowed with reason and inherent in their mode of relating to the 'other' in a communicative mode.

In addition, there are further instruments needed to explain how the normative mechanism works at all and why the normatively ideal path of development is normally not taken. In fact, we are confronted with uneven processes, characterised by ruptures and discontinuities, which show that the normative mechanism does not apply. This has already preoccupied proponents of the major theories of the public sphere when they have noted the silence of the public or even its wish to destroy itself as an actor with agency in politics (which happened, for example, under fascism).

To describe the failure or silencing of public spheres as a consequence of the increasing power of state apparatuses and market forces has even become a fashionable element in crisis scenarios of modern societies.

Two scenarios have dominated the sociological debate: the 'colonisation of the life world' through the instrumentalisation of mass media by states and markets (Habermas 1987); and the 'tyranny of intimacy', which has destroyed the autonomy of the public sphere (Sennett 1977). The first thesis joins the theory of the 'culture industry'; the second thesis defends the public sphere against the encroachments of private stories and against the public staging of private feelings and needs. Such empirical critiques do not do away with the mechanism built into the existence of a public sphere, as distorted as it may be. But they add a non-normative perspective which explains the real paths of the evolution of the public sphere. This is what can be called the post-Habermasian solution to the problem of relating the factual to the counterfactual, that is, of relating the factual paths of evolution to the counterfactual forces working through the mechanism of public communication, which provides permanent input into these processes. Deciphering such mechanisms in a comparative and processual way is what theorising about the public sphere can contribute to an explanation of European modernity in general, and to the 'new Europe' in particular.

Applied to the situation that characterises the new Europe, such mechanisms are equally at work. The post-national or transnational situation does not escape the institutional prescriptions that define political modernity. Yet it forces us to describe the mechanisms that foster the making of a public in this modern public space and that provide the ties that bind people together without identifying with a shared culture. This public is an actor that has agency by entering the public space and generating a kind of hybrid collective identity in which the cultural traits are recombined as the particular situation requires it. There is no collective identity fixed in time and space. We see, rather, collective identities formed and reformed in time and space.

That we have elements of such a collective actor has been shown by some research on collective action in Europe. The extent to which national or regional people will be drawn into the dynamic of transnationalisation within Europe offers a rather large set of options and opportunities to focus collective action and related collective identities on European issues. Yet these identities travel, away from Europe to the global stage and back to the local. What is important to know in terms of the legitimacy of the system of European governance is whether the diverse publics emerging in the – in principle unbounded – public sphere will stop at times at the level of the Union's system of governance, thus giving it the legitimacy it needs for its further evolution. It is not counter to the available empirical evidence that this public will grow and develop the bonds necessary to provide a counterweight to the power that is concentrating in systems of governance, not only in Europe, but well beyond it, thus making loose coupling work.

Notes

1 This system of representation in the nation state worked despite the fact that the social structure of parliamentary representatives did not coincide with the social structure of the people they represented. Lawyers and high public officials and other upper-class or upper-middle-class representatives always more or less represented the lower classes. This worked because of a special identification with the system of national representation.

2 The term 'public sphere' has differing connotations not only within European languages but also between European languages and non-European ones. The German term is *Öffentlichkeit* (an established term) as opposed to *öffentliche Meinung*; the French distinguish the terms *l'espace public* (an artificial term) and *l'opinion publique* (an established term) and the English between public sphere and public opinion (where the latter is the more usual). In Italian the same distinction between *la sfera pubblica* (artificial, as in French) and *l'opinione pubblica* is usually made. The term 'public space' offers a further option of naming this 'thing', but will be used here to denote the social space where public communication takes place. The *ulama* in the Islamic context describes cultural elites that specialise in the exchange of arguments, yet is tied closer to religious traditions than its European counterpart *Öffentlichkeit* (Eisenstadt 2002; Salvatore 2007).

3 This is the traditional approach to the use of survey data for constructing a 'political culture' or a 'public opinion' (Gunn 1995; Glynn et al. 1999).

4 Such approaches emphasise the rhetorical dynamics involved in creating a public opinion on issues (Page et al. 1987). See Gamson (1999) for the 'life world' embeddedness of public debate. The process character of the link of the media to public opinion is emphasised by McCombs (2001).

5 Legal and political support certainly has additional effects on rights to free speech, but historical research shows that public spheres were formed and reached their apex when censorship was still the normal reaction on the part of those in power.

6 One example is the nation as the people who succeed in generating a public opinion through coordinating the many voices in a process of public communication. National ontology would mean here that only nations are capable of creating public spheres. This at least is what we are used to when looking opinion polls: we look at what 'nations' think and compare the ways in which they think differently.

7 These distinctions have been developed by Neidhardt (1994).

8 Normally we assume political contention to be the basic type of action constituting a public sphere. This is due to the highly particular historical experience of the nineteenth century, namely the experience of absolutism, with attempts to censure an emerging public sphere, which provoked the reaction of defence against the state. Fascism turned this relationship upside down and thus provided a case where the public sphere was instrumentalised as a support-generating machine for fascist power and ideology.

9 The similarity between an individual actor and the 'public' as an actor is less irritating if we accept the argument of neo-institutionalists that cultural

orders make actors such as an individual, an organisation or a state (Meyer et al. 1997).

10 Any handbook of communication research gives a good overview of these traditions.

11 It is interesting to note that the early tradition of public opinion research has been interactionist and cognitivist. The idea of public opinion as consisting of nothing but individual opinion is an effect of the attempt to lay stricter scientific foundations for public opinion research. This has led to the exorcising of the idea of a group mind, which thus became the first victim of the positivistic tradition in sociology. Today, we observe the return of the question. Nobody is happy any longer with the idea of public opinion as a collection of individual attitudes.

12 With some notable exceptions – see Swanson (1981), Dervin (1989), Price and Roberts (1987).

13 This implies that recent theorising on individual identity is relevant also for understanding the self or the identity of collective actors, the 'public' being a case in point. Thus, we are not interested so much in the question of whether individuals in Europe act as Europeans but in whether there is process in which a collective actor emerges who does what the idea of a public sphere requires that actor to do: to protest when that is felt necessary, to be silent when that is appropriate and so on.

14 This does not exclude the fact that nation states tend to develop forms of governance too, in order to restructure their own capacity to act in a more complex world.

15 Legislators are no longer bound to God or some other transcendental reference, as in other civil traditions. See Salvatore (2007).

16 To speak of the evolution of a link between collective actors or of the co-evolution of two actors refers to the same phenomenon. These conceptualisations differ only with the respect to some action-theoretical assumptions which take either the actor or the link as the unit of evolutionary explanation. This will be left open within the limits of this chapter.

17 The term 'fourth power' refers to institutions such as supreme courts and central banks.

18 The debate on a European constitution shows to what extent the political thinking is organised by a conceptual map where ideas of a European demos, of a Europeanised representative system and a (culturally and linguistically homogeneous) European public space play a central role which easily leads to theorems on the unfeasibility and improbability of legitimate and democratic trans- and supranational institutions. The arguments of Grimm and Kirchhoff, both being German constitutional judges, stand for similar arguments in other countries.

19 This is not to argue that the link between the European polity and its economic environment has been better analysed – although there have been many more studies of that link. Nor is it to argue that the interaction between an emerging European polity and its cultural environment has received adequate attention. On the contrary, the latter is even less well known. The relationship of the EU to its cultural history is *terra incognita*, both for the policy-makers and for those observing it.

20 Empirical research corroborates this in its findings. Yet there is still no con-
    sensus on the 'meaning' of a transnational or post-national public sphere.
    See Eder and Trenz (2003) and Trenz and Eder (2004), and Gerhards (2001)
    for an opposing view. See also Pérez-Díaz (1998), who links this debate to
    the problem of a European civil society.
21 Habermas (2001) speaks of a post-national rather than a transnational situ-
    ation. A good discussion of how the Habermasian model might work on the
    European level is found in Kleinsteuber (2001).
22 Here the research of Barrington Moore on injustice is a good yet underrated
    piece of work (Moore 1978). 'Social movement' research has corroborated
    such findings (Tilly 1985).

Chapter 2

Governance and organised civil society at the European Union level: the search for 'input legitimacy' through elite groups

Justin Greenwood

Introduction

A central focus of the white paper on governance (Commission of the European Communities 2001b) and its aftermath has been upon the enhancement of the legitimacy of the European Union (EU), in terms both of inputs (to do with the ability of wider civil society to participate in EU decision-making and the consequent legitimacy which could arise from it) and of outputs (to do with the effectiveness of the results of EU decision-making and the corresponding legitimacy which arises), and in seeking a Pareto-efficient balance in the relationship between the two concepts.

Commentators such as Scharpf, Moravcsik and Majone (see Wincott 2002) have articulated widespread doubt about the structural ability of the EU to achieve input legitimacy. The core, structural problem is the absence of mechanisms to bring 'politics to the people', such as the agenda-setting power of adversarial debate, the absence of mass-membership political parties organised on a Europe-wide basis, presidential elections, voting to change a government (Hix 1999), an EU-wide media or simply a decision-making system which is readily intelligible to citizens.

That it is difficult to achieve input legitimacy is a conclusion shared by Majone, who argues that, in consequence, the EU should concentrate on efficiency-oriented regulatory policies which do not require democratic legitimation through citizen inputs because they aim at Pareto-efficient solutions that are in the collective interest (Majone 1996; see also Sudbery 2003). Some measures arising from the governance white paper, such as extended impact assessments, follow this line of thinking by broadening assessments of impact beyond those active in lobbying on them, to other stakeholders potentially affected. Sudbery's research records comment from members of the Commission team working on the governance white paper that 'perhaps the most effective way to link with the citizen is by more effective results' and that 'the issue about bringing in the citizen is for speeches, for the rhetoric. This organisation will never touch the citizen directly' (Sudbery 2003: 92).

The structural difficulties of achieving input legitimacy through other means have led to a focus upon elite groups organised at the EU level as a 'second best' substitute to pursue. The white paper itself, and the subsequent governance agenda, posit a series of measures aimed at such groups, in the explicit pursuit of input legitimacy. To what extent will these agendas affect the system of EU interest representation and have an effect on input legitimacy? To what extent will attempts to enhance input legitimacy interfere with the pursuit of output legitimacy, by overloading EU decision-making? To address these questions this chapter examines: the essential features which condition EU interest representation; the EU structural features conditioning EU interest representation; and the capacities of civil society organisations to meet the various agendas laid out for and by them. From the EU side, most of these agendas arise from the white paper on governance, which was initially greeted as a flop but which has since developed agendas of fundamental importance to the concept and operation of civil society organised at the EU level.

Essential features of EU interest representation

'Brussels' is a hive of activity of *organised* interests. This is because the EU agenda is principally regulatory, and regulation typically distributes costs and benefits narrowly, upon specialised constituencies of interest (Wilson 1995). Politics of the interest *group* type invariably results from these circumstances. Organised interests are also the natural constituency of the supranational institutions that are seeking partners for policy-making, monitoring and implementation purposes, and as demand constituencies for European integration. The European Commission, in particular, is notoriously short staffed to meet its needs for the first three of these tasks, and otherwise short of natural allies to help it achieve the last of these.

A typical pattern for the Commission in seeking to expand the frontiers of European integration (and therefore its own competencies) has been for it to select an area (such as equality) that member states find it politically difficult to resist, to fund a conference on the subject from which an interest group emerges, and to fund and nurture the group until it is strong enough to carry demands from its own national members to the doors of member state governments. Exactly this pattern helps to explain the extension of EU equality competencies in the Amsterdam Treaty (signed in 1997). Elsewhere, the role of the European Round Table of Industrialists in the creation of the European single market is a story which has been extensively told and cited as evidence of how civil society interests contribute to the very process of European integration (see, for instance, Sandholtz and Zysman 1989).[1]

Additionally, the Commission has historically seen groups as mediators that will help resolve its structural remoteness from European citizens, and therefore as key agents in its legitimacy. This aspect is present in the institutional definition of 'civil society' used by the European Economic and Social Committee, as 'organisational structures whose members serve the public interest through discussion and function as mediators between the public authorities and the citizens' (Economic and Social Committee 2000a: 107). Indeed, the Commission has argued that:

> belonging to an association provides an opportunity for citizens to participate actively in new ways other than or in addition to involvement in political parties ... organised civil society represents the views of specific groups of citizens to the European institutions ... and contributes to the formation of a European public opinion ... promoting European integration in a practical way and often at grass roots level. (Commission of the European Communities 2001a: 4)

For all these reasons, the Commission has been deeply active in the formation and maintenance of EU-level interest groups of all types, and provides much of the funding for those in the citizen interest fields, not infrequently to a level of 85 per cent of their operating costs. Interest groups are the lifeblood of the Commission, and in consequence it has steadfastly resisted any access barriers to it, such as schemes for accreditation. All comers are welcomed.

EU interest representation is principally, though not exclusively, centred around some 1,500 formal interest groups. Two-thirds of these represent business and one-fifth citizen interests, with the remainder representing professions, trade unions and public sector organisations at national and regional level. In addition to these interest groups, an estimated 350 large firms, 200 or so regions and 300 or so organisations supplying commercial public affairs services are active in engaging EU politics. All of these organisations – producer or otherwise – are embraced by definitions of 'civil society' in common use throughout the EU institutions. A policy document (Commission of the European Communities 2002) summarised the position in recording that:

Problems can arise because there is no commonly accepted – let alone legal – definition of the term 'civil society organisation'. It can nevertheless be used as shorthand to refer to a range of organisations which include: the labour-market players (i.e. trade unions and employers federations – the 'social partners'); organisations representing social and economic players, which are not social partners in the strict sense of the term (for instance, consumer organisations); NGOs (non-governmental organisations), which bring people together in a common cause, such as environmental organisations, human rights organisations, charitable organisations, educational and training organisations, etc.; CBOs (community-based organisations), i.e. organisations set up within society at grassroots level which pursue member-oriented objectives, e.g. youth organisations, family associations and all organisations through which citizens participate in local and municipal life; and religious communities.

So 'civil society organisations' are the principal structures of society outside of government and public administration, including economic operators not generally considered to be 'third sector' or NGOs. The term has the benefit of being inclusive and demonstrates that the concept of these organisations is deeply rooted in the democratic traditions of the Member Sates of the Union.

Thus, 'civil society' in this usage embraces producer and citizen interests alike, although to others the term is used as shorthand for the latter exclusively. A similar complication of terminology evident from the above definition arises with the term 'NGOs', which in popular use on the Brussels circuit refers to citizen interest groups, but which, when used in a more literal sense, can be used to refer, again, to producer *and* citizen interest organisations, in that they are all 'non-governmental'. Beyond these ambiguities are the terms 'private interests' and 'public interest', popularly used to refer, respectively, to producer and citizen interest organisations. These latter terms are problematic in that they convey the false impressions that all citizen interests always act in the wider public interest and that producer groups concerned with wider wealth creation (and thus public welfare) do not (European Parliament Directorate-General for Research 2003). For these reasons, the terms 'civil society' and 'NGO' will be used here to denote the entire spectrum of interests, while 'producer' and 'citizen' interests will be used to denote these respective differentiated interests.

The most striking feature of the system of EU interest representation is its elite nature: it involves a narrow dialogue between EU political institutions and organisations articulating a particular constituency of interest in wider civil society. Almost all EU interest organisations are confederated,[2] that is, are associations of other associations. Almost no associations of any type admit individuals as members. These factors mean that EU interest organisations have a structural remoteness from the grassroots interests they represent, but they do tend to embrace a broad range of European interests.

To play the 'Brussels game', you need a permanent presence on the Brussels circuit as well as expert knowledge both of how decision-making operates in the EU and of the cultural rules of the game. To a great extent, organised interests need to apportion rather little importance to 'public appeal' campaigning tactics, which form an important part of political communication for certain types of interests in other democratic systems. Such factors are typical of 'insider' relationships between interests and political institutions in other political systems, but are more or less universals about the Brussels system of organised interests. Producer and non-producer interests alike have proved adept at acquiring this knowledge and playing the game, with business relying upon its own resources and almost all other groups being supported by the resources of EU institutions. Demonstrations and the like are almost absent from the world of Brussels politics, because of the difficulties of organising transnational protest, and where public events do occur they tend to be symbolic stunts, designed to reassure the membership of continued activism. Newspaper campaigns are restricted to the *European Voice*, which has a narrow circulation (*circa* 40,000) and which is read almost exclusively by the Brussels players in EU political institutions and interest organisations, and those who study and analyse those players. Even traditionally activist organisations such as Greenpeace have policy offices in Brussels rather than campaigning offices, and are much more geared to building alliances and making private compromises with other policy players than their public marketing profiles might otherwise suggest.

Most groups are, thus, highly institutionalised in the elite world of Brussels EU politics. Organisations such as the European Women's Lobby (EWL) and the European Trade Union Confederation (ETUC) have become so highly embedded within the European Commission (in these cases, the Directorate-General for Employment, Social Affairs and Equal Opportunities, or DGEMP) that some commentators have pointed to their overdependence upon DGEMP to achieve their goals (see Martin and Ross 2001 on the ETUC) or point to a 'revolving door' type of relationship between them (see, for instance, Mazey 2000; Helfferich and Kolb 2001, on the relationship between the EWL and the equality unit of DGEMP). EU citizen interest dialogue is now substantially channelled through confederated 'family' organisations of EU NGOs. The most confederated level of organisation is the EU Civil Society Contact Group, a family of European NGO platforms. These include the Social Platform, Concord (relief and development), the Human Rights and Democracy Network, the Green 10 (environmental organisations), the European Forum for the Arts and Heritage, and the European Public Health Alliance. Many of these organisations are themselves highly confederated (for example, the Social Platform has thirty-nine EU NGO members), although they are not open to all comers; further, they have a *modus operandi* which privileges members and excludes non-members from their work, and thus have their own elite basis. The Social Platform, Concord and the Green 10 are highly institutionalised networks, at the least having highly formalised dialogues with their patron Commission service, ranging from high-level access through Council 'informals' to (in the case of the Social Platform) leader roles in the process of engagement with civil society in the treaty-drafting convention process (2002–3). The Social Platform has argued for a formalised, privileged status for 'family organisations' such as itself on the basis of their representativeness (Commission of the European Communities 2005b), although this may in turn cause access problems for citizen NGOs, whose legitimacy is not based upon criteria of representativeness but rather upon articulating a cause in civil society to EU political institutions.

Despite the apparent 'insider' nature of the EU political and interest representation system, another striking feature is that those who do approach the system as 'outsiders' in terms of familiarity with the system, and who seek dialogue, find themselves pushing at an open door. In general, this follows a typical pattern of political institutions welcoming opportunities for dialogue and to establish relationships, so that interests can see policy-making dilemmas and the need for moderation. The Commission welcomes and depends upon all comers for the reasons outlined above, and there is evidence that its clear policy statement to this effect (Commission of the European Communities 1992) is not just empty rhetoric. Former Commission official Bob Hull has described the typical rapporteur responsible for drafting legislation as 'a very lonely official sitting in front of a blank piece of paper wondering what to put on it' (Hull 1993: 83). Commenting on a draft directive on animal testing for cosmetic products, Baker (1992) and Fisher (1994), both activists in the British animal welfare movement, record their considerable surprise at the welcome reception they received at the Commission. Having proposed a directive with rather less protection for animals than exists in many member states, the Commission welcomed input from animal welfare groups and removed offending clauses, despite input from the European Cosmetic, Toiletry and Perfumery Association (COLIPA), US trade associations and individual firms.

Another initial sceptic was Goehring, who reaches the conclusion that the nature of the dialogue between the Directorate-General for External Trade and those groups seeking input to development policy from both 'inside' and 'outside' the established circuit resembles discursive democratic practice (Goehring 2002). In this dialogue, the

Commission has deliberately sought to reach out to groups that want no part of institutionalised fora, preferring to pursue critical 'outsider' strategies. These include anti-capitalist, anti-globalisation activist networks and groups that are implacable critics of the Commission. Ironically, a number of these groups seek, and obtain, funds from the Commission for their work. The Commission has done more than most governmental organisations to reach out to, and engage with, such groups. An open question is the extent to which such groups, over time, may become deradicalised by the process of such engagement.

Historically, the Economic and Social Committee has seen itself as the institutional outlet for organised civil society in EU public policy-making, and for discursive dialogue with such organisations. Its constitution stipulates that 'it shall consist of representatives of the various economic and social components of organised civil society'. Its self-perception is that of 'a key player as the representative mouthpiece for organised civil society … an essential bridge between Europe and its citizens' (Economic and Social Committee 2001: para 4.1). The Committee is undoubtedly a potential arena for mediation and discourse between different civil society interests. However, its role has been limited by its inability to reform itself, and in particular its inability to incorporate citizen interests within its official structures. The organisation remains dominated – some say gridlocked – by different producer interests, and by competing perspectives between business and labour on the desirability of formally including the organised EU citizen interest organisations which emerged and developed in the late 1980s and 1990s. Trade union interests organised at the EU level have recently made considerable efforts to pursue their goals by building alliances with sympathetic causes among the constituency of EU citizen interest organisations.

Also worth summarising in this overview are the features of regulation of EU interest representation. The Commission's historic opposition to a system of accreditation of the bodies it consults with (as described below, even this opposition may be in the process of being eroded) has led it to encourage self-regulation by 'lobbyists'. The issue has more frequently arisen in the European Parliament as a venue prone to policy entrepreneurship, with debates in 1992, 1996 and again in 2002/3 arising from initiatives of socialist Members. In 1996, the Parliament adopted an incentive system whereby those wishing to enter the Parliament building regularly could acquire a yearly pass that provided ease of access to the premises in return for signing a code of good conduct (originally formulated by public affairs consultants). Around 4,500 annual passes are now issued in this way, and the individual recipients are identified on the Internet.[3] Regulation is also based upon a system of disclosure on the part of Members of the European Parliament (MEPs), now extended to embrace their assistants. These debates have been richly laced with language invoking principles of transparency and with concerns to ensure a 'level playing field' between producer and citizen interests, although they have also been marked by the absence of specific 'scandal' events. As such, they reveal a number of wider issues about the system of EU interest representation and the wider political system in which it is embedded. These include: the tendencies within parliaments as a whole for 'solutions to search for problems' as MEPs seek issues to develop; the continuing pressures for a high level of transparency in the EU political system; the naturally elite nature of EU interest representation and periodic dissatisfaction with it as such; and the concern to engage with the member state citizen directly. These struggles find an echo in a number of the issues, debates and emerging concepts reviewed below.

The EU structural features conditioning EU interest representation

The fragmentation of power and decision-making within the EU machinery means that access is easy, to the extent that the system is approaching input overload. It also means that no one type of interest routinely dominates it. There are several dimensions of this latter reality. It is possible for civil society interests – producer or otherwise – to dominate a dossier as it is drafted within the Commission, because the technical nature of policy drafting results in expertise dependencies and the inaccessibility of issues to others. Those with technical knowledge and the capacities to develop established relationships with policy-making officials benefit from this scenario. Once a dossier leaves the Commission, however, it enters other decision-making arenas, where quite different rules of the game apply.

Most dossiers are now subject to the full decision-making powers of the European Parliament, including that of co-decision with the Council of Ministers. The Parliament has democratic credentials, and is a venue where citizen interests have successfully operated for some time; for example, Commission drafts are often amended and sometimes overturned. Once a measure has left the Parliament, the Council of Ministers exerts its own influence and produces its own amendments. Then there is a final scramble with the Parliament, and in part with the Commission, to find a compromise sufficient for a common position. Civil society interests of all types tend to get left out of these latter stages of the EU policy process – the inter-institutional scramble – as they often involve highly complex procedures or attempts to avoid them, to find common ground.

In other cases, the Council of Ministers rejects positions settled at earlier stages of the policy process; one example is a June 2003 decision by health ministers to reject the Commission's proposals to enable pharmaceutical companies to advertise directly to the public. In such circumstances, no one interest can routinely dominate EU policy-making. Whatever else its defects, the fragmented architecture and complexity of the EU decision-making system means that it is insulated from systematic domination. Grande has shown how the Commission has used this insulation for its own ends, by extracting compromises from civil society interests through pointing to the need to find an arrangement which will pass muster with the other decision-making institutions (Grande 1996).

The unique nature, and fragmentation, of the EU political system also prevents corporatist-type dominance of policy-making between political institutions and elite interest organisations. The lack of 'stateness' of the EU prevents the parcelling out of public authority to 'non-state' interests for governance arrangements, such as is common in the Germanic world. EU producer associations, in particular, lack the authority and membership appeal which comes from such recognition, and so they must search for alternative means of internal cohesion. The conclusion they reach is invariably to focus upon micro-specialisms, where members have interests sufficiently cognate to enable them to reach common positions. This may be good for individual associations, but the overall landscape, particularly among producer interests, is one of small organisations with low resource levels, and competition between narrow sectional interests. Thus, the predominance of business organisations among the constituency of EU interest associations should not be confused with influence. An additional factor contributing to the low resource levels of business groups is their narrow specialisation upon political representation. Their members are associations or large companies, neither of which require business services. Consequently, they are very dependent upon membership subscriptions and lack alternative income streams.

Some citizen interests are extremely well resourced and equipped to engage with EU policy-making. Environmental lobby groups have between them around 100 staff in Brussels, and in many cases the resources, technical expertise and populism of worldwide movements to draw upon. The Brussels offices of the World Wide Fund for Nature (WWF), the European Youth Forum and the EWL each have over twenty staff. Environmental policy-making is subject to qualified majority voting, and is 'mainstreamed' throughout every policy issue with which the EU deals. The work of these organisations is facilitated by a wider 'frame', which pervades every aspect of EU policy-making today, that of attempts to create a 'Europe of the citizens'; these attempts

date from the 'shocks' to the system provided by attempts to ratify the
1992 Treaty on European Union. Tony Long, executive director of the
WWF European policy office in Brussels since 1989, reflected that 'all
the talk in Brussels these days about the role of "civil society" and the
need to consult more widely is not just words' (Long 2003: 66).

This newly strengthened citizen policy frame has shifted the focus
from a preoccupation with output legitimacy in the period after the
single market legislation to a greater emphasis on input legitimacy.
This emphasis was initially pursued through EU campaigns such
as 'Citizen's First!' (later 'Dialogue with Citizens' followed by 'Your
Europe') and, more recently, through a raft of initiatives originating in,
or developed by, the 2001 white paper on governance. These include
the widest possible concept of transparency, a style of policy-making
which has eroded traditional bilateral discussions between the European Commission and certain civil society interests, through to open
consultation, by placing policy initiatives and drafts on the Internet for
comment[4] (Commission of the European Communities 2002; Vignon
2003). They also include the extended impact assessments of policy
measures, whereby selected policy proposals are to be assessed for their
impact upon the widest possible group of potential stakeholders, to
ensure that consideration of the effect of measures is not restricted to
an elite of those who are politically active in producing them.

One of the first dossiers to be subject to an extended impact assessment was the REACH Directive,[5] which attracted some 6,500 responses
in the initial consultation, as well as demands that the Commission
establish bureaucratic machinery to identify how it had responded to
the detailed input it had received. These calls demonstrate the ways in
which 'input' legitimacy can threaten 'output' efficiency. Nonetheless,
the Commission has pledged itself to provide an explanation of how the
results of consultations were taken into account in formulating the final
proposal, and in doing so has voluntarily extended its accountability.
These standards for consultation with outside interests have now been
adopted and implemented within the Commission (Commission of the
European Communities 2002). They seek to balance legitimacy with
effectiveness, by resisting demands for extended periods of consultation
and fixing the period in which to respond at eight weeks. While a legal
basis of dialogue is resisted, as is the softer 'compact' version between
governments and voluntary organisations originating in the UK and
now exported elsewhere, the standards promise to deliver similar *de facto*
outcomes. Attempts at institutional transparency are visible through the
Europa website, such as a listing of the Commission's consultative and
expert bodies.[6] Unlike the Council of Ministers, Commission transparency is strong compared with that of some member state governments,
and must be included in assessments of input legitimacy.

As is demonstrated below, transparency has also been a two-way agenda, for groups as well as institutions. For groups, the deal on the table from the European Commission since the white paper on governance has been clear: the promise of more participation in return for more transparency. While the elite nature of this deal prompted a reaction from the European Parliament and some backtracking from the Commission, the CONECCS initiative described below implies a *de facto* implementation of such a promise.

The capacities of civil society organisations

A number of parallel initiatives have been developed with the aim of enhancing the capacity of EU-level organised interest groups, or even to appeal directly over their heads, to citizens directly. Certain sections of the Europa website have been developed to facilitate and encourage interaction with citizens, and a range of EU funding programmes continue to provide benefit for those who can access them. As for the groups, the white paper on governance recorded that:

> civil society organisations need to tighten up their internal structures, furnish guarantees of openness and representativity, and to prove their capacity to relay information or lead debates in their member states. (Commission of the European Communities 2001b: 17)

This statement reflects an exasperation with the inability of civil society groups to perform the bridging role between the Commission and citizens in the member states, and a number of agendas have unfolded to address the problem, described below. The new Commission agenda on groups is one that business interests have actively supported, on the basis that it is one that has been relatively easy for them to respond to, yet one which puts citizen interest groups on the back foot. Consequently, business interest groups such as the Union des Industries de la Communauté européenne (UNICE) have been active in putting forward criteria for interest groups to meet, including some requirements for independence of funding which would be extremely challenging for many citizen interest groups, given the high degree of dependence of many of them on EU budget lines. The European Parliament, too, mindful of its own claims to legitimacy as the representative of the people, stresses the 'supplementary' nature of organised interests to that of its own role, as well as the need for groups to demonstrate their independence. Independence of funding is a point conceded by some leaders of citizen interest organisations, in acknowledgement that the sector has a weak record of seeking sources of funding other than EU institutions. On the wider issue of representativity, citizen interest groups have vigorously contested the agenda set for them, by arguing that they are organisations *for* a particular cause, rather than *of* it (Halpin 2001), whereas business groups have a readily identifiable constituency. Such reasoning implicitly concedes the point that citizen interest groups may well be in pursuit of a narrowly defined sectional interest rather than advocates of the wider public interest (Schlesinger and Kevin 2000). The natural tensions which exist between groups speaking for gays and lesbians, and those speaking for families, illustrate the point (Geyer 2001).

Research conducted among selective constituencies of citizen interest groups organised at the EU level has concluded that, on the whole, they do not act as agents of political socialisation in the member states, and that those who work for them have little interest in undertaking this role. For example, on the basis of his empirical research among them, Warleigh concludes that:

> Although it would be misleading to argue that all NGOs fail to demonstrate any such capacity, necessary structures to allow NGOs an EU socialisation function, such as the existence of methods of internal decision-making which allow supporter input into NGO EU strategy, are in general conspicuous by their absence. So too are mechanisms by which NGO supporters or members can hold these organisations to account, or make an input into their decision-making. (Warleigh 2003: 118)

Further:

> NGOs will be unable to act as agents of civil society Europeanisation unless they are internally democratic and willing and able to act as agents of political socialisation, with particular reference to EU decision-making and policy.... NGOs are as yet simply not ready to play this role, and ... it cannot be assumed that their capacity to act in this way will be improved.... their internal governance is far too elitist to allow supporters a role in shaping policies, campaigns and strategies.... Moreover, most NGO supporters do not actually want to undertake such a role ... NGOs are no 'magic bullet' which will automatically hit the target of political socialisation. (Warleigh 2001: 635)

Warleigh's research, findings and conclusions were replicated by Sudbery, who conducted interviews with the Liaison Committee of Development NGOs, the European Environmental Bureau (EEB), the Social Platform, and Amnesty International. A typical comment was that of a respondent from the Social Platform, who said 'we do not have direct contact with supporters, but rely on member organisations to bring the issues to their attention' (Sudbery 2003: 89). The respondent from the EEB commented that:

> While ideally it would be good to get people involved, time pressures mean that the most effective use of my time is to get on with advocacy. In

the end my role is not to encourage the most participatory governance, but to ensure the best results for the environment. (Sudbery 2003: 90)

Another of Sudbery's respondents stated that it was difficult to persuade colleagues in the member states to take an interest in the work of the Brussels office because the EU is seen as 'far away and fuzzy' and even as having 'negative overtones' (Sudbery 2003: 90).

Such concerns led to Commission initiatives, originating from the white paper on governance, aimed at upgrading the internal capacities of groups. The CONECCS[7] initiative includes a database of interest groups on the Europa website in which inclusion is contingent upon confirming that the interest group is formally constituted, operates across the EU, is active, has expertise and is prepared to provide information about itself. There are further compulsory questions about group establishment, objectives and post-holders, and, for those involved in EU consultative bodies, about sources of finance and details of members.[8]

While the site makes clear that inclusion on the database confers no special privileges, and there are at present no facilities – and little capacity – within the Commission for the evaluation of the information being presented by groups, an open question is whether it in fact represents the start of a *de facto* system of accreditation. This interpretation is supported by the observation that one motivation for the scheme was that it would be a means of keeping the Commission informed about the relevant groups to consult with in given policy areas.

The Economic and Social Committee has become the lead institution in putting forward criteria for EU interest groups to meet through its 'Opinion' on the white paper on governance (Economic and Social Committee 2002). Interaction between its members in the different sections produced the recommendations that a 'European organisation' must, in order to be eligible for institutional dialogue:

- exist permanently at EU level;
- provide direct access to its members' expertise, and hence to rapid and constructive consultation;
- represent general concerns that tally with the interests of European society;
- comprise bodies that are recognised at member state level as representatives of particular interests;
- have member organisations in most of the EU member states;
- provide for accountability for its members;
- have authority to represent and act at European level;
- be independent and mandatory, not bound by instructions from outside bodies;
- be transparent, especially financially, but also in its decision-making structures.

While these criteria were initially recommended as those to be applied in the event of adoption of a 'civil dialogue', they have an appeal which was recognised by the governance white paper, and they may become candidate criteria in any future discussions about the institutionalisation of EU interest groups. However, the criterion which demands that European organisations have member organisations in most of the member states would exclude those groups whose legitimacy is based upon the articulation of a cause, and is therefore problematic for democratic practice.

The institutionalisation of the principle of dialogue is proposed by the proposed Treaty Establishing a Constitution for Europe (TCE, signed in 2004), through article I-47:

> 1. The institutions shall, by appropriate means, give citizens and representative associations the opportunity to make known and publicly exchange their opinions on all areas of Union action.
>
> 2. The EU institutions shall maintain an open, transparent and regular dialogue with representative associations and civil society.

Article I-52 goes on to establish that 'churches, philosophical and non-confessional organisations' are to be included in this.

This does little more than codify existing practice, but the (unratified) treaty does include a number of other, new provisions which civil society interests organised at the EU level were active in developing, such as policy review and initiation mechanisms in response to petitions with a threshold of one million signatures from a 'significant number' of European countries.[9] While opinion is divided over the value of this 'citizen's initiative' mechanism, the world of Brussels-based citizen interest organisations is enthusiastic about it, not least because of the emphasis it will inevitably place upon them to operationalise it. In its most optimistic interpretation, it demonstrates both the wider responsiveness of the system to demands originating from organisations wearing the badge of civil society, and the wish for the system to reach out beyond organised interests directly to citizens, as a surrogate mechanism to overcome other structural limitations on input legitimacy.

Conclusion

Elite interest groups are clearly a second-best substitute in the absence of structural mechanisms which might otherwise endow the EU with input legitimacy, such as mass political parties, adversarial politics, an EU-wide media, voting which changes a government and a readily intelligible decision-making system. Within its own terms, however, the elite model of civic participation shows some signs of development, not least through the unfolding agendas originating in the white paper on governance. The agenda for groups to deliver more transparency and member accountability is a challenging one for civil society interests, whose legitimacy is grounded not in their 'representativeness' but in their speaking for a cause. For this reason, there will always be a limited supply of representative-based democratic legitimacy between themselves and citizens in the member states. While there is an elite basis of dialogue between highly institutionalised, Brussels-based NGO 'families' and the EU political institutions, the depth and breadth of the relationship between the Commission and civil society groups – and in some cases networks – and attempts by the Commission to reach out to 'outsiders' cannot fail to impress their observers. Some aspects of such attempts to find input legitimacy may, however, be at the point of interfering with output legitimacy. Where groups become a hindrance to output legitimacy and appear to add little value to input legitimacy, further development of a regulatory agenda aimed at them may become inevitable. The example of Birdlife International reveals how 'constituency representativeness' would be a blunt instrument indeed that would coerce groups to demonstrate their 'representative' basis when their legitimacy is grounded in their ability to articulate a cause. While the dialogue between NGO 'families' and EU political institutions will always have an elite ring to it, there is space for greater involvement of organised civil society based in the member states. The EU's Lisbon 'open method of coordination' process has thus far yielded limited results from the engagement of national interests in national agendas linked to EU policy issues (Armstrong 2003), but there is surely some scope for greater all-round engagement of these players, and with them the expansion of the European public space so critical to EU democratic legitimacy of the input kind.

Notes

1 Some caution should be exercised here, in that the Round Table was more a supportive agent than the causal one claimed by some accounts (see Greenwood 2003). Rather than it 'building the single market in six days and resting on the seventh', an impression left by accounts given by foe, self-propaganda and also by some observers, the single market was a project which already had wide support among member states at the time they agreed to it, and was one which member states would themselves have signed up to if left to their own devices.

2 This conclusion applies to virtually all non-business groups and even to the majority of business groups, although some trade associations have admitted

companies alongside associations (fewer still organise only companies). Some policy-making officials do prefer to deal with direct membership business associations to confederations, for reasons of their closeness to street-level business practice, the legitimacy carried by companies that are household names, and their ability to bring fresh thinking and to act relatively quickly. Others prefer the legitimacy which comes from the breadth of constituency which confederations bring, and this position remains the official one within the Commission.

3 See http://www2.europarl.eu.int/lobby/lobby.jsp?lng=en&sort=byname& index=L (accessed December 2006).
4 Open web consultations can be viewed at http://ec.europa.eu/yourvoice/ consultations/index_en.htm (accessed December 2006).
5 The Registration, Evaluation and Authorisation of Chemicals (REACH) Directive was adopted by the Commission on 29 October 2003.
6 See http://ec.europa.eu/civil_society/coneccs/organe_consultatif/liste_index_ cb.cfm?CL=en (accessed December 2006).
7 The acronym stands for Consultation, the European Commission and Civil Society.
8 See http://ec.europa.eu/civil_society/coneccs/question.cfm?CL=en (accessed December 2006).
9 Alex Warleigh-Lack, in chapter 3 of volume 1 of this work, looks at this provision from a critical deliberativist perspective.

Advocacy coalitions and the participation of organised civil society in the European Union

Carlo Ruzza

Introduction

All the institutions of the European Union (EU) have had an extensive debate on the role of civil society in the European system of governance. However, the wealth of the contributions to this discussion cannot be assumed to agree with each other or to be consistent with the institutional expectations of civil society organisations. The aim of this chapter is to examine the message that EU institutions are projecting through their official statements on the role of civil society in policy-making and through the use they make of civil society in concrete policy contexts. Civil society organisations also express views on what their roles should be, on how to improve the European system of governance and how they should interact with EU institutions; these views similarly need to be summarised and checked for consistency. These views are often complex and contradictory, reflecting the many directions in which civil society organisations are pulled in their multiple roles at various levels of governance (Keane 2003: 129). Views on such issues are typically formalised in written texts in institutionalised political systems, such as EU institutions, but also in the civil society organisations. These texts, then, constitute rich empirical material that can be utilised to examine relations between civil society and EU institutions.

The purpose of this chapter is, firstly, to focus on key institutional policy texts that discuss the role of civil society, to identify recurrent themes. A text analysis approach is then used to examine the documented interactions between civil society organisations and EU institutions. By systematically analysing these texts we can assess their internal consistency, their coherence across types of actors and the overall message that they attempt to convey. To be empirically viable, a text analysis approach that explores perspectives on civil society has to be delimited institutionally, chronologically and in terms of types of actors and policy sectors. The analysis here considers only environmental, antiracism and regionalist groups engaged in advocacy efforts; these have in common a reference to social movement organisations. As these groups are generally fairly institutionalised and interact with stable political actors, such as political parties, they will be referred to as 'movement advocacy coalitions'. By investigating their interaction with EU institutions, it will be possible to frame, in more general terms, concerns over governance issues and potential solutions, as they are perceived by both institutional and civil society actors. The results of course cannot be generalised to other types of civil society actors, for instance church groups, or to other policy areas, such as consumer policy. But as the three kinds of concern examined are among those where relatively large numbers of civil society groups are active and as they are related to important policy sectors, they do provide an overview of relations between governance and civil society at EU level. In addition, the first part of this analysis – institutional conceptions of civil society in policy documents – reflects institutional views and expectations from all types of organisations and, therefore, also provides an overview of institutionalised conceptions of civil society.

Conceptions of civil society in EU policy documents

A concern for the role of civil society has marked, albeit to differing degrees, the production of policy and legal documents of all EU institutions for several years. It was particularly expressed by the Economic and Social Committee (ESC), whose institutional role is defined in relation to functional representation (see for instance Economic and Social Committee 1999, 2000b, 2001) and more recently by the Committee of the Regions (COR). However, in terms of relevance, it is worth noting that civil society has grown most rapidly in the thinking of the Commission and the European Parliament.

The Commission consults widely in the development of policy in almost all areas and has reflected on its relationship with non-governmental organisations (NGOs) and other civil society organisations in a number of documents;[1] indeed, the policy of consultation and dialogue has itself been opened to a process of consultation and dialogue with the NGO and lobbying sectors. Several formal and informal reactions have been registered, including position papers by organised civil society (OCS) coordinating bodies (see for instance Crook 2000; Social Platform 2000). There is an evolving body of reflections by EU institutions and civil society organisations on reciprocal expectations and on the modalities of access to consultative activities.

The political values and the political socialisation of parliamentarians and senior Commission officials vary according to what model of Europe they favour and, consequently, what role they are prepared to attribute to OCS. However, in general, they tend to be supranationalists and to believe that Europe should be more than a common market; such views imply recognition of a role for OCS within the EU (Hooghe 1997) and even a constitutionalised vision of the EU in which the associational sector plays a key part.

Consultation with civil society takes place in the context of a broad range of activities, which also involve other EU institutions and national bodies. Consultation is generally guided by pluralist principles, which are frequently reiterated. For instance, a Commission website states:

> In its consultation policy the Commission applies the principle of openness. Everybody must be able to provide the Commission with input. Therefore, there is no general registration or accreditation system for interest groups. The Commission does not want to limit its consultations to a certain number of pre-screened or accredited organisations.[2]

Consultation takes place in the context of preparing green and white papers, consultation reports and communications. There are several types of fora for consultation, such as advisory committees, expert groups and *ad hoc* structures. There are also informal consultation events, such as occasional meetings with civil society representatives, and exchanges of documents. Consultation through the Internet is increasingly frequent, as reflected, for instance, in the Commission's 'Interactive Policy-Making' initiative[3] and a website that organises public consultations.[4]

The Commission has utilised the Internet to stimulate the growth of a public register of groups. In January 1997 a first version of the register was published, which comprised more than 600 non-profit organisations working at EU level and covering approximately 100 fields of activity. An electronic version was launched in 1999 which included over 800 organisations. Since 2000 the register has been automated and expanded; in 2005 the service, now known as CONECCS ('Consultation, the European Commission and Civil Society'), included over 700 civil society organisations and over 200 NGOs.[5] Since 2005, rules for inclusion have been tightened to ensure a broader European base, openness, transparency and better ability to provide input to the Commission's deliberations. The information is provided on a voluntary basis. The Commission also intends that the service provide a means to promote awareness and increase consultation of the less well known types of organisations.

Funds to support EU-level civil society are available from various sources. Some come from specific budget lines, of which there are many, but also some member states generously contribute to EU-level associations (Ruzza 2004). However, there is legal uncertainty surrounding the Commission's funding of certain types of civil society organisations, which first came to light in 1998 (Bates 1998). Yet there is great reluctance on the part of the Commission to restrict itself to the award of a set of small grants related to policy areas with uncertain legal bases. Several officials believe in the substantive importance of areas, such as support for minority languages, whose legal base is not apparent, and are aware of the strategic advantages of the Commission's involvement in the sector of public interest associations.[6]

In legal terms, a duty for the Commission to consult is established in the treaties, and ideal consulting principles have been codified in an attempt to achieve wide participation, openness, accountability, effectiveness and coherence (Commission of the European Communities 2002).[7] Consultation with OCS is sometimes referred to as 'civic dialogue' and is intended to complement the structure of social dialogue (which involves trade unions and employers). Consultation with civil society is mandatory only at the stage of policy formulation. Attempts to enhance the involvement of civil society are frequently conceptualised in institutional documents as being directly connected to a reform of governance structures. Calls for a deeper and clearer involvement of civil society were, for instance, reiterated in the white paper on governance (Commission of the European Communities 2001b), in the preparation of which a special group considered better ways of incorporating views from civil society (Commission of the European Communities 2001d), and in the Commission's 'Better Lawmaking' initiative, which is periodically reviewed to assess progress partly in terms of the involvement of civil society.

A more inclusive EU – particularly with reference to public pressure groups – is, in effect, what EU institutional documents have emphasised for several years. Its attainment is hindered by the disparity in resources between business and state-supported groups (such as regional offices and local councils) and public pressure groups. Although, in principle, the Commission does not distinguish between different kinds of organisations according to their purpose or sponsors, it realises that reform of its governance system should include the creation of a more level playing field, whereby the overwhelmingly imbalance in the resources available to business organisations would be compensated by grants and access structures specifically provided for public interest associations. However, allocation of resources and space to public pressure groups is slowed down by a dominant EU-level neo-liberal ethos, which limits redistributive state interventions and requires extensive financial reporting. This, for instance, hinders smaller and less professionalised NGOs. However, in recent years a compensatory factor has been the mounting attention to a more accurate representation of all civil society components and a growing concern for openness and transparency in the entire EU system of governance.

One particular development may provide insight into the trend of connecting civil society with democratic governance: the Treaty Establishing a Constitution for Europe (TCE, signed in Rome in 2004) and specifically Title VI of Part I of the constitution (articles I-45 to I-52 but see also article III-390), which focuses on the 'democratic life' of the EU, and particularly article I-47.[8] It includes articles on representative democracy, participatory democracy, transparency and the role of the social partners and the churches. These articles directly or indirectly point to a stronger involvement of associational life as a possible remedy to the host of problems collectively discussed as the 'democratic deficit'.

Thus, if we conceive the process of constitutionalisation in a broad and extended sense (even regardless of the ultimate fate of the TCE), it is clear that the role of OCS and specifically of citizens' associations has significantly grown and is in several ways connected to a widely advocated process of democratisation of the EU (see Craig 2001). At the same time, legal modifications to the framing of civil society keep occurring. In the TCE, the principle of participatory democracy is defined in broader and different terms than previously, which continues the recent trend of reversing the tendency to privilege the inclusion of EU-level organisations. It also clarifies some issues. It is reasserted that the foundation of democratic governance is in the principle of representative democracy, which is located in the Council and Parliament, thus ruling out interpretations that tend to set the basis for forms of associational democracy in which OCS has a direct decision-making role (Cohen and Rogers 1995; Hirst and Khilnani 1996).

Nonetheless, the formalisation of the emphasis on participatory democracy is important, as is the redefinition of consultation with civil society. Instead of significantly altering the Brussels-based institutions that articulate functional representation – the ESC and European civil society networks – with article I-47 the TCE introduces the right to a 'citizens' initiative', whereby a million EU citizens can petition the Commission to take legislative initiative – a function attributed and traditionally vigorously protected by the Commission. Also important is the reassertion of the principle of proximity (to which the COR makes frequent mention), which sets the stage for a stronger role of civil society organisations at the local level (see articles I-46 and I-49). Nevertheless, the existing structure of EU civil society consultation is not reduced, and it therefore continues to have a significant role.

This brief summary of the framework in which civil society operates in Brussels and its contribution to the EU governance system has to be interpreted in light of the actual interplay between actors with very different values, resources and interests in different policy fields. Briefly, we can conceptualise the EU organisational field in which relations occur as being shaped by the different concerns of political actors, business organisations, civil servants and public interest organisations. In order to do this, it is useful firstly to focus on the few central functions which define the role of civil society for different actors.

Civil society – a content analysis of EU policy documents

Views of civil society which are articulated in institutional documents cannot be assumed to coincide with how the role of civil society is actually viewed in specific policy areas. The presence of different ideologies, traditions of consultation and structural constraints in different policy areas make it necessary to investigate the role of civil society in specific areas. The strategies used to exert influence, the types of involvement and the mutual expectations of EU and OCS actors are likely to differ according to variables such as the type of legal base, the structure of policy networks and the interests mobilised.

To examine the construct of civil society, an analysis was conducted of a sample of sources in which it is used. The gradual and diffused process of constitutionalisation described above consists both of statements of principle, such as those reflected in the EU documents that set standards for consultation, and of the discursive practices that accompany policy-making activities. Through a textual analysis of EU documents it is possible to see how institutions conceptualise OCS. Further, it is possible to see how this process is echoed in civil society organisations by comparing a sample of documents from both EU institutions and civil society groups operating in different policy areas.

In concentrating on the functions envisioned for civil society, three types of public interest groups that seek to exert influence in Brussels were considered: environmental groups, groups active in social policy (specifically antiracism) and advocacy groups acting for ethnic minorities. Clearly, these represent only a very limited sector of civil society. However, they are crucial to the issues at stake – the democratisation of the EU, governance and the expansion of the role of civil society organisations. While the inclusion of business organisations is relatively uncontroversial at the EU level and dates back to the beginning of the process of European construction, the inclusion of public interest organisations is more problematic. Although they rank high in public opinion, they tend to be marginalised in the policy process.

In particular, the organisations selected for analysis are connected to popular social movements, which are positively regarded by public opinion, but because of their limited resources they find it difficult to exert any influence at EU level (Ruzza 2002).

The sample consists of Brussels-based organisations that are, on the one hand, connected to social movements involved with the environment, antiracism and the protection of minority languages. On the other hand, they are sufficiently organised and institutionalised to constitute broad advocacy coalitions with a wide range of supporters. They perform all the main functions of public interest associations, which range from policy research and advocacy to aggregation of interests in EU-wide networks and political action and media campaigns in member states. The political category of the 'social movement', which at the national level is typically defined in terms of political protest, takes on a broader, all-encompassing role when it is transferred to the international arena (Marks and McAdam 1996; Ruzza 2004).

To assess similarities and differences in policy discourse between OCS and EU institutions, a content analysis of policy documents was undertaken, specifically a type of content analysis known as 'frame analysis'.[9]

Frame analysis

Frame analysis consists of the identification and classification of recurrent concepts in policy documents. This analysis was performed by six researchers; it focused on the period 1993–2003. Here, only the aggregate difference between OCS and institutions will be considered.[10] Briefly, after a first reading of the materials, the main themes appearing in the set of texts are identified and listed. The occurrence of these categories is then counted by a team of analysts. This gives a more exact assessment of their prominence and allows a characterisation and comparison of different types of documents.

Of particular relevance was the comparison between the discourse of public interest associations and the discourse of EU institutional actors; therefore, a set of documents representative of the main organisations of each type active in environmental, regional and antiracism policy was selected for analysis. The documentary sources utilised for the EU field included the web pages of the relevant institutions,[11] the Commission's programmatic action plans, and institutional evaluations of those action plans.[12] For OCS, the primary materials consisted of: reactions to the action plans from EU networks as well as from large OCS organisations established in Brussels; submissions to the European Convention on the Future of the European Union; programmatic documents; and the websites of these organisations. A balance of sources was considered in each sector.[13]

The selected texts constitute a sample of those issues that are of concern to many policy-makers and activists; they incorporate agenda-setting efforts and preferred policy solutions.[14] The team of coders read the texts using paragraphs as the unit of analysis; in total, 134 documents were coded.[15] The findings consist of the identification of the dominant frames by type of organisation, and the results are articulated by type of actor and policy sector in table 3.1. After a general report on the dominant frames, we will focus here on one of the frames identified, that named 'importance of civil society', which refers to the reasons why civil society is considered important by civil society organisations and by EU institutions.

Table 3.1 Common codes identified in all policy sectors (percentages of documents)

Frames identified	Total	EU	OCS
Implementation	20.1	22.5	17.7
To improve knowledge	13.5	16.4	10.6
Horizontal diffusion	12.8	16.0	9.6
Importance of civil society	13.0	8.1	19.6

Overall, we can firstly note that EU actors and OCS tend to discuss the same topics as they engage in a dialogue at a distance on specific proposals and evaluations. Thus, policy documents of both institutional and civil society actors most frequently focus on issues of implementation, as this is the overarching concern of all actors. About 20 per cent of all paragraphs coded were about implementation issues, and there were no relevant differences between OCS and EU actors. Secondly, the two types of actors focused equally on how to improve knowledge of issues pertaining to their respective policy areas (13.5 per cent of frames identified). Thirdly, they discussed how to diffuse their areas of concern into other policy sectors (12.8 per cent of classified paragraphs). Fourthly, they discussed concerns with civil society, which constituted an important area of reflection in both EU and OCS documents. This is notable if we consider that the number of topics identified was obviously large – over two dozen – with a few topics (i.e. frames) attracting a lot of attention, but then with the number of references decreasing sharply.

Predictably, attention to civil society was not as evenly distributed as were other topics of attention: civil society organisations were much more concerned with their contribution to the EU than vice versa (19.6 per cent versus 8.1 per cent). But the same range of concerns appears in the documents of both types of actor.

Conceptions of civil society in environmental, antiracism and regional policy

A few examples from the documents examined will clarify how civil society is conceptualised. A frequent concern of both OCS and EU actors is with the *effectiveness* of EU policies. Thus, for instance, in the mission statement of the EU-level environmental network the European Environmental Bureau (EEB) there was the following statement:

> Co-ordinated actions by EEB members and existing and potential allies can bring positive change, a change of direction in EU policies towards sustainability.... As a result, the mission of the EEB is to become an effective instrument in visibly improving EU's environmental policies and realising sustainable development by effectively integrating environmental objectives in horizontal and sectoral policies of the EU.

A similar results-oriented approach was evident in views of the role of OCS in fostering the *horizontal diffusion* of policies. Thus, antiracism organisations attempt to diffuse antidiscriminatory concerns throughout all common policies, as do environmental organisations, as shown in this example taken from the website of the WWF:

> Major policy areas where the European Union has strong powers – for instance, agriculture, fisheries and regional development – will be decisive in whether the environment is protected. Influencing these other policies that make up over four-fifths of the EU's annual budget is a crucial challenge for WWF.

In these texts, OCS legitimises its presence in terms of help in achieving policy results – this concern can be described as *results oriented*. Considered in the light of the crisis of legitimacy of EU governance, this focus on results can be classified as amounting to an attempt to pursue *output legitimacy*.

A different function for OCS, which was emphasised by both OCS and EU actors, is as a direct connection with *citizens' participation*, which was exemplified on a website of Friends of the Earth Europe (FoEE):

> FoEE aims to raise public awareness, enhance the participation of people and environmental citizens' organisations in political processes, and influence political decision-makers, especially at the European level.

Several excerpts similar to this one stressed participation specifically at local level, emphasising a role of civil society as a link between different levels of governance. OCS is often linked to attempts to engender desired values at the grassroots level. In this excerpt from the Commission's 1998 antiracism action plan, the praise of OCS is motivated by its function of *bringing the EU vision to the local level* – in this case of a racism-free society:.

> Non-governmental organisations have long been instrumental in carrying forward the fight against racism. They play a crucial role in both stimulating action at a grassroots level, and in ensuring that the problem of racism remains on the political agenda. The Commission supports the Migrants' Forum in its broad role of providing representation at European level for immigrant and ethnic minority organisations.

Other concerns that OCS stressed and that Commission documents also identified were the need to counterbalance economic interests and the need to advance a process of EU democratisation. Both concerns are reflected in this excerpt from an EEB document – a response to the Commission's Sixth Environmental Action Programme. Also exemplified in this excerpt is a fundamentally different view (common to many OCS groups) of the role of the state from that prevalent in the institutional realm (where the 'minimal state' seems to be favoured):

> The Commission is determined to work closely with stakeholders in coming to decisions on policies. In principle the EEB supports this. However, it wants the Commission to realise that stakeholders in society have different strengths, and that in particular multinationals, federations of business and industry, banks, etc. have much more possibilities for dominance over decisions and implementation than organisations that work for the common good. As this inequity is structural, the EEB is not in favour of a withdrawing state, it sees the state as having an important role in steering society and bringing balance between stakeholders. This is also a matter of democratisation, as citizens' organisations usually can count with more confidence with the public than governments or business. The EEB wants the Decision to include concrete commitments to address the structural inequity between stakeholders.

The principles of accountability and of representativeness are frequently asserted in EU documents and emerge in the interaction between institutions and OCS, often with recommendations for improvement. It is not only a construct emphasised by the EU domain to 'discipline' OCS. In the following example, from a letter from five environmental groups to the Commission after the Gothenburg summit, the principle of accountability is introduced and institutions are found to need the help of OCS:

> An important contribution to achieve sustainable development can come from civil society, its organisations and individual citizens. They need to

be given the opportunity ... to create a culture of accountability to citizens, to ensure that citizens can hold businesses, governments and other institutions accountable for sustainable development in a democratic manner.

To sum up this section, EU and OCS actors concur in stressing the importance of improving the implementation of policies, improving policy knowledge with the help of OCS, and emphasising the importance of horizontal diffusion of policies and the general importance of civil society. Both kinds of actors stress the information-providing, monitoring and ideational role of OCS, its contribution to policy deliberation, its connections with marginalised sectors of the EU population and its ability to represent them. They also stress the communication potential of civil society and therefore its media impact, as well as its implications for the legitimation of policies in the public sphere. They reiterate the need to have a counterweight to business dominance.

In addition, a contextual reading of the excerpts (and a separate quantitative analysis of the same data – see Ruzza 2006a) shows that OCS shares the views of the EU institutions, but it differs in demanding greater access. It also criticises the Commission for insufficient attention and for being 'pro-business', and it advocates a stronger state.

Discussion

The findings of the frame analysis show that, overall, the three movement advocacy coalitions engage in a policy discourse which, while being compatible with the dominant neo-liberal policy discourse of European institutions, stresses some factors more and underplays others. This suggests a constructive role of EU OCS and specifically of its institutionalised social movement component. In particular, the neo-liberal values of the European institutions are criticised and a more interventionist role for the state is advocated in two key areas: to redress what they perceive as discrimination against peripheral locations and racial minorities; and to strengthen regulations to protect the environment, in contrast to what they see as a purely market-oriented approach taken by the Commission.

In general terms, on the basis of these findings it can be argued that there are dominant and converging elements that allow us to define an EU model of civil society involvement, albeit from which there are deviations. This model is characterised by an overarching emphasis on participation, mainly in terms of a consultative role and an information-providing role. To a lesser extent there is evidence of a desire to include OCS in debates on the merits of proposing legislation in a dialogical role inspired by models of deliberative democracy. There is, though, little evidence of a desire to include OCS in decision-making, where the preference is for it to remain both autonomous and unencumbered. In addition, an EU model of civil society also includes an emphasis on its role in connecting different levels of governance and in relating to other non-state actors in horizontal governance structures.

Deviations from this model include the perspective of several OCS associations which emphasise a stronger state as a guarantor of their inclusion in deliberative fora, and as a guarantor of their role of representing weaker social constituencies and of channelling state resources to their client groups. Similarly, deviations from this model, but in the opposite direction, are expressed by EU institutional actors who dissent from any interventionist agenda to redress the imbalance between private and public associations, and occasionally from institutional actors (mainly in non-social policy roles) who dissent from any perspective that promotes the inclusion of non-state actors in policy-making.

This EU model of civil society and its functions constitutes a set of rules and practices which are part of an articulated 'constutionalising' project in which an input from OCS is sought to shore up the European project in several connected ways. The features of this project, that is, the different functions attributed to civil society by OCS and EU institutions, can now be aggregated and presented in a typology.

A typology of conceptualisations of civil society

The most frequent role attributed to civil society is as a support in guaranteeing the high quality of EU policies. Firstly, OCS can redress (at least to some extent) the insufficient input legitimacy (traditionally rooted in principles of representative government) by way of increasing 'output legitimacy' (established by implementation of effective policy) (Scharpf 1999). This in turn means utilising civil society to several different ends: to address policy-makers' information deficit, as well as their need to aggregate interests; to formulate efficient and accepted policies (Greenwood 1997); to monitor outcomes; to help with implementation; to help policy-makers approach crises in a coherent manner; to enrich decision-making with new policy ideas; and to spur collective processes of policy learning. All these areas can benefit from the direct input of civil society, as is acknowledged by EU institutions, and such input demands the inclusion of a broad range of civil society organisations, from business organisations to churches, NGOs and public interest groups, although sometimes the same organisations will take on different roles, such as research institutes, advocacy organisations and fundraising.[16]

Secondly, connected to this approach is the realisation that a deeper involvement of civil society is necessary simply because, in some respects, states are no longer the main locus of political authority. With globalisation, control over a growing range of issues increasingly eludes the state and is instead associated with civil society (Dryzek 2000: 5). It is for this reason that the involvement of civil society is essential: in monitoring functions that the state cannot afford; in ensuring compliance through non-state sanctions; and in fostering the transposition of legislation through sectoral pressure on policy-makers in member states.

Thirdly, a different function of civil society relates to the fact that, increasingly, 'democracy' is being conceptualised in terms of deliberation. As Dryzek argues, the essence of democracy is now widely held to be deliberation rather than interest aggregation, constitutional rights or self-governance (Dryzek 2000). In this sense a project of democratisation of the EU, together with a continuation of European construction and a connected project of increasing its legitimacy, takes the form of integration through deliberation. This means seeking to create the equivalent of a demos outside the framework of the nation state (Eriksen and Fossum 2000), even while acknowledging (and attempting to overcome) the difficulties of this approach (Brunkhorst 2003). This approach is particularly relevant at EU level, as civil society here, as a differentiated component of the demos, can provide an inter-mediating civic sphere to connect European societies to transnational governance (Armstrong 2001).

Fourthly, another approach involves attempts to build a demos through the shaping of the European public sphere (see for instance Eriksen and Fossum 2001) or other influences of OCS, such as the supposedly beneficial impact of associationism on the formation of social capital and the democratic attitudes of the population.

To sum up, civil society can be used by a range of actors to pursue different types of objectives. These can then be clustered into four types. That is, civil society can be utilised by EU institutions:

- to improve output legitimacy;
- to address the globalisation-driven relocation of ambits of power;
- to construct the 'European citizen';
- to construct a European public sphere.

Taken all together, these objectives aim to increase the political legitimacy of the EU through a stronger involvement of civil society. These uses of civil society constitute ideal types. They are clearly interconnected, but for analytical purposes it is useful to consider them separately. The remainder of this chapter will expand and elaborate on the implications of these uses of civil society within the EU system of governance. They will be conceptualised as resources that different actors employ according to their perceived political goals and opportunities, the policy areas in which they operate, and the specific problems that they face at different points in time.

Output legitimacy

The Commission welcomes the role of NGOs in a number of contexts and assesses their performance with reference to a set of criteria which often relate to the contribution of OCS to improvements to the policy process. As mentioned above, it stresses the information-gathering abilities of OCS, as well as its feedback on policy implementation (e.g. monitoring transposition) throughout different levels of governance. Among this list of virtues attributed to civil society, output democracy issues are the ones that stand out most frequently in EU documents; that is, civil society is generally praised for its potential contribution to the improvement of EU policies. This emphasis has been interpreted as an attempt to replace 'input legitimacy' with 'output legitimacy' (Scharpf 1999).

In enlisting civil society to improve performance, EU institutional actors declare their readiness to increase inclusion and support, but also express a concern with current NGO performance when assessed through the institutionally sanctioned criteria of participation, openness, accountability, effectiveness and coherence. This raises important issues of co-optation and institutionalisation for the civil society sector. While some NGOs are ready to trade access and funds for cooperation with EU institutional objectives, others are more reluctant. For instance, Greenpeace refuses to accept Commission funds, while EU umbrella groups are fully dependent on them. In effect, the EU straddles the line between including NGOs as competent allies and including them as critical voices that contribute to a democratisation of the system. A choice between the two models is problematic and politically controversial. It is also associated with different views of European governance. It touches upon the divide not only between co-optation and confrontation, but also between a pluralist approach and a neo-corporatist one, whereby political control of civil society remains more attainable.

Responding to a globalisation-driven relocation of power

Much of the EU structure has been created to respond to the fact that policy needs to be conducted beyond the state. This was clear in all the policy areas examined. For instance, the Europeanisation of environmental policy resulted from concerns with issues such as trans-border pollution, preventing a competitive lowering of environmental standards, and the need to spread and coordinate environmental policy both cross-nationally and across policy sectors, such as agriculture, energy or tourism (Ruzza 2000). If EU policy is already policy beyond the state, it is also increasingly becoming policy conducted through agreements between non-state actors. Examples of attempts to promote self-regulation of non-state actors include the emphasis on the open method of coordination (OMC), which has emerged in recent years as a philosophy, a key set of proposals and a field of sustained academic attention (de la Porte and Pochet 2002; Radaelli 2002; Armstrong 2003; Chalmers and Lodge 2003).

'Doing less and doing it better' is a concept often heard in Brussels these days. Right and left have different visions of the EU, but they often concur in criticising EU performance and in seeing its functions as overstretched. A relatively small bureaucracy, which increasingly feels under attack, is often more than willing to enlist external help. This is to improve the quality of policies – output legitimacy – but also because the idea is currently discredited that in complex societies it is the proper role of the state to regulate an increasing number of sectors. This is one reason behind the important aggregating role accorded to business lobbies (Greenwood and Aspinwall 1998). In 'hollowed out' states, public authorities often lack the means and the will to regulate society and prefer to leave difficult tasks of interest intermediation to composite policy networks, and with them to the OCS sector. Similar processes are taking place at EU level. In areas of social policy a similar role is given to public interest organisations.

Constructing the 'European citizen'

The Commission seems to advocate an interventionist role on the part of public authorities in fostering embryonic forms of civil society. For instance, a key document reads:

> It should not be assumed that less-advantaged stakeholders are already in existence as relatively easily identifiable entities, and organised to a greater or lesser extent. It may be the case that, as an issue arises, important stakeholders are not at all organised, and may not be at all well-informed about the potential impact of them. Redressing material and cognitive imbalances may therefore, first and foremost, involve public actors in assisting the emergence of stakeholders as organised entities in order that they may make a meaningful contribution to the policy process. (Commission of the European Communities 2000b)

Here, we can identify a kind of social engineering, whereby if civil society is absent it could, and maybe should, be created. On the other hand, and particularly in recent times, when state interventionist approaches are seen as unjustified, many institutional actors dissent from this approach.

In this respect, we can also identify an institutional desire to further a process of European democratisation that goes beyond the European political systems and sees civil society as an independent factor in the democratisation of everyday life. It is in this sense that the concept of 'social accountability' comes to play a role. Civil society would then become a component of a process of societal constitutionalism (Sciulli 1992), that is, of democratisation of public life, that EU institutions could support with funds and political space. This articulates the social scientific view that a rich associational life promotes social capital and results in good governance by instilling altruism, collaboration and respect for democratic rules. It also reveals a state-like preoccupation with citizens' values, which could be construed as a further indication of a constitutionalising intent of the EU.

Creating a public sphere

A connected but distinct aspect is the creation of an EU public sphere and therefore a European demos. The Commission and OCS emphasise their contribution to European integration through their contribution to the creation of a European public sphere (Commission of the European Communities 2000a), thus linking satisfaction with EU policy performance to moves to promote the construction of a European demos.

This democratising concern is not restricted to member states. The Commission welcomes the democratising impact of NGOs in Europe, but also in the developing world, and for this reason it also funds development NGOs, and values their contribution to project management, particularly their abilities in monitoring and evaluating projects financed by the EU. In this concern for a broader democratising role, we can identify a continuing concern for the general attainment of fundamental rights – another marker of a constitutionalising intent (Weiler 1995). In interviews undertaken to contextualise the textual analysis reported above, we noted that while the first dynamic did not necessarily result in stronger European identities, the second was specifically and frequently articulated in strategic pro-European terms.

Civil society, governance and legitimacy

These conflicting and cross-cutting expectations on the part of the EU institutions and OCS cannot be easily generalised. The positive attributes of involving civil society will naturally vary with the value orientations and specific contexts of the different institutions. For instance, within the Commission, the Directorates-General have always had clearly different ideologies and tend to operate differently in their consultation procedures (Michelmann 1978). Thus, the specific role of civil society actors can be elucidated only by reconsidering them with reference to empirical case studies (Ruzza 2004; Smismans 2004). Nonetheless, the political legitimacy of the European project is the overarching concern; it brings together different views of what the contribution of civil society should be. It is a concern that emerges both in EU-wide documents and in actual interviews with civil servants and political actors – a concern with legitimacy. Thus, concerns with the quality of the policy output, with delegating to civil society some functions that the EU does not accomplish satisfactorily, with creating a European demos, and with stimulating citizens' participation have in common an ultimate desire to salvage the European project by injecting it with new forms of political legitimacy.

Tensions in EU models of civil society

With the above-mentioned fourfold model of civil society functions, it is now possible to reflect on internal tensions and strains in the role that OCS and EU institutions have envisioned for civil society at EU level.

Ambiguities surrounding the accountability and representativeness of OCS

Representativeness is emphasised by several EU institutions, not only the Commission. For instance, the ESC stresses that a 'basic precondition and legitimising basis for participation is adequate representativeness of those speaking for organised civil society' and that 'when consulting civil society organisations, the European institutions should check how representative these bodies are' (Economic and Social Committee 2001).[17] However, there is also ambiguity in the institutional discourse. If the dominant view emphasises representativeness, there is also an awareness that good policy advice is, in principle, a different issue from representativeness. For instance, the Commission recognises that:

> representativeness, though an important criterion, should not be the only determining factor for membership of an advisory committee, or to take part in dialogue with the Commission. Other factors, such as their track record and ability to contribute substantial policy inputs to the discussion are equally important. (Commission of the European Communities 2000a)

In other words, good policy ideas are not necessarily representative ones – and the Commission recognises and acknowledges this fact. Thus, considerations of output legitimacy can conflict with considerations of political legitimacy.

In the same vein, the often reiterated emphasis on representativeness as a deciding criterion for the inclusion of particular civil society organisations led the Commission to argue that, in principle, consultations with representative bodies such as trade unions and employers' organisations have to be considered more important than consultations with non-representative organisations.[18] But while this is possible in the context of the social dialogue, it is less attainable with the civic dialogue, where representativeness cannot be easily checked. Nonetheless, this criterion can be utilised instrumentally to justify a preference for large umbrella organisations, which include the possibly more controllable European networks. The choice of peak associations in the social dialogue and of EU-level associations in the civil dialogue indicates a preference for a centralised, neo-corporatist model of state–civil society relations, in which the task of aggregating preferences is left to civil society itself. It is, however, a preference that conflicts with stated objectives. The dispersion of power along vertical and horizontal lines that recent EU documents emphasise may in fact merely reflect aspirations.

In any event, there is no agreement within the NGO community on what constitutes evidence of representativeness, or on whether only representative organisations should be consulted (Economic and Social Committee 2000a). Some OCS actors point out that, increasingly, civil society expresses fluidity in the types of formation that represent its values and opinions. New organisations often emerge quickly, with strong popular support, and dissolve or change into different organisations in a short time. Therefore, an insistence on calculating memberships would exclude an important part of civil society.

There is also an acknowledgement of the difficulties that OCS encounters in developing good ideas without appropriate resources. The extent of involvement with state authorities is, however, problematic, as a high level of support might induce excessive compliance. For this reason, there is a debate in political theory between authors who recommend the sponsoring of representative organisations – for instance Schmitter suggests an EU-level voucher system in which citizens select from a list of OCS groups which ones to support – and theorists – such as Dryzek – who believe that the state should limit itself, to protect OCS autonomy (Dryzek 2000: 107–21; Schmitter 2000).

In addition, there is a conflict between seeing the role of OCS as primarily one of negotiating or as primarily one of deliberating. If it is a negotiating role and the representation is oriented by a binding mandate, which relies on structures of internal democracy, the allocated period of eight weeks for consultation is clearly insufficient.[19] And even in the NGO community, there is much ambivalence about whether to participate in policy-making or to take on the role of a 'critical conscience', possibly threatening protest and using other social movement tactics. The current emphasis on participation in state institutions is seen by some OCS actors as masking continuing centralisation and merely legitimising vested interests (Cooke and Kothari 2001).

The same ambiguity that emerges with representativeness also emerges with accountability. A first important question is, accountability to whom? Here the Commission distinguishes different forms that may well be at odds: political and social accountability. For instance, one of the teams involved in the preparation of the white paper on governance argued that, 'in addition to the traditional forms of accountability, public administrations are accountable towards society as a whole' (Commission of the European Communities 2001d). Here, as the EU public administrator, the Commission seems to imply an acceptance of a responsibility to European society, which is different and presumably broader than accountability to elected representatives and institutions. Through civil society, it seems to be attempting to bring the EU presence down the levels of governance and into a direct relation with EU citizens.

However, in the same document accountability is ultimately subordinated to the mechanisms of representative democracy, which implies an output legitimacy function for civil society and a conception of relations with OCS in which they are seen as mainly channels of information in the policy-making process. The document reads:

> It is nevertheless apparent that the decision-making process in the EU is first and foremost legitimised by the legislator, i.e. the elected representatives of the European people.... However, consultation, if carried out properly, can provide valuable expertise laying the ground for – technically – sound decisions. In particular, consultation helps reconcile the views and concerns of different actors throughout the policy-cycle (i.e. in policy-shaping, implementation and evaluation), thereby obtaining wide support and social acceptance for decisions. (Commission of the European Communities 2001d)

The Commission, in frequently emphasising accountability, as well as the 'need to respect diversity and heterogeneity of the NGO community' and the 'need to take account of the autonomy and independence of NGOs' (Commission of the European Communities 2000b), assumes that the two concepts can be combined. But in many ways the two categories are different and not easily reconciled.

Civil society, pluralism and neo-corporatism

The EU has often been conceptualised as largely a pluralist system with neo-corporatist pockets in sectors such as agriculture. While pluralism remains the stated standard for including civil society, the Commission has traditionally favoured European networks of public interest associations, both in granting access and in funding. It has often encouraged, if not directly created and sponsored, umbrella groups based in Brussels (which, some informants argue, effectively discriminates against NGOs from member states). Observers have seen this approach as amounting to a strategy to increase the scope of common policies (see Justin Greenwood's contribution to this volume – chapter 2). In interviews, Commission officials justify this approach by noting that coherence in consultation is best achieved if organisations are represented at EU level (for speed of response, global perspective, understanding of the EU policy process, etc.).

Some NGOs see this EU-centred approach as practically equivalent to a system of accreditation without the formal guarantees of such a system, and they advocate a broader consultation process. The Commission has sought to dispel the view that 'Brussels is talking to Brussels' and so has encouraged broader consultations, for example including organisations based in member states, as well as a more proactive input from the public at large. Thus, in the choice of inclusion, the attempt to dispel the negative image of an inward-looking EU governance system has played a deciding role. In this contrast between criteria for preference in consultation lies another ambiguity. It is debatable to what extent practical considerations of effectiveness, time and resources – that is, of output legitimacy – should override attempts to reach out directly in member states and to their civil societies.

However, Internet technology may in this respect redefine the situation. Several interviewees from civil society organisations emphasised the role of the Internet and the new initiatives mentioned above. These have facilitated the work of NGOs, firstly by making information previously restricted to policy-making bodies widely accessible, and secondly by lowering the cost of participation in the policy process. The European Parliament allows petitions through the Internet, by both individual citizens and associations.[20] For this reason, smaller NGOs find that a stable presence in Brussels is increasingly less important and cost-effective, since they are now able to acquire relevant information on funding and can contribute position papers directly from their bases in the member states. A similar development – but for different reasons – has been reported in the business lobbying sector. As growing importance is increasingly attributed to EU lobbying, large firms prefer to conduct it from headquarters rather than decentralising it in Brussels-based offices or using functional representatives (Greenwood 1997).

OCS and its conflicts

Doubts about the present functioning and proper role of OCS are also present in the EU-level NGO community. NGOs are not fully satisfied with their relations with EU institutions. In particular, the policy process is seen as too unpredictable and fragmented to give them the possibility of performing their role appropriately – however conceptualised. In particular, the *ad hoc* forms of inclusion of non-governmental actors and the haphazard quality of consultation are singled out for criticism. The Commission is aware of these criticisms, as evidenced by the report of the working group on civil society (Commission of the European Communities 2001d), which notes that, in the course of the team's consultation:

> All the representatives of civil society stressed the need for the Commission to adopt a more systematic and coherent approach to consultation. They felt that existing formalised or structured consultation procedures should be made more transparent.

However, if there is general agreement in the OCS community that the frequency and relevance of consultation with OCS should both be increased by the Commission, it is less settled how this should be done. Suggestions have included: a treaty article that would give a legal basis to dialogue with associations; activating an accreditation system; and opening the consultation process to smaller NGOs, which, it is argued, would better represent emerging sensibilities and ideas in society (Commission of the European Communities 2001d).

There are also doubts within civil society about the selection of those NGOs to be included in consultation. One view is that the Commission should reverse its inclusive approach and move towards some kind of accreditation system, similar to the one operating in several other international organisations, whereby inclusion is conditional upon recognition by other NGOs or evidence of size of representation. This approach is, however, rejected by some other NGOs, which see it as potentially institutionalising a system that would marginalise smaller NGOs in favour of larger and more well established organisations. This approach could defeat the purpose of including NGOs as sources of alternative policy solutions, of less utilised expertise and of unpopular but innovative and useful proposals. For smaller NGOs, the principle of inclusion should be that all relevant voices on a specific policy area are heard, regardless of claims of representativeness. However, this view appears difficult to accept by a Commission which frequently faces accusations of lack of representativeness itself. Rather than being streamlined according to clear criteria, overall the consultation process remains fairly unorganised, even haphazard. For a perception of increased efficiency to come about, the Commission would have to be more selective in its choice of which organisations to consult.

In summary, there is much ambivalence about the working of the present consultation framework and we may be seeing the beginning of the unravelling of the Brussels-based consultation system, largely organisationally based, and its replacement by a more mixed system, in which organised and non-organised actors interact with policy-makers in a variety of fora and through a range of technologies. The exercise of political authority may be acquiring new characteristics of decentralised steering conducted jointly by social and political institutions, which is performed in cooperation with networked centres of power that criss-cross territorial levels and include multifarious types of organisation (Kohler-Koch 2000). This diffused, networked structure is the element emphasised by several key EU documents through the invariably positive use of the concept of 'governance' and the inclusion of actors from civil society (on 'governance' as an ideology see Della Sala 2001).

Nonetheless, the involvement of OCS and its role in European governance remain attractive. OCS involvement constitutes an opportunity for EU elites because it supports the claim that an unachievable concept of democracy fully based on representative mechanisms can be replaced by the inclusion in the policy process of a set of independent and conflicting voices (Majone 1996: 286), which at times come to be construed as the functional equivalent of a European demos and at other times as a tool in the transformation of representative government into a government of expertise.

Conclusion: OCS as an EU constitutionalising factor

This chapter has documented the various ways in which OCS has been recruited in the project of European construction. In concluding, we can note that so much is expected of civil society that, without a further institutional clarification of its role, it will be difficult to overcome the stalemate resulting from the conflicting functions which different actors advocate. There is a tension between representativeness and innovative policy ideas, a tension (and a lack of clarity) in the contrast between institutional and social accountability, and a tension between good output performance and consultation at all levels of governance, including the fragmented and unstructured local level. There are also tensions between a representative role and a deliberative one, and between internal democracy and speed of decision-making. There are different views on the amount of institutionalisation to be supported. There are worries that a publicly funded civil society could become too compliant to be innovative, and that an independent but weak civil society may simply legitimise the strategies of economic vested interests. However, if we look at civil society as a structured field, it can be argued that, while different types of organisation may stand uneasily on one or other side of the tensions identified, the field *as a whole* will have enough balance to make it useful in all the functions considered. Thus, the EU institutions should protect the internal difference of civil society rather than prescribe universal attributes.

Although they compete, different types of organisation constitute an integrated ecology of associations (Ruzza 1996; Warren 2001). As Warren (2001) notes, in some circumstances they balance each other and provide different democratic goods to governance structures. For instance, business associations can provide useful technical knowledge and information on the preferences of an important sector of society; they may effectively guarantee internal democracy, as there are no identity barriers that stimulate internal consensus and push out dissenters, as may be the case with some identity-oriented groups (Warren 2001). But their ability to represent society may be limited. This limitation could be counterbalanced by the inclusion of public pressure groups. And it would be the task of decision-makers to ensure that a good mix of organisations are represented. Any such mix should, at a minimum, include a balance of vested interests and public pressure groups, but also of churches, trade unions, advocacy groups and social movements, which is why EU institutions should continue to take an inclusive approach.

Notes

1 Some important examples have been Commission of the European Communities (2000a, 2001b, 2001d, 2002)
2 See http://ec.europa.eu/civil_society/apgen_en.htm (accessed October 2006).
3 The European Commission's 'Interactive Policy-Making' (IPM) initiative consists of two Internet-based instruments reachable from the 'Your Voice in Europe' website (http://ec.europa.eu/yourvoice/, accessed December 2006), which is itself a 'single access point', aimed at collecting citizens' opinions to improve EU-level policy-making.
4 See http://ec.europa.eu/yourvoice/consultations/index_en.htm (accessed October 2006).
5 See http://ec.europa.eu/civil_society/coneccs/index_en.htm (accessed October 2006).
6 In this case, the European Bureau for Lesser-Used Languages (EBLUL), a minority-languages European network, was closed as it lacked a proper legal

basis. The Commission was forced to close EBLUL because the checking procedure was started by a member state (the UK). The uncertainty concerns only those lines of funding that pertain to policy areas which are not common policies and therefore have no clear right to be funded.

7 This document also provides guidelines for consultation activities. It emphasises that: the content of consultation needs to be clear; relevant parties should have an opportunity to be heard; the scope of consultation should be broad; the access points should be easily reachable, such as the website 'Your Voice in Europe' (http://ec.europa.eu/yourvoice/index.htm); participants should be given sufficient time for responses (eight weeks for open consultation); and feedback should be provided.

8 Article I-47, 'The principle of participatory democracy', begins:

> 1. The institutions shall, by appropriate means, give citizens and representative associations the opportunity to make known and publicly exchange their views in all areas of Union action.
> 2. The institutions shall maintain an open, transparent and regular dialogue with representative associations and civil society.

Article I-50, 'Transparency of the proceedings of Union institutions, bodies, offices and agencies', begins:

> 1. In order to promote good governance and ensure the participation of civil society, the Union institutions, bodies, offices and agencies shall conduct their work as openly as possible.

Article III-390 reads:

> The members of the Economic and Social Committee shall be appointed for five years. Their term of office shall be renewable....
> The Council shall act after consulting the Commission. It may obtain the opinion of European bodies which are representative of the various economic and social sectors and of civil society to which the Union's activities are of concern.

9 The technique of frame analysis comes from a central tradition in social movement research and also in policy analysis. Key texts are: Snow et al. (1980), Rein and Schon (1994), and Alink et al. (2001).

10 For a more complete description of the frame analysis, see Ruzza (2004). For a more extensive analysis of EU policy documents see also Ruzza (2006a, 2006b).

11 These consisted of: Directorate-General (DG) web pages presenting the specific policy remit (DG Environment, DG Regional Policy, DG Employment, Social Affairs and Equal Opportunities); the websites of agencies and consultative institutions (the EU Environment Agency, the COR, the European Monitoring Centre); and the European Parliament's web pages describing the thematic areas.

12 In the field of the environment, the two most recent action plans were examined (the fifth and sixth plans). One plan (the first) was looked at in relation to antiracism. Programmatic documents in regional policy were the used. The reaction to the Commission's action plans on the part of

the European Parliament (in the form of resolutions, including those only indirectly connected to the action plans) and the opinions of all consultative bodies on the action plans were also considered.

13 The environmental sector included: the European Environmental Bureau (EEB), Climate Network, WWF Europe, Greenpeace Europe, Birdslife, Friends of the Earth Europe, International Friends of Nature, and Transport and Environment. The regionalist sector included: the European Bureau for Lesser-Used Languages (EBLUL), the Association of European Regions (AER), the Association of European Border Regions (AEBR), the Council of European Municipalities and Regions (CEMR), and the Congress of Local and Regional Authorities of Europe (CLRAE). Also considered were associations of regions and a sample of regional offices from the type of regions examined in the text – regions with prominent ethno-nationalist advocacy coalitions such as Sardinia, Veneto, Catalunya and Pays Basque. The antiracist sector included: the European Network Against Racism (ENAR), the Starting Line Group and the Migration Policy Group.

14 All classified documents and database files are available online at www.soc. unitn.it/users/carlo.ruzza (accessed December 2006).

15 A paragraph – our unit of analysis – was classified into one or more of the 'frames' identified after the first reading when it matched a central defining statement. Thus, when two or three frames were present in a text, two or three occurrences were counted. A total of about 1,000 paragraphs per sector were coded (environment, 1000 paragraphs from 47 documents; regions, 998 paragraphs from 43 documents; antiracism, 1074 paragraphs from 44 documents). In addition to the frames identified, other variables were coded. These were: policy sector, type of actor (the various OCS organisations or institutions), type of document, and year of selected texts. These variables are not utilised in this analysis but are considered by Ruzza (2004).

16 For instance, a Commission documents states: 'European public policy research organisations can provide ideas and reflections to feed the debate at European level. They can also provide a link between the European institutions and the citizens, and should therefore be supported' (Commission of the European Communities 2005c).

17 The ESC also stresses that 'representativity must be qualitative as well as quantitative … meaning that representatives are able to participate effectively and constructively in the opinion-forming and decision-making process through the provision of appropriate organisational structures and expertise' (Economic and Social Committee 2001).

18 See, for instance, Commission of the European Communities (2002), note 7.

19 Eight weeks is the length of time the Commission will wait for responses to proposals.

20 See www.europarl.europa.eu/parliament/public/staticDisplay.do?id=49&page Rank=3&language=en (accessed December 2006).

Chapter 4

Meeting the European Union's environmental challenge

Anthony R. Zito

Introduction

The environmental policy of the European Union (EU) is held to be one of the major success stories of the integration process, a prime example of how the responsibilities for protecting the environment against complex pollution problems has gradually been shared between the member states. Until 2000, environmental policy was one of the fastest-growing areas and now comprises well over 500 measures in its *acquis* (Jordan 1999a). Nevertheless, the success achieved in this policy area raises issues of how effective environmental governance actually is, in all of its dimensions, in the EU context; it also challenges us to consider how much power and legitimacy over this area have been ceded by the member states.

This chapter examines how the EU's institutional logic, combined with diverse sets of ideas and knowledge, poses fundamental challenges to governance, as well as opportunities for the EU environmental policy arena and for environmental non-governmental organisations (ENGOs). The chapter's larger objective is to question how the policy process can strengthen the effectiveness of governance while ensuring a substantial role for civil society. The complexity of the EU structure, with its chains of institutions, which often have conflicting ideas and policy values, can create both difficulties and opportunities for civil society when it seeks to engage with the environmental governance process.

This chapter defines 'governance' as the capacity of authorities with public responsibilities to steer their economy and society in a goal-oriented way that differs from what the spontaneous cooperation of actors in the markets and society would achieve on its own (Kooiman

1993; Peters 1997). The challenges of the EU decision-making structure shape the coping strategies of ENGOs in particular ways. Because of the acknowledged importance of civil society actors to the governance process, EU decision-makers have used various means to bring the ENGOs more fully into this structure. The involvement of members of civil society provides substantive and symbolic contributions to the environmental effort.

The chapter utilises a 'thick' institutional and ideational analysis to examine these mechanisms. There is already a substantial literature that explicitly examines environmental governance at the level of both the EU and the member states (note particularly Butt Philip 1998; Lenschow 1999; Weale et al. 2000), but this literature generally has not focused on the interlocking challenges and how they have affected governance and civil society in particular. This chapter argues that the institutional and ideational complexity of the EU leads to both regulatory and network patchworks (i.e. a complex web of actors and norms) that are new, and that provide both opportunities and constraints for the wide array of actors involved. The same ENGOs can be surprisingly effective in some circumstances and not others. Because of space constraints, the discussion concentrates on the ENGO perspective but acknowledges the importance of other civil society actors.

The next section outlines some of the key institutional and ideational concepts, and applies them to the EU. The third section presents a list of the challenges to EU governance that are created by the interplay of complex institutions and conflicting policy ideas. The fourth section examines in more detail the relationship of civil society to the political process. The fifth section investigates the efforts the EU has made to overcome the governance challenges, and illustrates the range of tools that could be used to do so.

Conceptual distinctions

Governance

The 'new' governance literature offers several conceptual distinctions that raise important points about the rise of complexity in societal organisations, the increased importance of technology, the ambiguity of cause-and-effect relations and more diverse relationships within the political process; all these points are incorporated into the understanding of the challenges to governance raised in the next section (Kickert 1993; Kooiman 1993). Certainly, these pressures are affecting the ability of the state to govern society by traditional means (Rhodes 1996). Nevertheless, we must be wary of some of the implications of the new governance approach and, accordingly, this chapter adheres more closely to the second particular notion of governance of the two described by Pierre and Peters (2000). With this approach to governance there is a recognition of the blurring of the boundaries of what is political but also the realisation that power struggles occur at all levels of the political arena. In the EU context, this political struggle is occurring in a number of new areas beyond the state, but also beyond the supranational process in Brussels – for example in the role of individual regions within a state and the role of international and local interest groups.

Civil society

There is a rich literature on social movements and the importance of civil society, particularly at the national level. In the specific area of democratic transition and consolidation, Linz and Stepan (1996) provide a useful definition of civil society: 'that arena of the polity where self-organizing groups, movements and individuals, relatively autonomous from the state, attempt to articulate values, create associations and solidarities, and advance their interests.'

Although this is a useful starting point, the nature of environmental problems and policy requires us to push the civil society concept beyond its traditional domestic boundaries (Wapner 1995; Keck and Sikkink 1998). Notions of global civil society in world politics may encompass both domestic and international participation by individuals and organisations. Equally important, actions to influence government policy and citizens' perception of civil society itself may come from domestic and international sources. Thus, we must look at how institutional structures and policy ideas at all levels of the environmental area (i.e. subnational, national, EU and international) shape each other and constrain the nature of governance and civil society.

This chapter acknowledges that many of the claims made for global civil society are problematic. There is an assumption in some of the literature that such civil society necessarily empowers groups; at the same time, however, there are real questions about whether the empowering happens for some members of society but not others (Amoore and Langley 2004). The concept may mask the contradictions and tensions felt by the included and excluded members of society within this political activity (e.g. the anti-capitalist movement). While acknowledging this danger (the EU Commission has stressed that civil society organisations need strong forms of openness and accountability), the fact remains that institutions such as the Commission have explicitly acknowledged that some form of civil society is necessary to improve European governance (Commission of the European Communities 2001b). The Commission views this entity as one of the most significant means of giving voice to citizens in the EU policy process. Obviously, the European Parliament and the national parliaments provide representation, as do the Committee of the Regions and the national governments within the Council of Ministers, but civil society is one direct means of more actively involving groups in the EU policy process, in a way that promotes some steering by societal actors (through feedback and criticisms) and which thus enhances the legitimacy of the EU process.

Theoretical explanations

This chapter combines a 'thicker' institutional approach with a focus on ideational explanations. 'Thick' is a shorthand for arguing that policy analysis should move away from the purely formal notion of institutions (i.e. rules that rational actors create to advance their interests, as formulated by Riker and others – see for example Riker 1980). Instead, we move towards a more sociological understanding of the independent effect that institutions, and the values they contain, may have on environmental actors. While rules are important and define actors' choices, over the longer term the implicit norms within the institutions also define the identity and views of reality for the actors that operate them. Over time, actors are less able to set goals independently of the institutional context (Aspinwall and Schneider 2001). Accordingly, this chapter borrows from more formal and rationalistic perspectives in terms of thinking about 'veto points' and the opportunity structures that actors can utilise (Kitchelt 1986; Immergut 1992) but emphasises the institutional ability to shape decision-making paths and identity, as argued in more sociological analyses (March and Olsen 1989).

Embedded in the EU policy process are also ideas and ways of viewing the world (Goldstein 1993). Ideas provide the means for making choices and establishing the rules of the game, and serve as the focus for new policies and political coalitions (Goldstein and Keohane 1993). Ideas need particular actors to push and promote them in the policy process. In comparison with institutional analysis, ideational explanations have a greater focus on the potential for significant, non-incremental policy change.

To bring these institutional and ideational elements together, Hall (1993) provides a useful outline of the components of a policy area, differentiating between structure, style and content. For Hall, policy structure covers the administrative structures of government and the procedural arrangements that develop and implement policy.

Policy style refers to the way in which institutional actors normally go about making environmental policy decisions and how they involve interested societal actors; this value encompasses both rules and the attitudes of institutional actors. Policy content has three aspects. The first is the goals of the policy; these are centred on a framework of ideas that explain how the goals operate and that indicate the means of attaining these goals. As Goldstein (1993) discusses, those policy goals/ ideas can become embedded in the institutional structure. The second aspect is the instruments or means of achieving the policy goals. The final aspect is the precise calibration of the policy instruments. These concepts are heuristic notions that often overlap; they provide a more systematic way of studying how civil society is engaged in the EU process and what solutions the EU is developing to handle the larger governance question.

The governance challenges

As with Hall's notions of policy structure, style and content, the governance challenges offered here need to be understood as heuristic concepts: they encompass a number of factors that impinge on effective EU environmental governance. It is expected that these factors interact to create even stronger challenges for the players in the EU arena. While there are other governance tensions that might be considered, the four studies looked at here are more focused on the challenges from the civil society perspective (Zito 2005). There are also important governance tensions, such as the tension between the territorial and supranational political authority within the EU, and that between more central political authority and the more local authorities. This type of tension cuts across more of the EU policy process and is not considered here (Flynn 2003).

The epistemic effect

Environmental scholarship has closely examined the concept of 'epistemic communities'. Haas (1992) defines these communities as networks of professionals with recognised expertise in a particular domain and an authoritative claim to policy-relevant knowledge in that area. In circumstances of policy uncertainty (due to lack of knowledge or ambiguous linkages to other issue priorities), the arguments of the epistemic community can persuade decision-makers to alter their policies substantially. The real impact of epistemic communities is arguably quite limited in the EU context; even where they exist, their influence may be limited to very particular circumstances. For example, the influence of the epistemic community tends to be stronger in helping to define problems and the policy agenda than in helping to sway political negotiations over policy (Zito 2001). Furthermore, knowledge of policy problems and solutions does not necessarily require a sophisticated understanding of cause and effect to be useful to policy-makers; a practical solution that incorporates past environmental policy experience can prove equally important.

Accordingly, 'epistemic' is used here to label a broader set of knowledge than Haas's (1992) definition. Whether or not they use epistemic knowledge, the EU and member states face a number of complex issues that must be decided under conditions of uncertainty, with global warming perhaps being at the head of the list. However, knowledge of such issues is not distributed evenly or widely within the EU. There are too many complex environmental issues that require enormous technical resources to study and to develop a response for a regional organisation and its membership to manage in a completely independent fashion. This leads to the involvement of international organisations, particularly those that have specialised in particular issue areas. Young (1994) notes a tendency of international organisations developing new environmental regimes to 'piggyback' on the expertise and efforts of other international organisations. There is an explicit desire to avoid duplication of effort. It is natural in this context for the EU member states and Commission, especially given the small resource base of its Directorate-General for the Environment, to embrace the policy ideas and experiences of international organisations.

Simultaneously, it is important to realise that many environmental policy areas are more routine, but even so a tremendous amount of information is required in order for European policy to be effectively implemented and monitored. The sheer number of regulations in place has led the Commission to emphasise the need to pursue implementation issues in its strategic documents (e.g. the Fifth Environmental Action Programme – Commission of the European Communities 1993), financial schemes and other instruments (Jordan 1999b).

The situation represents both a challenge and an opportunity for different environmental actors. Care must be taken to emphasise that knowledge has an intensely political and conflictual role; the assumption that a rational, scientific decision-making calculus will determine the issue outcome is problematic. Distributive gains and losses for domestic interests occur when this knowledge triggers a particular regulatory response. Those actors with the ability to contribute (if only by providing information) will gain a greater voice, but other actors may find it more difficult to wield influence. As an illustration, the Commission must carefully listen to all technical advice and information concerning an issue when it is developing a policy proposal. As will be discussed below, typical civil society actors like NGOs and consumer groups only in very rare cases can provide such information. This is more likely only if the technical arena for the debate involves inter-national institutions, which have their own problems of legitimacy. Both the Commission as well as those representatives of other interests face a major resource issue of trying to attain the knowledge required to steer EU policy towards particular goals.

The Schattschneider effect and forum shopping

In *The Semisovereign People*, Schattschneider (1960) noted how key political decisions can rest on whether or not groups seeking to change the status quo succeed in expanding 'the scope of conflict'. This thesis posits that most policies have an established group of actors surrounding them and that they will seek to keep the issue defined on their terms. Actors who wish to end the status quo have to broaden the debate to include other interested actors who are also dissatisfied with the status quo, who might tip the political balance against the established network. Thus, when particular actors seek to gain support for their effort to modify the EU agenda, they may go 'forum shopping': the arena is widened to include other actors who favour changing the status quo. This may involve switching arenas by going to other institutional bodies (Dudley and Richardson 1998; Kellow and Zito 2002).

The stark complexity of the EU institutional process is clear, as is its continual evolution (Sbragia 1993). This complexity holds true more for issue areas – such as the environment – that have been included in the Community legal framework within the EU. Because the environ-mental policy rules of the game largely have been fixed in treaties, the supranational institutions (the Commission, the Parliament and European Court of Justice) have a very significant policy role alongside the more territorially oriented Council of Ministers.

This creates an environmental policy process in which a significant number of institutions help to define the agenda and can help to block particular decisions. Consequently, certain actors strive to enhance the territorial interests of particular states while other institutions promote other priorities, which may reflect more supranational or narrower interests of the institutions or their clientele. Actors must promote their policies across this complex chain of institutions and build a supporting coalition at each of these veto points in order to achieve any regulatory output (Weale 1996; Zito 2000). This enables actors who perhaps have been excluded from the Council's or Commission's deliberations to build a base of support and to expand the scope of conflict in a European Parliament armed with co-decision power.

However, the picture for individual actors is even more complicated. Given what international institutions contribute to the addressing of policy issues, environmental actors have the opportunity to expand the scope of conflict within the EU process by acting at the international level. For example, in 1995, during negotiations over the 'Basel Ban Amendment' to the Basel Convention on the movement of hazardous waste, Denmark, Greenpeace and allied ENGOs wielded disproportionate influence, and essentially sabotaged an agreed position by the Commission and Council (Kellow and Zito 2002). In the wake of the successful 1989 negotiations at the United Nations Environment Programme on the Basel Convention, a substantial split emerged between the waste-exporting industrialised countries and the developing countries and ENGOs. In the 1995 Basel conference, the Danish government broke ranks and joined the ENGOs and developing countries in calling for an outright ban on all waste exports. The EU position, as promoted by the Commission, which would have banned the export only of waste intended for disposal, was completely undermined, resulting in an outright EU ban in 1997 (Kellow 1999).

Both international involvement and actual international policies can give European environmental actors more leverage for the same issue area and more general influence in the EU and in domestic politics. At the same time, economic interests may seek to loosen EU regulations by raising the issue at the level of international organisations. The complexity of the EU process, which is linked closely to the efforts of international institutions, provides a different layer of uncertainty (in contrast to scientific uncertainty about the nature of environmental problems). Actors who have a greater understanding of the EU process will have an advantage. Nevertheless, the uncertainty remains for all actors: the Basel waste negotiations are a clear example of the Commission being ambushed by its fellow EU actors. This makes it more difficult for actors to steer towards particular goals.

The cross-cutting regime effect and problems of integration

Much of the complexity inherent in environmental policy results from its nested status in other important global issue areas, particularly economic ones. We must not forget that the common market was the heart of the historical European integration process and the roots of EU environmental policy. Before the Single European Act (SEA) of 1987, environmental policy had no treaty basis and could not be considered as a European policy area in its own right. The European Community's environmental policies reflected the fact that the main priority for much of the legislation was to harmonise national regulations that would otherwise restrict trade, or to protect the health and life of the EU biosphere – provided the measures did not restrict trade in an unfair manner. The dominant policy idea of this period was the protection of the common market.

Over time, starting with the SEA and continuing with the 'Danish bottle case' (a landmark ruling in 1988 that accepted the principle that environmental concerns might outweigh common market concerns – see *Commission* v. *Denmark*, C-302/86), environmental priorities have played a greater role in the EU's constitutional basis; this has also been reflected in a number of the member states – particularly the more pioneering northern states. Even with the full inclusion of environmental issues within the treaties, the increasingly competitive international trade arena places heavy competing demands on EU policy officials, who have to consider all the variables that might affect the EU's trading position and economic growth. Since the Maastricht Treaty of 1992, the Amsterdam and Nice Treaties have given a greater place to the concept of sustainability, which extends to the integration of environmental concerns into other policy priorities. Nevertheless, the actualisation of a sustainability policy idea/world view in the policy outputs and processes of EU environmental policy has been more limited in reality (Lenschow and Zito 1998: 429–31).

It is possible to take a too pessimistic outlook on this development. Justin Greenwood and others have noted the relative success of environmental campaigners in forcing the EU agenda to prioritise the environment.[1] Certainly in relation to biotechnology, environmental actors have had a considerable role in providing the direction in areas of high economic growth, where EU nations have hoped to take the lead. More generally, particular national governments and EU bodies may have pushed successfully for stricter environmental legislation at the EU level in the past. However the balance may appear to environmental and economic actors, the overall fact remains: the prioritisation of both economic and environmental objectives raises the constant possibility of tension. In 2005, this was seen most dramatically in the discussion of the EU chemical policy reform regulation (known as REACH – Registration, Evaluation and Authorisation of Chemicals). The initial Commission vision was seen as far too onerous for business; nevertheless, the green lobby fought hard to protect parts of the regulation, such as the rules concerning the authorisation of chemicals of high concern (*ENDS Environment Daily* 2005).

The policy tensions are reflected in the functional organisational structure of the EU. The individual Commission Directorates-General, the European Parliament committees and the individual Council meetings and smaller group meetings contribute to a specialised policy process in which it is difficult to integrate perspectives and priorities within and across institutions. This functional reality creates the possibilities for conflict within organisations motivated by bureaucratic self-interest (e.g. the desire to protect their own clientele, such as ENGOs) or by policy ideas oriented around the particular views and priorities of those who dominate the issue area. Given the longer historical standing of more traditional policy areas at both the member state and EU level, particularly centred on fiscal/economic management and the common market, the economic Directorates-General of the Commission and the economic Councils generally have more prestige and influence than their environment counterparts. Thus, when political conditions indicate a tension between protecting economic growth (the common market policy idea/principle) and more sustainable development, relative influence can become critical. In this vein, it is the Competition Council that has negotiated the key aspects of the REACH legislation.

The sectoral differentiation and various ambitions of the EU lead to a further pervasive problem directly relevant to environmental policy-making. The ideational principle of sustainable development suggests that there must be an integration of environmental concerns into the other EU policy areas (Commission of the European Communities 1993). The deeply sectoral nature of EU decision-making in the major institutions makes this a difficult hurdle. For example, elements of the Commission, Council and Parliament have been able to take decisions that benefit agricultural interests in a way that has been detrimental to the environment.

Recognising this situation, the Commission pushed the principle of sustainable development in its Fifth Environmental Action Programme (Commission of the European Communities 1993). The Commission, more concretely, decided to make a number of changes to its own organisational structure, such as the creation of 'integration correspondents' in each Directorate-General (Schout and Jordan 2003). Far greater legal and constitutional validity was given to this proposal by its incorporation into article 6 of the Amsterdam Treaty of 1997. Nevertheless, the fact remains that the increase in horizontal coordination has been problematic and requires some remedy as well as leadership to increase the flow of information across policy-making units (Schout and Jordan 2003).

Given how the tension between different policy arenas and interests manifests itself both in the macro policy negotiations and in the more micro administration found within the EU process, it becomes potentially more difficult to steer towards environmental objectives. Indeed, conversations with Commission officials in 2003 revealed how the non-environment Directorates-General have used the concept of policy integration to force the Directorate-General for the Environment to take into consideration other EU policy values.

Problems of political authority and legitimacy

Perhaps the most significant governance challenge facing EU environmental policy and the EU more generally is the problematic linkage between the 'community method', with its focus on good policy outputs, and European society at large, which confers legitimacy and authority to the EU. As this has already been addressed in this chapter and in the other contributions to these volumes, the discussion here is brief. The Commission's white paper on governance makes this issue the point of departure for its discussion of the governance problem (Commission of the European Communities 2001b). By the Commission's own estimation, the gulf between the EU system and its people is widening and has substantial implications: the inability of the EU to act effectively in areas where it is clearly needed, the lack of credit given to the EU process for improving quality of life, the lack of communication by the member states about the EU process, and a general ignorance about EU institutional actors and what they do (Commission of the European Communities 2001b).

The heavily technical nature of EU environmental policy requires early discussions among policy experts, where the presence of a democratic representative is unlikely to be influential. Furthermore, the Commission has used the knowledge and arguments of expert groups to overcome objections raised by economic and political interests in order to create environmental policy – so there is a strong political dimension to the nature of this process (Héritier 1997). This EU reality is only strengthened when one takes into account the role of the international arena in shaping actual EU policies.

ENGOs and civil society

Having laid out the specific governance challenges that confront policy actors in the EU environmental arena, it is now time to explore how these challenges affect the position of civil society actors. Because of space constraints, this chapter looks solely at ENGOs. ENGOs certainly do not represent all aspects of civil society, but they are typically the most active voice; their constraints and opportunities illuminate what scope all of civil society can have in trying to steer the EU towards stronger environmental protection. ENGOs must surmount all the governance challenges mentioned previously, usually with very limited resources.

The first subsection below explores the more constitutional, structural aspects of EU environmental policy. The second looks at the institutional opportunity structures that the EU system allows for the involvement of civil society. The third subsection examines the ENGO response to this situation and how the EU process is being used to link civil society more to the environmental policy process.

Constitutional, institutional and ideational foundations

As was the case with its effort to enhance policy integration and coordination, the Commission has used explicit recognition of the stakeholders in the Environmental Action Programmes, particularly the Fifth (Commission of the European Communities 1993), to contend that wider societal participation is necessary for effective environmental policy. Consequently, the Commission has proposed various new policy instruments and directives to involve society. For example, the EU has created an eco-label[2] and introduced the 1990 Information Directive to empower societal groups and, through this widening participation, to increase the EU's legitimacy (Héritier 1999a). The EU has a clear incentive to do so because the treaties significantly limit the scope of EU policy power: member states continue to control EU financing and policy implementation in areas such as the environment. While the states must implement environmental policies with some Commission oversight, their dominance of this process is even stronger because the Commission's limited resources make it difficult for it to monitor implementation (Jordan 1999b). These substantial institutional constraints have led the EU to focus on regulatory environmental policies (Majone 1997).

Mapping the actors and opportunity structures

Given the complex web of EU institutions (and their relations with other international institutions, as well as with the democratic political regimes in the member states), it appears that the opportunity structure for ENGOs is considerable. However, the actual opportunity structure is more contingent on the policy and political context. The institutional multiplicity gives ENGOs numerous chances to insert their voice into the process. Nevertheless, while the complex institutional chain allows actors to have influence on the agenda, the long link of bargains requires a truly significant effort to *maintain* the issue on the agenda. This difficulty in maintaining a favoured definition of a problem and its solution intact (the problem of agenda maintenance – see Zito 2000) through the complex chain creates considerable limitations on how ENGOs can affect outcomes.

Policy stage analysis reveals how EU opportunity structures may vary during the development of policy. For instance, the Commission has a particularly significant role in problem definition and the setting of the EU policy agenda. With its very limited staff and budget, however, it requires substantial input from the knowledge communities based at both the national and regional levels. The Directorate-General for the Environment, traditionally perceived as being less prestigious and more junior within the Commission, has sought to build an actor network to assist it. The network provides essential material and knowledge support, but also confers legitimacy on the Directorate-General for the Environment *vis-à-vis* the other institutions and other Directorates-General, and pre-empts opposition from these same groups in the network.

While the Commission still retains the dominant role in formulating legislative proposals, it requires information and resource support to develop proposals; it also needs to build consensus with the other veto players, the Council and the European Parliament (Bomberg and Burns 1999). If we combine this consultation dynamic with the process of deciding proposals, both the Parliament and the Council, as well as the member state representatives acting individually, provide important opportunity structures. The opportunity structure in the Council varies for each national ENGO in terms of how open the national structure is to the ENGO's interests and policy world view. The European Parliament has several access points through its pan-European parties, including a substantial green party presence, and its highly prominent Environment Committee (Judge 1993; Bomberg and Burns 1999). There are, however, numerous constraints that limit the impact of the Parliament: lack of a coherent party system, lack of voter interest in both the parties and the body as a whole, and lack of resources to provide truly independent policy viewpoints. The lack of resources actually makes the European Parliament more receptive to ENGOs, which can provide knowledge and even develop amendments and other legislative wording that Members can simply adopt.[3]

The Economic and Social Committee, created in 1957 with the Treaty of Rome, represents another institutional effort to incorporate civil society into the EU process. It is also the formal channel for interest groups to insert their views. Nevertheless, the Committee remains a consultative body that the supranational institutions have largely ignored (Jeffery 2002). Moreover, the Committee reflects the initial common market orientation of the EU in the organisation of its membership, although the presence of environmental groups in one of the horizontal groups and the existence of an environmental section has made the institution relatively green (McCormick 2001; Jeffery 2002).

Although ENGOs have opportunity structures throughout the policy stages, there are significant limitations. EU agenda maintenance requires knowledge and political exertion at each stage of the process and with regard to each veto point. Given the immense range of environmental issues discussed in the governance challenges section above, as well as the EU's institutional complexity, not even large and powerful ENGOs such as Greenpeace can take on more than a limited set of issues.[4]

The ENGO reaction to the EU environment

As environmental policy has become increasingly important for the EU, ENGOs have made greater efforts to influence the policy process and organise their strategy. However, because other societal interests have also gained awareness of the need to lobby the EU, ENGOs face greater lobbying competition. Nevertheless, relatively few ENGOs have a permanent presence in Brussels, and those that do tend to have small offices. Most ENGOs concentrate their presence and influence at the national level (Rucht 1993). This reality leads the groups to cooperate relatively closely, in the manner described below (Grant et al. 2000).

To reiterate, the ENGOs' opportunity structures in the policy process have significant limitations. Agenda maintenance at the EU level requires the knowledge and the exertion of political resources at each stage of the process and with regards to each veto point. Moreover ENGOs traditionally (though the next section notes the potential changes in this area) have lacked the kind of rights they would find at the national level, including the right to information (Rucht 1993). Thus, their provision of information and the early and sustained consultation about the EU agenda has occurred in a largely *ad hoc* and arbitrary fashion, and on an informal basis. ENGOs do not have the right of standing before the European Court of Justice (Grant et al. 2000).

The Directorate-General for the Environment, in its efforts to build an environmental coalition to support its position, has even gone so far as to provide a substantial amount of financial support for certain ENGOs, such as the European Environmental Bureau (EEB) (Mazey and Richardson 1992). Even as recently as 2003, the Commission, for example, provided over 42 per cent of the EEB's funding, which the EEB leadership has interpreted as giving the Bureau some responsibility to act as the ENGO representative across a wide range of policy issues, often less well covered by ENGOs (European Environmental Bureau 2003). The Directorate-General for the Environment also funds the Health and Environment Alliance.[5] However, various actors have criticised this Directorate–ENGO interdependence, arguing that both parties have lost autonomy and independence of thinking as a result of it. Another consequence has been the tendency for both parties to neglect other important (e.g. economic) institutions and interest groups. Nevertheless, Grant et al. (2000: 52) argue that ENGOs tend to suffer from fewer conflicts within the group than their economic counterparts, which enables more cooperation and unity in presenting policy views.

The factors mentioned above have led the ENGOs to pool their resources and divide the European effort among themselves (Long 1998; Grant et al. 2000). A few umbrella groups have been created that operate in Brussels, such as the Greenpeace International European Unit and the EEB. ENGOs also tend to participate in single-issue coalitions, such as Climate Network Europe (Grant et al. 2000). When ENGOs have difficulty in moving the political system towards their perspective they can engage in leverage politics by playing the EU institutions, particularly the Commission, against the member state governments. Thus, lobbying action and participation occur at both national and regional levels. The more organised and better resourced ENGOs have sought to build networks and orchestrate campaigns. Such campaigns have involved the simultaneous lobbying of different EU institutions, as well as efforts to mobilise national groups to influence policy in their own countries. Larger ENGOs such as the WWF and the Royal Society for the Protection of Birds have made a point of creating programmes to provide information for various national groups and to represent these in Brussels (Corrie 1997).

The multiplicity of issues and the complexity of the EU system have led some of the major groups to form the Green 10 (which started out as the Green 4 but grew). This loose, informal grouping, which includes Greenpeace and the Health and Environment Alliance, helps to coordinate the regional ENGO effort.[6] There is a tendency for the group members to specialise rather than attempt to cover all issues. While the Green 10 has an important and very visible presence because of its membership, Warleigh (2000) argues that loose, fluid and *ad hoc* coalitions consisting of more actors are often the key means by which NGOs influence EU policy.

Nevertheless, the knowledge/capacity building and leverage linkages have remained a major ENGO priority because of the enormous impact of EU enlargement. Organisations like the EEB have recruited new members, covering all of the accession countries.[7] The EEB, the WWF and other groups have sought to promote workshops and other learning activities to train accession ENGOs; besides educating them in knowledge strategies, there is a conscious effort to train the groups and enhance their role as members of both the national and EU civil society (Bomberg 2003).

Turning to the specific policy stages at which ENGOs can influence the EU process, there is the important agenda-setting role of providing information and lobbying support to the definition of environmental problems and the selection of solutions (e.g. the Blue Flag for water quality). They have sought to target member state representatives, Commission officials and Members of the European Parliament (MEPs) with specific policy information and amendments. They have mustered their constituents to voice their opinion and used media occasions to attack their opponents' positions. ENGO research suggests that successful past collaborations, recognised expertise and a large membership are the criteria that make certain ENGOs more attractive to EU policy actors (Warleigh 2000).

At the same time, however, ENGOs seem to lack the knowledge and resources to fully lobby member state delegations and the Council secretariat, even when circumstances lead these actors to welcome ENGO activity (Warleigh 2000). In the EU negotiation process, ENGO position and support may change the opinion of institutional actors, but this is less likely; the more likely scenario is that they provide support and ammunition for the coalition of actors that shares a similar position. Thus, other actors adopt the ENGO position to assist their campaign and perhaps use the ENGO position to mask their own position from attack (Warleigh 2000).

The ENGOs' resource problem makes it difficult for them to have a sustained policy presence throughout all the steps of the institutional policy-making process; they also often lack the detailed expertise needed to calibrate and evaluate policy instruments (Grant et al. 2000). ENGOs have striven hard to influence the EU policy-selection process, not only in terms of taking positions on specific policy instruments such as regulations, but also in terms of pushing for the adoption of wider principles and policy attitudes to regulation.

Turning to the issues of implementation and monitoring of policy, the ENGOs have played a substantial role in particular aspects of these stages. One obvious role is the reporting of what is happening at the national level – Keck and Sikkink's informational and accountability politics (Keck and Sikkink 1998). This effort can also involve coalition-building and leverage politics. For example, in trying to increase the emphasis on sustainable development in EU regional policy, the WWF coordinated an effort to build awareness of the topic and to provide opportunities for discussion among the various interests (Corrie 1997).

Throughout all the policy-making processes, ENGOs struggle with institutional complexity, limited access to particular negotiating arenas and the sheer resource demands of playing a significant role in the development of a technical policy. This position is only heightened when considering policy areas where the EU is negotiating international treaties and interacting with international institutions, which tend to have very limited opportunity structures for civil society. Nevertheless, an ENGO with a good understanding of the EU and international process is able to play the Schattschneider game, as Greenpeace and other ENGOs have demonstrated. Focusing strategically on media-friendly angles on complex negotiations occurring at the international level may allow ENGOs to define aspects of the debate, as was seen in the Basel negotiations. Nevertheless, the complexity of the issues and the process ensures that ENGOs tend to intervene on very specific points and that means that the civil society dimension to the EU process is potentially lacking for a whole host of issues.

Bridging the governance challenges

This section samples the range of policy solutions that the EU has at its disposal to address these governance challenges to the involvement of civil society. It concentrates on Hall's differentiation between the structure of the policy process and the content of the policies (i.e. macro versus more micro approaches), subsuming policy style into the more structural argument (Hall 1993). There is no attempt to argue that there is one solution or method of governance. Indeed, the dominant metaphor of this section is to argue that the EU consists of an evolving patchwork of governance. Some of the patchwork is based on the evolution of formal institutions and law, while some is based on what Héritier (1997) calls 'second order' (i.e. more informal) policy structures. At the same time, there will be both formal interactions between institutions and society and more informal networking. Finally, the EU environmental policy will reflect a mixture of 'hard' regulatory measures – those that involve specifying certain defined activities on the part of stakeholders – and 'softer' environmental measures – those that give greater flexibility and sometimes even a greater role to other policy actors. The expectation is not that this basket of instruments and processes will fully overcome the governance challenges listed; one model is unlikely to provide all the solutions. Rather, there should be an incremental path of building layers of process that involve civil society and protect the environment.

Policy structures

In discussing processes and networks it is sometimes easy to forget the importance of law. Nevertheless, the EU does have some opportunities to create rules by which to force greater environmental policy integration and civil society involvement. An important example is the constitutional convention that agreed a treaty draft in June 2003. The convention was a clear opportunity for all EU actors to shape the institutional rules of the game at the highest intergovernmental level. The EEB, representing the Green 9 (as it was at the time), joined the Contact Group of Civil Society, which was formed to promote the involvement of civil society in the work of the convention (European

Environmental Bureau 2003). Its membership included a range of NGO networks – social groups, human rights groups as well as the European Trade Union Confederation. Besides acting as a conduit for the opinions of national and regional social groups and seeking to influence the opinions of convention secretariat, the group sought to inform and mobilise its constituency.

The Green 9 wished to put forward a coordinated submission to the convention and proposed the insertion of various references to the principle of sustainable development in the draft constitutional treaty. Repeated lobbying by pro-environment actors managed to get some environmental principles included, such as an environmental policy integration principle into a specific section (Hallo 2003). Nevertheless, the Green 9's other proposals to enhance the presence of sustainability in both the EU process and its institutional principles met with less success. The convention did introduce an article on the broad aims of 'participatory democracy' (which included the environmental concerns) but the ENGOs found it too vague and would have preferred stronger language (Hallo 2003). Given the mixed results and the clear continued priority given to economic over environmental objectives, the ENGOs face an uphill struggle. At present, the EU constitution is in hiatus (as a result of the French and Dutch referenda); however, the outcomes of the convention suggest that any *ad hoc* attempt to negotiate a solution to the constitution would not advance ENGOs' position with respect to opportunity structures.

Much less publicised but perhaps a much more critical development, if US environmental history is at all suggestive, is the EU effort to implement the Århus Convention, an international agreement which was signed in 1998 to enhance citizen access to information and participation in environmental decision-making. It is important to emphasise the role that another international institution has had on civil society's relationship to the EU process, as in this case a clear opportunity to enhance the ENGO position has resulted. As a result of the obligations the EU undertook in signing this international treaty, the Commission has drawn up several pieces of legislation to implement the Convention, including a directive under the rubric of 'Access to Justice', which would allow ENGOs to go to the European Court of Justice (Commission of the European Communities 2003). Officials of the Directorate-General for the Environment have sought to involve ENGOs in this discussion, in order to help the development and build a political coalition in support of the legislation.[8]

The Council and European Parliament have agreed two directives proposed by the Commission to implement the Convention: Directive 2003/4/EC, on public access to environmental information, and Directive 2003/35/EC, on public participation (Commission of the European

Communities 2005a). The most interesting directive has been proposed but not yet adopted, namely that on access to justice. Given the potential role of NGOs and other actors in redressing environmental failures through the court system, as seen in the United States, which organisations will be able to seek justice is one of the contested issues in the EU formulation.[9] The EEB believes that the member states are moving very slowly on the proposal for the directive on access to justice (European Environmental Bureau 2005: 3).

In addition to this proposal, the Commission adopted two more, one for a regulation to apply the Århus Convention to EU institutions and the other for a decision to ratify the Convention (Commission of the European Communities 2005a). In December 2004, the Environment Council agreed for the Commission to ratify the Århus Convention, which the Commission proceeded to do in February 2005. This ratification came in spite of the opposition of the ENGOs, particularly the EEB, which were calling for a delay to the ratification. The EEB argued that the ratification violated the spirit of the Convention because the modifications made by the Environment Council to the draft regulation to implement the Convention conflicted with the objectives of the Århus Convention (European Environmental Bureau 2005).

Policy content

The more 'macro' provisions for access to information and the prominence of environmental concerns in the EU constitution have the potential to have a far-reaching impact on environmental policy and civil society, and accordingly have occupied the lion's share of this section. Nevertheless, given the protracted and contingent nature of this structural evolution, as witnessed in the negotiations over both the constitution and the Århus Convention, it may well be the case that the more substantial governance change will result from the promotion of democratic legitimisation at the level of policy content. The EU has built its substantial policy platform through traditional means of command and control regulation (Jordan et al. 2003). Since 1992 there has been a change in the philosophy behind this regulatory tool. In part, this effort has involved a recognition by the Commission and other EU actors that EU policies must address some of the governance challenges mentioned above, for example the integration of both economic and environmental concerns and the process of sharing responsibility in a way that enhances involvement and thus helps legitimisation.

In terms of more traditional, legislative tools, this process involves integrating principles of transparency, for example with the inclusion of clauses giving the public a right of access to information (Héritier

1999b). The Water Framework Directive is a good example of the evolution of traditional regulation in this regard, as it specifies that member states' implementation plans must involve public information and consultation (Commission of the European Communities 2001a). Essentially, the member states have an obligation to encourage all interested parties to be involved in the planning, with the potential for the creation of local networks interested in the management of a particular river. The directive grants the possibility for member states to use a second type of instrument – an economic one – that helps with the sectoral/integration governance challenge. The EU and the individual member states are increasingly turning to these instruments (Jordan et al. 2003). A third type of EU instrument that increasingly is being used is informational instruments, such as eco-labels and environmental management standards. There is some doubt about the actual environmental impact these instruments have, and there are further concerns about how well civil society groups are incorporated into the process (i.e. in the actual specification of the standards). Nevertheless, these instruments do have the potential to involve societal actors in a way that spreads responsibility for environmental choices and that gives ENGOs potential benchmarks to target politically.

Conclusion

This chapter has presented four major challenges for EU environmental policy and looked at how to ensure an effective role of civil society in the policy process. The picture painted is of the actors facing a situation rather analogous to Keohane and Nye's idea of complex interdependence and nested issues (Keohane and Nye 1989). The fact that difficult issues are nested in other political issues and the fact that unforeseen linkages are made by other actors have made the job of steering the EU towards specific goals much more unpredictable. Power and influence most decidedly do exist in this governance system, but they are more likely to manifest themselves in unpredictable ways. However, this should not be viewed necessarily in a negative light, as it may lead to political opportunity.

The chapter then examines, by way of illustration, the specific position of ENGOs, which represent only one kind of actor within civil society's engagement with EU environmental policy. ENGOs confront numerous EU environmental issues but possess very limited organisational resources. In this context, the many technical issues and the complexity of the EU process, which may involve diplomatic negotiations between international actors, make the ENGOs' position even more difficult. Nevertheless, the complex reality of the policy process (in terms of both the epistemic and the Schattschneider effects) does allow the strategic coalition of actors the opportunity to make use of veto points and gives them new arenas in which to shape the governance agenda in their own way. There are chances to exert influence on the steering of the EU policy.

Because of resource constraints and the complexity of the challenge, it is difficult for ENGOs to sustain such effort across both many issue areas and all the policy stages. In terms of evidence of ENGOs shaping the EU process, the fact remains that key ENGO actors see their organisations as mainly *reacting* to the EU institutional process, although they attempt to take an active strategy in their reactions (Rucht 1993). However, cases such as the Basel Convention suggest that all EU actors are suffering to some degree from these challenges. This creates a dependence on the part of all actors, such as the Commission, and it gives actors with the necessary strategic skill the opportunities to exploit the system.

The EU does have opportunities for addressing these governance challenges; some involve formal processes while others are more informal. The basic reality of the EU environmental governance process is that it is both a regulatory and a political patchwork. The process of addressing these governance challenges is more likely to be incremental, but moves such as the change in institutional access to information and the incorporation of public involvement in EU legislation represent significant possibilities for civil society engagement in environmental protection.

Notes

1 For this part of the discussion, I am grateful to Justin Greenwood and the other participants at the workshop 'Multi-level Governance and Civil Society: Comparing the Influence of Non-state Actors in the United Nations and the European Union', Berlin, 14–15 October 2005, as well as Carlo Ruzza.

2 Eco-labels may engage civil society actors in the creation of the label, but more generally they create informational incentives for producers and consumers.

3 This was evident in interviews the author undertook with ENGO and European Parliament officials in 1992.

4 This was reported by ENGO officials in interview with the author in 1992 and 2001.

5 See www.env-health.org (accessed December 2006).

6 Author's interview with ENGO official, 23 September 2003.

7 Author's interview with ENGO official, 23 September 2003.

8 Author's interviews with Commission and ENGO officials, 23 September 2003.

9 Author's interview with ENGO official, 23 September 2003.

Chapter 5

The role of civil society organisations in written consultation processes: from the European Monitoring Centre to the European Fundamental Rights Agency

Emanuela Bozzini

Introduction

Written consultation, which constitutes a formal channel for the participation of citizens and associations, is gaining relevance at both the European and the national level. Together with petitions to the European Parliament (EP), committees, public hearings and so on, it offers opportunities for indirect participation at the European Union (EU) level and for the input of public preferences and knowledge in EU policy-making (Nentwich 1998). In terms of institutional design, participatory devices utilised at the EU level are not innovative *per se*; rather, it is their role in policy-making processes that is changing. Such a change may be understood as a consequence of the need to find an innovative balance between efficient and timely decision-making and the basic requirements of transparency and responsibility on the part of European institutions. As the literature on new forms of governance shows, one way to achieve this new balance may consist of enhancing the contribution of civil society in decision-making processes. Accordingly, an understanding of written forms of participation may shed some light on the role of civil society in European governance and on its implications for established notions of representation and accountability.

In this chapter, this topic is addressed by using the example of consultation over the establishment of the new European Fundamental Rights Agency (FRA).[1] The new Agency will replace the European Monitoring Centre on Racism and Xenophobia (EUMC), but will also extend its remit and tasks. The decision to convert the EUMC into the FRA proved controversial: as a first reaction, civil society organisations stressed the danger of diluting the fight against racism and criticised the European institutions' lack of commitment to the issue. In the autumn of 2004 a public consultation on the decision promoted by the Directorate-General for Freedom, Security and Justice took place, and this specific case constitutes the empirical study presented here. Through an analysis of policy documents and written contributions to the process of creating the new FRA, the functioning and the potential of the process of written consultation as a channel for organised civil society to access and influence the Commission is assessed.

In the first of the following four sections, the relevance of the institutionalisation of new forms of public participation is set with reference to the current debate on the embeddedness of deliberative practices in policy processes. In the second section, the focus is on the process of written consultation as a specific tool for enhancing civil society participation in decision-making. The case study is presented in the third part, and in the final section some concluding remarks on the potential of consultation processes are presented.

New institutional devices for public participation: theoretical issues

The need to strengthen public participation arises for a number of reasons, often linked to the so-called 'crises of politics', which suggest that states are no longer the only repositories of political authority and which question the legitimacy of traditional institutions for citizens' participation in political life (Maier 1987; Pierre and Peters 2000). In this light, a number of models for citizen participation have been proposed, particularly in the context of the debate on deliberative democracy. In general terms, the need to institutionalise 'deliberation' emerges from the need to enhance both equality and deliberation in collective decision-making; equality among voters and deliberation among elected representatives no longer guarantee the quality of policy processes and, at the end, the quality of democracy (Fishkin and Luskin 2000). Models of deliberative democracy are highly differentiated; in terms of prescriptions, they range from the institutionalisation of fora on specific issues for enhancing the effectiveness of decision-making (Cohen and Sabel 1997) to wide-ranging and spontaneous debate in the transnational public sphere of an open set of issues (Dryzek 1999, 2000).

There is a perception that democracy needs to be improved, and an innovation in the form of public participation is claimed to hold the most promise (Saward 2000). In this context, special attention is given to the role played by civil society organisations, because, particularly at the EU level, participation of citizens is equated with participation of *associations* of citizens (Nentwich 1998). The literature lists a number of advantages that derive from the inclusion of civil society in political processes: engagement in dialogue with civil society is seen as a viable way to enhance public participation, in the context of decreasing trust in political institutions (Pharr and Putnam 2000); civil society organisations can supplement political parties in informing debates and aggregating preferences (Budge 2000); and they can take account of the increased cultural and ethnic differentiation of European countries. Civil society organisations should also be involved in the implementation of policies, because public authorities are no longer able to deliver services that meet the needs of an increasingly differentiated population (Hirst 1997). At the EU level, the participation of civil society is said to be a useful way to address the perceived democratic deficit of the Union, and in this context organisations would be required to act as agents of political socialisation (Warleigh 2001).

Whatever the merits of and the expectations for the involvement of civil society, evidence is emerging of innovation in political practices of participation; for example, new institutional designs have been developed in many European countries, at both local and national levels. It is of note that even a cursory analysis of different experiences highlights the great variety of solutions that have been implemented in different contexts and in different policy areas within the common framework of civil society and citizens' participation. Reflections on the topic have a predominantly normative orientation; and systematic comparative research on institutional arrangements for public participation at different territorial levels and in different policy areas is still lacking. A partial exception consists of the so-called 'argumentative approach' in public policy studies (Fischer and Forester 1993), which has paid specific attention to deliberative practices in policy-making (Fischer 2003) and in planning (Forester 1999) at the local level. In this context, research has attempted to analyse the democratic potential of deliberative experimental devices, such as town meetings, citizens' juries, consensus conferences and deliberative polls (Fishkin and Luskin 2000), and to show under what conditions the direct involvement of citizens and stakeholders in decision-making can help to deliver solutions to 'intractable' policy issues, thanks to their local knowledge and their capacity to reframe problems in innovative ways (Hajer and Wagenaar 2003).

However, the use of written consultation – the focus of the present chapter – has received less attention; indeed, the 'status' of the tool of written consultation is not clear. It does not represent an innovative institutional design and it does not easily fit the theoretical framework of deliberative democracy.[2] Yet the relevance and the frequency of written consultation are growing. It is of note that it appears to be a channel for participation that is increasingly used by EU and national institutions in a variety of policy sectors, and its procedures have been recently regulated.[3]

From a normative point of view, the characteristics (for some scholars the very existence) of new institutional devices pose a number of challenging questions. We can concentrate on two main features: the criteria for the process of selection of citizens to be involved; and the existing formal and informal linkages between the deliberative forum and the institutions that are called to make binding decisions over an issue.

Empirical research suggests that, in terms of criteria for selection, a large variety of arrangements can be found. The main division, defined by the consequences inherent in each mode, is between institutional devices for the inclusion of individual citizens and those for the participation of associations, and examples of both can be found in different contexts. Town meetings and citizens' juries rely on self-selected people. In citizens' fora, members can be elected, or can be appointed by political authorities or by associations with an interest in the field. In deliberative polls, citizens are randomly sampled, while in written consultations the process can be either open to almost all citizens, associations and institutions; or focused, that is, open to a particular constituency or to selected stakeholders. Members can be involved as experts, as representatives of a particular territorial constituency or of a social group, as representatives of influential organisations, or as citizens with an interest in the issue. The main point here is the acceptance of the assumption that a group of twenty citizens or a selection of associations involved in a forum or in a jury has the legitimacy to represent the whole population, or at least all those citizens affected by the outcomes of a decision. If this assumption holds, deliberative devices should have a recognised role in the policy process.

This leads to the second dimension mentioned above. Generally, participatory devices such as citizens' fora, committees and so on have an advisory role and are not entitled to make binding collective decisions. This is in line with normative arguments: deliberative devices are generally considered complementary to established representative institutions and not an alternative to them. It is, therefore, essential to understand the role given to participatory devices in the policy process, the stage at which public participation takes place, and the use of outputs made by politicians. In particular, the transformation of the outputs of deliberative fora into binding collective decisions is a very sensitive issue, which is somehow neglected in theoretical reflections on deliberative democracy. As Gould points out:

> presumably because of Habermas' separation of communicative discourse from decision-making, these discursive interpretations of democracy focus exclusively on participation as talk or discussion or deliberation. In effect, it becomes all talk and no action, in the sense of effective decision-

making. We may say that while decision without deliberation is blind, deliberation without decision is empty. (Gould 1996)[4]

It is debatable whether the creation of deliberative devices really makes a difference in decision-making processes. From an empirical point of view, both successes and failures are emphasised: the creation of a forum for citizens' deliberation can lead to an effective empowerment of citizens (Fischer 2003) or to the marginalisation of an issue on the political agenda of representative institutions (Vertovec 1999).

Decisions over the institutional devices to be employed for including citizens and associations are themselves matters of political controversy, and it is of note that the demand for inclusion and participation is growing at all territorial levels. Research on the role of civil society organisations in European governance shows that formal channels for participation, such as public hearings and written consultations, are appreciated, although their effectiveness is perceived to be quite low and they tend to be considered a supplement to lobbying activities. In the next section, the general characteristics of the procedure for written consultation at the European level are presented, with particular attention paid to the consultation on the creation of the FRA.

Characteristics of the process of written consultation

General standards for consultation processes at the EU level were set by the Commission in 2002. The aim was to make practices for consulting civil society consistent, by laying down general principles and practices to be shared by all Directorates-General. Until 2002, each Directorate could adopt its own mechanism and procedure to engage in consultation with relevant sectoral interests; with the aim of guaranteeing transparency, the Commission proposed a common procedure and stated that 'the overall rationale of this document [Communication 704] is to ensure that all relevant parties are properly consulted' (Commission of the European Communities 2002).

The process of written consultation, as established by the Commission standards in 2002, can be subdivided into four stages:

1 the launch of the consultation by a Directorate-General;
2 the delivering of contributions by citizens and associations;
3 the summary of received contributions;
4 the results of the consultation being used in the decision-making process.

At each stage specific questions are presented, which in the rest of the section will be highlighted with reference to the consultation on the FRA.

In the first stage, the Commission drafts a policy and launches a consultation exercise with the production of a document that sets the areas for discussion and lists questions to be answered by civil society organisations and citizens. In discussing deliberative practices, Hajer and Wagenaar (2003) note that the definition of the issue has a crucial impact on the subsequent discussion, and on the way in which different topics are linked and causal mechanisms among phenomena are drawn. This argument applies to written consultation as well, and it is particularly relevant in the case study under analysis, as the initial decision, that is to the transform the EUMC into the FRA, was never a topic for discussion: rather, contributions were sought on how to proceed with it. Such considerations can be linked to the debate about the role that civil society organisations are expected to play in EU policy processes. The Commission stresses that it is important for the quality of EU policy to 'ensure wide participation throughout the policy chain – from conception to implementation' (Commission of the European Communities 2001b), but consultation generally takes place at the formulation stage of the decision-making process, and written contributions are not an exception. Thanks to its local knowledge and expertise, civil society is often able to produce policy solutions that match specific needs and to input innovative ideas into policy-making.

However, the potential for participation is a matter for debate at the theoretical level, and there are different opinions on whether citizens should be asked to deliberate over the general ends of a policy or over the specific content of policy measures. The argument here is that most citizens lack the specific knowledge to make decisions on highly technical or legal matters, and consequently their input should be limited to the broad directions of the policy sector. The counter-argument is that, if appropriately informed, citizens can discuss all issues in a fruitful and reasonable way.[5] In this light, civil society organisations are asked to play an important role in collecting and disseminating information, and, more generally, in socialising citizens to political issues. Indeed, the questions for the consultation on the FRA were quite complex and required a deep knowledge of the EU Charter and of the rather limited powers of the Commission in the field. The list included questions about how to structure the relationships between the new Agency and European and national institutions in the field of human rights protection (in particular, the Council of Europe, the EU Network of Independent Experts on Fundamental Rights and national bodies already operating in the human rights field), questions about methods of data collection, and questions on the formal role played by civil society organisations in implementation (for the full list of questions, see the appendix to this chapter).

In the second stage of the process of written consultation, civil society organisations submit their comments on the policy document proposed by the Commission and more specifically answer the questions listed. This can be a highly demanding task. As noted above with reference to the list of questions on the FRA, citizens and organisations need a high degree of specific knowledge on the European political environment to take part in the consultation process in a meaningful way. This is particularly difficult for local and national organisations, as research on the relationship between the national and European level highlights: the EU system is perceived to be highly complicated, and it seems to be necessary to focus 'full time' on Brussels policy processes in order to have an impact on them.

The large majority of contributions from civil society focus on (some or all of) the topics raised by the listed questions.[6] They present their arguments in a detailed way, giving reasons for their preferences, as we will see in a more detailed way in the next section. Ideally, in order to deliver a written contribution, each organisation should start an internal process of deliberation, involving its membership in a debate on the issue. Here, time is an important issue, affecting in a decisive way the number of participants and the quality of contributions. The Commission allows a period of eight weeks from the launching of the consultation exercise for the receipt of contributions. Eight weeks has been regarded as sufficient for the preparation of position papers and in the view of the Commission represents a good balance between the need to consult properly and the need to take timely decisions. Civil society organisations objected to the eight-week time limit at the time it was established (Commission of the European Communities 2002). In the specific case of the FRA, activists welcomed the process of consultation but at the same time stressed the need for more consultation, for widening the discussion and noted that it was not possible to organise a wide debate on the issues in two months:

> This seems to confirm the regrettable trend that the minimum standards for consultation are now, in practice, the maximum we can expect from the Commission, even in such an important case, that is the establishment of a new Agency with an entirely new mandate. (Social Platform)[7]

The process of written consultation is open to everyone, without limitation. In setting its procedures for consultation, the Commission stressed its willingness to adopt an inclusive approach and not to restrict the number of potential inputs. From this point of view, the selection of participants, which is a crucial stage in deliberative processes, appears not to be problematic, although it is important to assess the results, that is, who participates. In the consultation on the FRA, the Directorate-General for Justice, Security and Freedom received a total of 102 contributions: fifty-seven from civil society organisations and NGOs, twenty-nine from national institutions, four from international institutions and twelve from private citizens. It is interesting that seventy-five of the contributions were in English and that, in terms of countries, there was a predominance of contributions from the UK and an absence of documents from new member states. It is important to note that the process of written consultation is more accessible than public hearings in Brussels and can play an important role in involving associations and citizens in different countries. Indeed, in practice it is often the only available channel for locally and nationally based civil society organisations with limited contacts to make their preferences known at the European level. However, differences in resources, knowledge and perceptions about the relevance of the EU in the sector and about the effectiveness of participation are all factors that influence willingness to take part in consultation and more generally to get involved at the EU level.

Is a total of fifty-seven contributions from civil society organisations a large or a small number? And does it constitute an appropriate sample of civil society in the field of protection of human rights at the EU level? The communication from the Commission on the general principles and minimum standards for consultation makes clear that representativeness is not to be considered the only relevant criterion for organisations to gain access to the consultation processes and for evaluating the relevance or the quality of contributions (Commission of the European Communities 2002). Rather, Directorates-General are asked to adopt an active approach to consultation, and to seek out contributions from relevant target groups, marginal groups in particular. One important criterion for evaluating the contribution of civil society organisations relates to the expertise they possess and can input into the policy process. As briefly noted above, groups are sources of policy ideas, are repositories of expertise and can help to make decisions legitimate. All these reasons explain why political institutions might have the need for and the interest in including civil society organisations, even when their representativeness cannot be clearly ascertained. It is widely recognised that the Commission is understaffed and often lacks knowledge on specific issues (Greenwood 2003). According to organised civil society, in the case of the creation of the FRA, the need to gather information was particularly urgent. The Directorate-General for Justice, Freedom and Security was in charge of the process of converting the EUMC into the FRA. In this instance, the consultation process led it to deal with, for the first time, antidiscrimination and antiracist issues, an area that had fallen within the remit of the Directorate-General for Employment and Social Affairs, which was also the institutional reference for the EUMC within the Commission. Civil society organisations stressed the point, saying that within Directorate-General for Justice, Freedom and Security there was little experience with the issue and more particularly with the fight against racism and xenophobia; and they regretted that the Directorate-General for Employment and Social Affairs had no role in the process of constituting the FRA.

In the third stage of the process of written consultation, all contributions are taken together and are processed by the Commission or by an external organisation. In order to meet the need for transparency, all received contributions are published on the web. The Directorates-General are not required to respond to the comments they receive, and in this sense it is arguable that contacts between the Commission and associations are unilateral.

In the case of the consultation on the FRA, an independent organisation, EPEC (the European Policy Evaluation Consortium), was in charge of drafting the summary report (European Policy Evaluation Consortium 2005). It was a highly sensitive task. The analysis of responses to the public consultation on the FRA was made public in the spring of 2005 and it was submitted to all relevant decision-makers to ensure they were informed about the issues and about stakeholders' preferences. Civil society organisations, or more generally contributors, were not allowed to comment on the feedback document – as is the case with all written consultations – so that, at least from a formal point of view, their role ended at that stage. The summary report went through all the documents, highlighting the content of answers to each question and their frequency. The report tended to focus exclusively on answers to the initial list of questions; it is possible to say that the potential for innovation that is supposed to derive from the inclusion of civil society organisations was thereby severely undermined. The 'asynchronous' discussion expected in written consultation processes (Fishkin and Luskin 2000) is limited in scope, as the range of positions to be taken into account and topics to be addressed are clearly delimited and filtered in the process of summarising contributions. In addition, the strength of an argument is mainly evaluated on the basis of the number of organisations that subscribe to it; thus, the summary report gave the frequency of each answer and tended to emphasise arguments where a consensus could be found. It therefore makes sense for civil society organisations to coordinate their contributions and their contents. Networking and building alliances have always been perceived to be fundamental strategies for organisations to gain relevance at the EU level (Greenwood 2003; Ruzza 2004). In the case of the written consultation on the FRA, there is evidence of coordination among antiracist associations and networks. In these instances, supranational umbrella organisations play a fundamental role, trying to facilitate the delivery of contributions and providing their members with information and position papers. Interviews with key actors in the UK and Italy showed that umbrella organisations actively encourage their national members to participate in consultation processes, in order to strengthen the relevance and the salience of their arguments; and that they try to find a common position with other groups, such as organisations dealing with disabilities.

In the fourth stage, the results of the consultation are used in the decision-making process. As noted above, consultation exercises have a purely advisory role. There are no obligations to respond, although minimum standards for consultation establish that, with legislative proposals and in the impact assessment, the consultation procedure has to be mentioned and an explanation of how the results have been taken into account must be included. The problem here is the possibility that politicians or the authorities in charge of the summary of the results 'cherry pick only the favourable recommendations and judgements from citizens' forums' (Budge 2000). Indeed, civil society organisations stress that political institutions act instrumentally and tend to engage in consultations with the purpose of gaining legitimacy. The search for legitimacy is said to be one of the main reasons for EU institutions including civil society in policy processes. From the point of view of activists, factors determining their willingness to participate and potentially grant legitimacy to the process are the transparency of the procedures and the perception of effectiveness.

From the EUMC to the FRA

In this section a more detailed analysis of the written contributions is presented, with specific attention paid to arguments advanced by civil society organisations. The analysis focuses on a specific issue, namely the different positions on the remit of the new Agency. This was one of the most controversial aspects of the debate, as it focused on extending the mandate of the EUMC.

At the EU level, a broad antiracist advocacy coalition has been active since the 1990s, lobbying for the adoption of antidiscrimination legislation and specific antiracist measures. The antiracist advocacy coalition is said to have been quite effective in taking advantage of all the political opportunities it had: 1997 was declared the European Year Against Racism; also in 1997 the EUMC was set up in Vienna; in 2000 an Action Plan Against Racism and two crucial directives were approved – the Racial Equality Directive and the Employment Equality Directive. In subsequent years, the antiracist advocacy coalition demanded more effective implementation of EU directives and monitoring of the situation in member states. The antiracist advocacy coalition developed strong linkages with the Directorate-General for Employment and Social Affairs, which was responsible for the implementation of the EU agenda in the field. The decision to extend the remit of the EUMC and to create the FRA was taken in December 2003 by the European Council (more precisely, at that time the European Council decided to create a 'human rights agency') and followed a debate about the effectiveness of the EUMC, and more precisely about how to provide institutions with consistent and comparable data on racism, xenophobia and Islamophobia. As the Directorate-General for Justice, Freedom and Security rather than that for Employment and Social Affairs was in charge of the creation of the FRA, it proved difficult for the antiracist advocacy coalition to influence the process. New contacts with both institutional and social actors involved in human rights protection had to be established, which opened up new opportunities for building alliances but also new potential for conflict.

In the content analysis of the written contributions it was possible to identify two different advocacy coalitions in the broad field of protection of fundamental rights: on the one hand, a coalition with a strong commitment to antiracist values; and on the other, a coalition advocating the adoption of a broad conception of individual human rights. The former, antiracist coalition advocated prioritising the fight against race discrimination and making racism and xenophobia the main focus of research and campaigning activities of the new Agency. For example, a document submitted by the UK Race and Europe Network stated:

> Whilst we welcome an integrated approach to tackling discrimination, we do feel it is important to acknowledge the specificity of combating racism, which could not be addressed within a single model applied to all equality grounds.

Consequently, the call was for the identification of precise thematic areas to be explicitly prioritised in the remit of the FRA, as the idea of taking into account all fundamental rights simultaneously was 'a surreal development', which would undermine the overall effectiveness of the Agency.

The need to reframe the specific issue of the fight against racism and xenophobia within the broader context of human rights led the (former) antiracist coalition to emphasise the concept of equality, as the goal of the protection of fundamental rights.[8] In this light, the goal of the new Agency should be to 'use a human rights approach to address equality issues' (Birmingham Race Action Partnership 2004). In so doing, racism (including institutional racism) and xenophobia should have the priority, as racism is said to be 'at the roots of human rights violation' (in the written contribution from the European Network Against Racism).

Interviews with key UK actors indicated that efforts were made to build a coalition, in order to present a unified position from the antiracist sector and to extend the network to other groups, such as the European Disability Forum. In their documents, activists gave evidence of the need to pay specific attention to vulnerable groups, such as racial minorities, people with disabilities and gypsies. In addition, antiracist organisations stressed that a strong focus on racism would avoid the danger of duplication of efforts, as the Council of Europe, the EU Network of Independent Experts on Fundamental Rights and a number of national institutions were still working on the issue of human rights protection; consequently, they stressed the need to maximise the expertise of the EUMC and its network of national focal points (the EUMC had established national branches in each of the member states) in tackling racial discrimination.

The second coalition of actors, that which favoured the new Agency taking on a broader conception of individual human rights, focused on the protection of human rights with reference to all areas covered by article 6 of the 1992 Maastricht Treaty on European Union and the EU Charter of Fundamental Rights. Extending the remit of the new Agency to cover all thematic areas was deemed essential, because setting priorities would lead to a 'hierarchisation' of rights, which was perceived to be unacceptable. Here the concept of 'human rights' has a broader meaning and the protection of human rights can have multiple goals, in relation to, for example, discrimination, rights of victims, minority rights, access to justice, conditions of detention, the right to asylum, counter-terrorism measures, racism, fundamental social rights, gypsies and gender issues (in fact a new Agency dealing specifically with gender issues is due to be established in 2007). For instance, a number of large organisations, such as Amnesty International, and professional organisations, such as the Council of the Bars and Law Societies of Europe (CCBE) and Fair Trials Abroad (FTA), all underline the need to pay attention to the rights of prisoners, suspects and those under investigation in European countries. Although they recognise the salience of racism in general terms, they do not prioritise the fight against racism, and equality as a policy goal was seldom stated in their documents. Rather, they focused on, for example, the introduction of antiterrorism legislation in different EU countries, the protection of personal data of all EU citizens, concern over detention without trial and freedom of expression; these are all sensitive areas and quite distinct from discrimination on the ground of race. Whereas human rights are mainly seen as the protection of individual citizens from abuses of political power, the fight against racism implies a focus on both vertical relations among individuals and institutions and horizontal relations among individuals. From these viewpoints, the work the FRA would be expected to undertake is different.

The two coalitions of civil society organisations did, though, have some common ground. In particular, they both advocated the new Agency having powers under article 7 of the Maastricht Treaty, which enables the EU to act against a member state in case of violation of fundamental rights. They also advocated giving the FRA the independence to comment on the fundamental rights situation in the EU and in member states. Civil society organisations stressed the need for a strong role for associations in the work of the Agency, on the basis that human rights protection is a broad and demanding task, and only close cooperation with organisations can guarantee the delivery of results.

The summary report drafted by EPEC emphasised that all the contributions received welcomed the creation of the new Agency. Indeed, only one document expressed a negative reaction to the transformation of the EUMC into the FRA, even if the decision came as a surprise and was initially criticised by antiracist organisations (for instance in press releases published on their websites). However, the report also contained evidence of shared concerns regarding both the effectiveness of the new Agency and guarantees of adequate resources in terms of funds and staff. The summary report emphasised shared arguments made by NGOs, particularly about the powers and the independence of the new Agency, while also giving evidence of divisions among them concerning the overall goals of the FRA, where they listed different sets of priorities.

The final proposal for the FRA, presented by the Commission on 30 June 2005, rested on the idea of linking the remit of the FRA to the Charter of Fundamental Rights; it did not set areas to be prioritised in the FRA's remit, but instead formulated a 'multi-annual framework' for defining the main thematic areas to be addressed in the subsequent five years. The fight against racism and xenophobia must always been included in the thematic areas to be addressed. The proposal contained a summary of the EPEC report, and stated that 'this proposal takes on board those issues on which there was a broad consensus' (Commission of the European Communities 2005d). The FRA will be based in Vienna, as was the EUMC, and will have around 100 members of staff (the EUMC had thirty-five). The main task of the FRA will be to gather reliable information on the protection of fundamental rights in five selected sectors in order to assist European and national institutions in their duties on fundamental rights, to draft an annual report on such themes and to perform research on behalf of the Commission and the European Parliament. In addition, it is expected to have an active role in networking activities, facilitating contacts and sharing information among different institutions involved in different countries.

Conclusion

The use of written consultation has been described as a success by the Commission. The analysis of written contributions performed for the research presented here showed that civil society organisations took the task seriously, and engaged their resources to deliver well reasoned position papers. Overall, it revealed a high level of technical expert knowledge of the characteristics of the EU legal system and of the EU institutional structure. The effort to clarify preferences in an articulated way seems to be an important feature of the consultation exercise in the context of the debate on institutionalisation of different forms of deliberative practices. Consultation *per se* is nothing new: what is of interest here is the role given to consultation in policy-making. Civil society organisations have increasing expectations, and the efforts made in coalition-building and frame alignment highlight the intention to gain relevance in the EU. However, written consultations were said to be only partially effective for gaining influence; personal and informal contacts with institutional actors were preferred. In addition, as several organisations noted in their position papers, the severe time limit for delivering written contributions has a negative impact on the ability of civil society organisations to take part effectively.

In the specific case of the FRA, the Commission's original preference was refined as a result of the process of consultation. Its proposal published on 30 June 2005 agreed to include a strong commitment to the fight against racism in the activities of the new Agency. More or less all the written contributions contained an invitation to maintain the focus on racism, or at least to stress that the fight against racism is of central importance in Europe. The EUMC itself and national political institutions emphasised the need to build upon existing knowledge and to avoid the dispersal of the expertise gained in the area. However, most of the requests advanced by civil society organisations – such as the possibility for the Agency to deal with individual complaints – were not taken on board.

The levels of participation were hardly satisfactory, and in this sense a crucial issue is how to get associations involved in EU governance. The Directorates-General need to gather information from different sources and from different territorial levels; that proved difficult in the case of the FRA consultation, as indicated by the lack of documents from locally and nationally based organisations in the consultation processes, as well as by the lack of feedback from new member states. Umbrella organisations played the main role at the supranational level, mediating between their members in different countries and the European political environment, but their ability for coordination was not uniformly diffused across EU countries, and their capacity to get associations involved in consultation processes varies according to network relationships between supranational and national associations and between organisations within a country. Consultation was mainly focused on the task of recording levels of agreement and disagreement over a defined range of proposals, rather than on collecting new ideas on how to proceed with the monitoring of protection of fundamental rights in Europe. If, as noted at the beginning of the chapter, the role of civil society organisations in policy processes is to bring knowledge, diversity and innovation to policy-making, the approach to consultation should be more open. In this sense, consultation was limited in scope and the role of public consultation in the policy process was marginal. In particular, time constraints and the lack of feedback from European institutions to the written contributions led to criticisms of the procedures for consultation. In addition, the use of contributions made by decision-makers and the substantial link between public consultation and formal decision-making are not entirely clear. The effectiveness of consultation and the overall possibility for enhancing public participation are closely tied to the transparency of procedures and to a perception of the effectiveness of participation. The adoption of a participatory approach is not sufficient *per se*. However, delivering written contributions could allow the EU to overcome its geographical remoteness, and it is important to note that, whatever the disagreements over the procedures, both civil society organisations and European institutions express a willingness to use written consultation and have high expectations of it.

Appendix. List of questions for the Commission's consultation on the FRA

1 How can the remit of the Agency be defined in order to ensure both added value for the EU institutions and member states and its efficient operation?
2 In which areas should the Agency operate? Should these areas be defined in relation to the Charter of Fundamental Rights of the Union and if so how (by article or by chapter?)? Should certain priorities be established? If so how? How can we ensure that the current remit of the EUMC (racism and xenophobia) is maintained and built on?
3 How can the geographic coverage of the Agency be best defined, bearing in mind the need to avoid overlap with existing organisations and the need to ensure that the Agency operates in the most efficient manner possible?
4 Which tasks should the Agency be given? How can the Agency gather objective, reliable and comparable data at European level? How can cooperation with member states and civil society to obtain

this information be best assured? How should the Agency present its conclusions and recommendations? How should the work of the Agency be disseminated?

5 How can a meaningful and efficient dialogue between the Agency and civil society be established?

6 How can close cooperation with other stakeholders be assured, notably with the Council of Europe? How can the Agency capitalise on the wealth of experience of the national bodies for the protection and promotion of fundamental rights and other similar national agencies? Following the creation of the Agency, how can the added value of the Network of Independent Experts be assured?

7 Which structures should be put in place to ensure that the Agency operates in an independent and efficient manner? Who should be represented on the Management Board of the Agency? Should a scientific advisory committee be established?

Notes

1 More formally, the new Agency is termed the European Union Agency for Fundamental Rights, and it was due to be operational from January 2007.

2 Whether written consultation does fit the framework of deliberative democracy, though, depends on the definition of deliberation. Fishkin and Luskin (2000) argue that when broadly defined as 'the serious consideration of arguments and counter-arguments for and against policy alternatives', even synchronous or asynchronous online exchanges and written digests of the full range of arguments should be taken into account as deliberative tools. The main point here is that it is misleading to equate 'deliberation' with 'discussion in assemblies' (Cohen and Sabel 1997), which is but one of the potential institutional devices that can be implemented according to deliberative principles.

3 In the UK written consultation processes have particularly gained in relevance. The British government produced a *Code of Practice on Written Consultation* in 2000 (see http://archive.cabinetoffice.gov.uk/servicefirst/2000/consult/code/_consultation.pdf, accessed October 2006) and assessed its performance in 2002 (see http://www.cabinetoffice.gov.uk/regulation/documents/consultation/pdf/2002.pdf, accessed October 2006). Further, a specific administrative unit for consultation processes has been set up, in order to coordinate consultation processes. More than 600 exercises have been carried out by central government departments, and representatives of organisations find it difficult to answer all requests.

4 Even well known examples of experiments with deliberative polls, such as the debate on prison sentencing in the UK in 1995 involving citizens in a wide and well informed process of deliberation and with the participation of representatives of both government and opposition and extensive media coverage, did not lead to a binding decision.

5 The most famous examples are the citizens' fora on nuclear power (see
   Fischer 2003).
6 An analysis of contributions received showed that in some cases organisations did not take into account the list of questions, and in a few cases
   documents amounted simply to a self-presentation of the organisation and
   an expression of its interest in the activities of the FRA.
7 See www.socialplatform.org/module/FileLib/ENSPresponseFundamental
   RightsAgencycommunicationFinal.pdf (accessed December 2006).
8 The need to emphasise the commitment to fight racism emerged in relation
   to suggestions for the name of the new Agency, which it was felt should
   contain the word 'equality'. If we consider that naming is an important
   indication of beliefs (see Hajer and Wagenaar 2003), it is of interest to note
   that a number of different names were proposed: 'Equality and Human
   Rights Agency', 'Equality and Fundamental Rights Agency', 'European
   Equality Agency', 'Human Rights Agency', 'Human and Fundamental
   Rights Agency', and so on.

Chapter 6

Social capital and civil society: governing outside the state at the local level

Fortunata Piselli

Introduction

Since the beginning of the 1990s, numerous studies have shown that globalisation has radically reduced the nation state's role as the epicentre of politics and social order. New global actors have arisen (e.g. the North America Free Trade Agreement and the World Trade Organisation) and have assumed ever greater importance, in part through the acquisition of new statutes and instruments with which to condition the power of nation states. Structures and approaches, such as government and pluralism, have been replaced by the concept of 'governance', a term that encapsulates the major changes which, concomitant with globalisation and European integration, have occurred in the objectives, functions and procedures of governing (Streeck and Schmitter 1985; Hollingsworth et al. 1994; Stoker 1998). 'Governance' refers to a form of governing which emphasises the diffusion of political authority along vertical and horizontal dimensions; its political epicentre is no longer the state (Trigilia 1998; Hirst 2000; Crouch et al. 2001). It reflects the reality of a complex order of relations and interconnections structured through and within various levels of government: local, regional, national and supranational. It involves numerous individual and collective actors external to the formal political arena.

These phenomena give particular salience to the local dimension of civil society in political and economic development and democratic participation. It is true that global politics has restricted the regulatory scope of the nation state and generated a system of global governance that consists of numerous international and transnational organisations. It is equally the case that it has also fostered decentralisation and regionalisation, giving renewed vigour and significance to the local dimension as a regulatory context able to engender processes of economic and social development and to compete in the new circumstances of the global market (Porter 1998; Streeck 2000; Burroni 2001). The term 'governance' also refers to forms of government which enhance the role of civil society in decision-making. The flexible and informal strategies characteristic of governance entail a restructuring that gives not only greater autonomy to domestic structures, but also and especially – at both transnational and local levels – greater willingness to cooperate with all the organisations which link the political-institutional and social spheres together. This is civil society as the third level of political participation between citizens and the state (Ruzza 2004).

In these processes of what the literature terms 'global localisation' (Beck 1997), both local development and the role of civil society are closely associated, theoretically as well as empirically, with a further concept: that of social capital (Organisation for Economic Co-operation and Development 2001; Commission of the European Communities 2001d; United Nations 2001). The literature has shown that, in the post-Fordist economy, the endowment of social capital has a crucial bearing on policies for local development, and especially on the production of what have been called 'local collective competition goods' (Crouch et al. 2001). New interpretative paradigms centre on the optimisation of endogenous resources, both institutional and social, and therefore on local social capital as a crucial element in an area's locational advantages. The ability of firms, and multinationals in particular, to move from one country to another in order to exploit local advantages, and to combine inputs from sub-suppliers located in diverse areas in their manufacturing processes, has not only deterritorialised production but has also generated greater competition among regions, in which social capital is crucial (Trigilia 2001, 2005). In other words, these processes have made firms more dependent on the local environment in which they are embedded (Becattini 2000; Crouch et al. 2001), so that their success depends not only on their internal organisation but also on the cultural, social and institutional context in which they operate – or, in other words, the external economies which constitute an area's social capital.[1]

The literature has also shown that social capital underpins the processes by which civil society organises itself into firms, networks, associations, schools, clubs, churches, trade unions and so on (Cohen and Arato 1992; Gellner 1994; Alexander 1995; Giner 2000). These 'public interest' groups and associations, institutionalised and otherwise, perform a crucial role in representing diffuse interests, and they are important intermediate institutions of democratic representation and legitimacy. It is therefore social capital – the willingness of people to associate and act for the common good – which explains spontaneous capacities for self-government and self-discipline at the level of social organisation. Again, the concept of social capital enables exploration of civil society's role in governance, and therefore the ability of actors (individually and collectively) to influence the development policies of a particular territorial area.

This chapter has two aims:

1 to analyse the concept of social capital and its contribution to our understanding of the nature and role of civil society in decision-making processes;
2 to examine recent examples of local-level governance in order to highlight the newly acquired importance of civil society in local development policies.

Governing outside the state is not solely a matter of transnational forms of government like the European Union (EU): it just as importantly concerns forms of local government. Indeed, analysis of the production of local-level public policies enables us to identify the new forms of democratic legitimation made available by the diffusion of political authority: in particular, the role of interest groups and associations in decision-making; and more generally, the contribution that civil society can make to a decentralised political authority. In short, by narrowing the focus it is possible to study processes and interdependencies that are difficult to grasp in broader contexts. Comparison can thus be made between abstract principles and generalisations and the concrete action of actors in specific situations.

The remainder of the chapter consists of five parts. The first analyses the concept of social capital in its two main versions – as a relational resource and as a property of the social system – with particular regard to Coleman's formulation. Then examined are a number of recent examples of local-level governance (territorial pacts and urban strategic plans) in which the role of civil society has proved to be especially important. The third section shows how different configurations of public and private actors come about in different situations, so that diverse forms of democratic participation arise. The fourth section argues that political-institutional actors still perform a crucial role in these innovative modes of governance, notwithstanding their differences from traditional ones. The article concludes with some methodological suggestions regarding how the concept of social capital can be most fruitfully used in empirical analysis of the role of organised civil society.

Social capital: a relational and culturalist concept

The concept of social capital enjoys increasing currency among sociologists and political scientists. Its principal merit is that it directs attention to the importance of social relations – especially informal and solidaristic ties – in economic and political organisation. However, the concept has been applied to such a wide variety of problems and settings, and within such different theoretical frameworks, that it is often ambiguous. Given that the purpose of this chapter is to specify the relation between social capital and civil society, it is advisable briefly to consider the two main definitions of social capital.

The first definition, which is couched in relational terms, was introduced by Bourdieu (1980) and then taken up and systematised by Coleman, whose formulation has provided the template for all subsequent studies. Coleman (1990) concentrates on the social structures that facilitate individual action, his explicit purpose being to correct the individualistic bias of neo-classical economics. According to Coleman, the concept of social capital concerns the structure of social relations between two or more persons. Like other forms of capital, social capital is productive: it is a resource for action which enables an (individual or collective) actor to attain ends which would otherwise (or only at great cost) be unattainable (Coleman 1990: 302). Social capital is the result of intentional or unintentional investment strategies designed to create and reproduce enduring social relations and to yield material and symbolic profits over time.

The social relations in which actors are embedded are both components of the social structure and resources for individuals. Coleman distinguishes the resources possessed by an individual as physical capital, human capital and social capital: physical capital consists of tangible (material or monetary) instrumental goods; human capital comprises the capabilities and skills that people have acquired over time; and social capital is the set of relational resources which a person partly inherits and largely constructs by him/herself within the family and in other social settings. As a component of the social structure, social capital acquires concrete form in the structural and normative features of a particular social system: organisations, norms, institutions and so on.

According to Coleman, an essential feature of social capital is that, unlike private capital, it is a public good. It benefits not only the persons who put effort into creating it but also all those who belong to a particular structure or organisation, whether or not they participate in it. For example, a neighbourhood association set up by a group of residents in order to improve the amenities in their area usually involves a small number of people. Yet those people who have created and then run the association are not the only ones who enjoy its benefits, because these also extend to the residents of the neighbourhood who have not contributed in this way. In short, for Coleman social capital may be an individual resource or a collective one; but even in the latter case, he considers it from the relational point of view and in terms of the benefits that it yields for individuals.

The situational nature of the concept is evident from Coleman's argument. Social capital, precisely because it inheres in the structure of relations among people, is not tangible. Like physical and human capital, it is not entirely fungible; it is so only with respect to specific activities (Coleman 1990: 302). Social capital may assume the most diverse of forms, each of them productive with respect to one specific purpose. It has different costs and benefits in different situations: a form of social capital which favours one type of action may be a constraint on another; in one context social capital may facilitate innovation, while in another it may impede it; it may furnish resources which are useful for one purpose but useless or damaging for another.

Social capital is not only situational; it is also a dynamic, diachronic concept. This is evidenced in particular by the fact that social capital is often a byproduct of activities undertaken for other purposes. That is to say, it may be directed towards goals other than those for which it was formed. An association or organisation set up for one purpose may be useful for another. Social capital is the result of a process of dynamic interaction: it is created, maintained and destroyed. It can be intentionally or unintentionally created, but it can also be destroyed by individual behaviours (e.g. people leaving an organisation and therefore weakening it) or by the onset of external factors which make people less dependent on each other (perhaps by increased wealth, or government projects which render the individual less dependent on reciprocity relations with others, mobility, ideologies that place greater value on individualism and egoism, and so on). Like any other form of capital, it requires constant investment.

Social capital, therefore, is not an 'object' or an 'entity' that can be identified, isolated, circumscribed by a formula or given precise definition. It is a general concept that acquires concrete form in the creative action undertaken by actors in the performance of practical projects. It is an array of resources which become social capital only when they are activated for instrumental purposes. And every move, every action, changes the interweaving pattern of interactions; they change the strategic situation and thus condition the subsequent choices of actors. Coleman (1990: 304) writes: 'social capital ... is created when the relations among persons change in ways that facilitate action'. In other words, when actors establish new relations or combine existing ones in different ways, they always produce new forms of social capital. For this reason, social capital involves an infinite range of phenomena. Coleman constructs his theory by citing examples taken from the most diverse of contexts and situations: primitive societies, market organisations, voluntary associations in contemporary metropolises, and so on. The ambiguous, multiple and even contradictory forms that social capital assumes – and which have induced some authors to criticise it for vagueness and imprecision (e.g. Portes 1998: 5) – are only a result of the situational and dynamic character of the concept.

Very different to Coleman's relational perspective is the culturalist (or systemic) approach adopted by authors, most notably Putnam and Fukuyama, who have stretched the concept of social capital so that it becomes a property of the overall social system which favours democracy and economic development. For Putnam (1993), social capital (which he often reductively equates with 'civicness') consists of features of social organisation such as trust, reciprocity rules, and the networks of civic associations that promote cooperation and collective action and thereby increase efficiency within society. He identifies a close link between social capital and the performance of institutions, with the former as the independent variable. Context and history determine a particular society's endowment of social capital, and this in turn profoundly influences the workings of institutions: the greater the amount of social capital, the better the institutions – and, by extension, the economy – will function. For this reason, the regions of northern Italy, with their strong civic traditions and large social capital endowments, have achieved economic development and have well performing political institutions. The regions of the south, by contrast, where civic traditions are weak and social capital is deficient or non-existent, are characterised by nepotism, clientelism and illegality. As a consequence, they have suffered from ineffectual government and economic stagnation.

The same conclusions are reached by Fukuyama in his comparative analysis of the institutional structures of international capitalist systems (Fukuyama 1995). Fukuyama stresses the increasing importance of culture in the construction of economic society and he links national performance, in terms of democracy and capitalism, with countries' differing endowments of social capital. His notion of social capital is closely connected with trust-based cooperation. Social capital exists when people are able to work together in groups and organisations in the pursuit of common goals, and when they subordinate their individual interests to collective ones. This propensity to cooperate – or social capital – is formed and transmitted by the cultural mechanisms of religion, tradition, ethical codes and customs. The accumulation of social capital is a 'complex cultural process' which depends on spontaneous capacities for self-discipline and self-government in civil society – in other words, on capacities for spontaneous association. Fukuyama's thesis, therefore, is that the vitality of political and economic institutions depends on the health and vitality of civil society. The latter is based on the values, habits, norms and moral

attitudes acquired within the family through socialisation. In general,
a society's efficiency, economic success and wellbeing depend on inherited ethical codes, on shared values that fuel trust and people's
capacity to associate and cooperate. Depending on the social capital
endowment – that is, the array of trust relations – inherited along
with culture, countries assume different economic configurations and
occupy particular niches in the market. We thus have the small and
medium-sized family-based enterprises of north-eastern Italy, and the
large corporations of Japan, Germany and the United States, countries
where the family has not impeded the development of extended associative forms (these being also favoured by other cultural factors). The
Mezzogiorno region of Italy and certain countries, Russia for instance,
are instead examples of a restricted familism, without extended trust
networks, which explains their economic backwardness and the in-
efficient workings of their institutions.

Social capital and civil society: some clarifications

Various authors, following Portes (Portes and Ladolt 1996; Portes
1998), have criticised Putnam and Fukuyama's theory of social capital
for envisaging only its positive effects and for producing tautologies
or self-evident truths. In fact, the theory accounts for the economic
success or failure of a community or nation *a posteriori* in terms of
the presence or absence of social capital, using a circular explanation
in which social capital is both the cause and effect. The same applies
to the notion of civil society, which for both Putnam and Fukuyama
is closely connected with the notion of social capital. Only an ample
endowment of social capital makes a civil society healthy and dynamic;
without a healthy and dynamic civil society there is no social capital;
consequently, there is no economic development or democracy. Social
capital and civil society may be two concepts best kept theoretically
and empirically distinct. Although the concept has evolved over time,
there is a consensus that civil society is a set of intermediate institutions between citizens and the state, which consists of a wide variety of
groups and associations (formal and non-formal). The concept of social
capital, on the other hand, is much broader, more ambiguous and more
complex than emerges from Putnam's and Fukuyama's paradigms.

   Firstly, social capital is not necessarily a resource for development
and democratic participation. A distinction must be drawn between
positive effects of social capital for local development, on the one
hand, and its positive effects for certain possessors of capital but negative effects for local political and economic development, on the other.
That is, we must also consider the 'dark side' of social capital, its

negative and undesired effects. Particularist networks and trust within a group (social capital) sustain criminal groups like the Mafia or the Camorra, which certainly obstruct democratic life and development (Trigilia 2001).[2]

Secondly, the concept of social capital embraces a variety of meanings, which differ according to the situation, so that it may have positive effects on people's wellbeing even in the presence of what we may call a weak and fragmented civil society. Notwithstanding the various definitions that Putnam offers, he privileges one particular dimension of social capital: networks of civic commitment, or associationism. This is a conception which he reaffirms in his monumental work on the decline of social capital in the United States (Putnam 2000). Yet the positive connection between social capital and associative participation (civil society) is not automatic. Consider the emblematic case of Italy's Mezzogiorno, where research has amply documented that local communities characterised by widespread and pervasive particularist bonds (and therefore by a feeble and lethargic civil society) have ample endowments of social capital, which have produced benefits coherent with the goals pursued by actors and the contexts in which they act. In some areas they have prompted the central state to introduce redistributive measures, which have considerably improved the quality of life for their inhabitants (Arrighi and Piselli 1987). In other areas they have stimulated horizontal and vertical processes of cooperation oriented to self-sufficiency. Hence, rather than an insurmountable obstacle, particularist ties have become a resource for economic and political modernisation (Mutti 1994, 1998; Piattoni 1999).

Thirdly, for both Putnam and Fukuyama, social capital is the expression of a propensity to collective action by actors in civil society. It is measured by the level of associationism and cooperative behaviour, with roots in the distant past; it is the persistence of cultural codes transmitted by socialisation. But Putnam and Fukuyama overlook the intentional and creative action of actors, especially institutional ones, and therefore the role of politics, in reproducing and shaping social capital. Fukuyama claims that government policies have eroded social capital without having devised measures with which to reconstitute it. Recently, however, a number of authors have returned to Coleman's paradigm, to stress the importance of strategic action and the active role of individual and collective actors (especially institutional ones) in the production of integrative resources like social capital (Bagnasco 2001, 2003; Trigilia 2001). Consequently, in light of these considerations, we cannot establish *a priori* the coincidence between social capital and civil society and their effects on economic development and democracy. These connections should be analysed as they evolve in a particular setting.

Examples of local-level governance

Territorial pacts

Territorial pacts (negotiated strategies for local development) are a particular type of public policy intended to promote the endogenous development of an area through the active involvement of local-level actors – individual and collective, institutional and social. Launched in Italy in the 1990s, they have now spread throughout Europe. They may be financed by individual countries or by the EU. On the basis of complex regulations, territorial pacts aim both to achieve concrete objectives of local development and to promote specific decision-making procedures.[3] In other words, they are intended not only to achieve economic objectives measurable in terms of efficacy and efficiency indicators, but also to promote, through specific decision-making procedures, the propensity of public and private actors to take collective action, build reciprocal trust, and collaborate. The signatories to a pact undertake to coordinate their actions and to pool their capabilities and resources. They must therefore adopt new forms of behaviour, relinquish egoistic and parochial interests, adopt the logic of cooperation, and be willing to assume (material and non-material) costs with a view to fulfilling a collective interest. The purpose of pacts is to have public policies impact on the area's social and institutional context, namely, promoting and optimising its latent resources and directing them towards new goals of territorial development.

Firstly, the projects pursued under the pact seek to be congruent with the area's specific features, and be based on its priorities, on its sectoral specialisation and on its capacities for adaptation and evolution. These, therefore, are not interventions planned from outside; rather, given adequate incentives, they are integrated projects for local development which mobilise all the area's resources – economic, social and cultural – and gear them to new business opportunities. Secondly, territorial pacts must foster the development of cooperative action between public and private actors, and create new horizontal relations among local institutions, interest organisations, associations and voluntary organisations. In other words, they must boost the resources and self-organising capacity of local society and produce new forms of social capital. The purpose of a pact, in fact, is to promote not only informal kinds of social capital, like networks of relations and communication among individual actors, but also forms of organised social capital among firms, interest organisations and public institutions. Finally, the aim of a pact is to ensure that the behaviours acquired become permanent: that once the actors have learnt the rules of the pact, they are able to transfer them outside the context of the pact in a cumulative process.

These are the aims; but what about the results? Although a large number of pacts have not yet concluded, which makes it difficult to assess their results, there is a good body of documentation available (Cersosimo 2000; Sviluppo Italia 2000; Di Gioacchino 2001; Barbera 2001; Cersosimo and Wolleb 2001; de Vivo 2004; Cerase 2005, Magnatti et al. 2005). Completed and on-going research demonstrates that the pacts have produced concrete improvements with respect to the initial conditions. It is true that the results differ considerably among pacts, and that predominant in some situations – owing to social and economic factors, geographical isolation, the local culture and leadership, the weakness of interest organisations, and so on – have been opportunism and coalitions formed solely to tap into public resources. It is also true that in some cases errors have been made when designing the pact's organisational strategies (separation of the concertation and management phases, for example, or incorrect specification of the management company), and that bureaucratic inefficiency or default or delay in the payment of funds have discouraged some of the actors involved. Overall, however, the pacts have had positive outcomes and have proved essential for local governance.

Research shows that territorial pacts have changed the interpretative criteria of actors, making them more willing to cooperate and to sustain the (monetary and non-monetary) costs of undertaking collective actions with a view to the production of collective goods. Even in cases where the results have fallen short of expectations, the pacts have encouraged aggregation among actors and stimulated at least some form of cooperation. The actors involved have constantly engaged in dialogue, exchanged opinions and expanded their cognitive horizons. And in cases of success, these new attitudes have been transferred externally, giving rise to further concrete actions once the pact has concluded: agreements have been reached among firms, while cross-shareholdings, consortia and other forms of long-term partnership have been created.

Admittedly, in some cases the local institutions have been unable to achieve a leap of quality by relinquishing corporative and parochial forms of behaviour. But in other cases pacts have created the conditions for dialogue and cooperation among mayors and laid the basis for joint initiatives by municipalities. In general, pacts have seen a good level of involvement by public administrations (municipalities, provinces and regions) and a strengthening of horizontal relationships among collective actors – in particular, between public institutions and interest organisations; they have improved infrastructures and services and thus encouraged investment in the area by both local and external firms. In conclusion, by fostering cooperation and trust, territorial pacts have given the actors concerned a new perception of their local reality and awareness that concertation is indispensable for the promotion of local development. Concertation has favoured communication in the public arena, thereby stimulating participative forms of democracy.

Some case studies

An examination of specific cases will provide the basis for discussion of the performance of pacts in the various contexts considered – and in particular of the aspect of greatest interest here: the endowment of social capital and the role of civil society in the new processes of local governance.

Two pacts in Italy's Mezzogiorno are considered: the Locride Pact (in Calabria) and the Caltanisetta Pact (in Sicily). Both areas are characterised by an extremely weak economic and social context: their unemployment levels are among the highest in Italy, there is social malaise, a lack of a culture of cooperation among institutional actors (the municipalities in particular), a weak associative tradition and widespread organised crime. These are fragile societies with little dynamism, scant or no positive social capital, and the presence instead of forms of negative social capital, like the networks of reciprocal trust internal to criminal groups, which, rather than favouring development, obstruct it. And yet, despite similar initial conditions, the outcomes in these two areas have been very different. The Locride Pact has been an outright success, generating substantial improvements at both the economic and socio-institutional levels, as well as a notable increase in the quality of local governance. In the case of the Caltanisetta Pact, although some success has been achieved, the results have been generally modest.

The Locride Pact (which covers forty-one municipalities) has been pursued with determination since 1994 by two trade unionists, who first involved the head of the young entrepreneurs' association (Missione di Sviluppo) in the project and thereafter aggregated around a joint development strategy both political-institutional actors (regional politicians and mayors) and private ones (individual firms, cooperatives, consortia, etc.) (Perri 2003). A decisive role has been played by local politicians, who have set partisan-political issues aside and joined forces in a shared project. The level of participation among institutional actors has been high. The process of formal concertation, launched with creation of the supervisory body Locride Sviluppo S.p.A. (of which one of the above-mentioned trade unionists was appointed president), involved fully sixty-three actors: the municipalities, the mountain communities, all the trade unions and employers' associations, two cultural associations, banks and consortia, and individual firms. Trust and cooperation relations were immediately established between Locride Sviluppo (acting as a local development agency) and the company furnishing technical assistance, Nomisma S.p.A. There has consequently been full integration between political concertation aspects and technical managerial ones. The presence of a strong and stable leadership recognised by all the actors, and its ability to start up cooperation processes with clear and transparent rules, have been the main factors responsible for the success of the Locride Pact. Significant in this regard has been stipulation of the 'Protocol on Legality', which has prevented Mafia infiltration of the concertation process. Both the start-up and implementation phases of the Pact have been based on partnership and concertation, so that the Pact has brought together actors (firms especially) which previously operated separately, and has created and reinforced links among them. Not only has the Pact stimulated private initiative, strengthened the local production system and increased employment, it has also induced positive changes in the workings of the public institutions and the relations among them. It has created a network of horizontal relations among institutional actors, mayors in particular, who have begun to undertake joint initiatives. The Pact has generated numerous positive externalities, thereby setting off other growth processes. It has promoted various complementary initiatives and activities, such as a Pact for the Environment, and the creation of two consortia (Consorzio del Turismo Verdi and Arredi Artigiani) and an Integrated Development Project; and thanks above all to the Protocol on Legality, it has attracted investments from outside.

The promoter of the Caltanisetta Pact (Wolleh 2003) since 1993 has been a civil society actor, an industrialist (and director-general of Assindustria, the industrialists' association), who has involved other leading entrepreneurs and the trade unions in the project. The mainstays of the pact have been Assindustria and the trade unions. The memorandum of understanding was signed in 1996 by thirteen municipalities in the province of Caltanisetta, the Consorzio A.S.I. of Caltanisetta, four professional bodies, eight employers' associations and trade unions, and by various other bodies, institutions and associations. The concertation process, led by the director-general of Assindustria, was initially characterised by great enthusiasm, which continued through the creation of the management company (the managing director of which was the director of Assindustria) and the implementation phase.

The Pact has undoubtedly favoured the creation of forms of horizontal partnership between local institutions and local entrepreneurs. It has fostered awareness that the concertation method is indispensable for local development, and it has created a new working method which will bear fruit in subsequent projects. But from the outset it has encountered various problems, two in particular. Firstly, difficult relations with the Treasury and delays in the payment of funds have had harmful consequences for projects. After initial enthusiasm, participation waned and entrepreneurs began to withdraw from the concertation committee. Secondly, there has been no commonality of intent between the management company, in the person of its managing director, and the local political institutions. On the one hand, the programme of the Caltanisetta Pact, which came into being on the initiative of members of civil society, is markedly production oriented and in a certain sense seeks to keep politics out of the Pact, in order to ensure its efficiency and transparency. On the other hand, the institutional actors have failed to take political responsibility for the process. It is true that the Pact has fostered activity by the local authorities and cooperation among them: indeed, seven of the municipalities that signed the Pact have created an association for the joint management of certain services. But the political institutions have not played a central role in carrying the Pact forward, nor have they been able to overcome partisan interests and create a single point of reference for the devising and implementing of strategies for local development. Some municipalities have withdrawn from the Caltanisetta Pact; others have participated only marginally, in the belief that it is of no benefit to them. Each institutional actor has sought to create its own area of influence, thereby hampering collective action. Proof of this is that, in an area of such economic weakness, there are two general territorial pacts, a thematic territorial pact, two integrated development projects and an area agreement, and a distinct management company has been created for each of them. All this has undermined the Pact's management company and in particular its bid to become the local development agency for the entire province, as is the case with the company managing the Locride Pact. We can conclude, however, that the Caltanisetta Pact, even with all the limitations described above, did have some positive impact on the local area, albeit less than the one in Locride.

Hence, similar initial conditions in Locride and Caltanisetta led to different outcomes. The same is the case for two pacts in northern Italy: the Canavese Pact (in Piedmont) and the Ferrara Pact (in Emilia-Romagna). Both areas are somewhat backward or in decline relative to the regions in which they are situated, which have among the highest rates of development in Italy. Characteristic of the two areas are previous experiences of cooperation between local actors and institutions, and relatively dynamic associationism, with a consequent substantial endowment of social capital (especially in the surroundings of Ivrea in Piedmont, the town where the headquarters of the Olivetti electronics company are located). But once again, although the initial conditions have been similar, the outcomes of the Pacts have been different. In the Canavese area, the Pact has strengthened institutional relations, which have proved to be effective for local governance, and collective action has produced public goods internally and externally to the Pact. In the

Ferrara area, by contrast, although the Pact has achieved some success, the results have been disappointing.

The Pact for the Canavese area was initially promoted by the municipality of Ivrea, which in 1997 convened a 'concertation table' that involved the most important institutional and collective actors in the area, the purpose being to initiate joint action to counter the area's industrial decline (Barbera 2001, 2003). The signatories to the Pact were 122 municipalities, five mountain communities, the provincial administration of Turin, the three trade union confederations (CGIL, CISL and UIL), sixteen sectoral associations (firms, third sector, etc.), eight vocational training centres, and twenty-five economic/social bodies, institutions and associations. The Pact has established links among zones of the Canavese area which previously had few contacts. Concertation has led to the creation of robust partnerships, both political-institutional and social, and to the generation of cooperative relations among individual actors. The mayor of Ivrea has provided constant and vigorous leadership, with the backing other local actors, addressed the needs of other municipalities as well, and optimised the use of technical resources. However, although the public institutions (which, as noted above, in addition to the municipality of Ivrea included the provincial administration of Turin) have made crucial contributions, they have not dominated the decision-making process: important roles have also been performed by a private actor, the Canavese Industrial Association, the technical secretariat of the Pact, which has mediated the interest of local actors, the API (the small business association), the CGIL and the Consorzio per il Distretto Tecnologico. There has been continuity between the start-up and implementation phases of the Pact, and the political concertation and technical aspects have been well integrated. The 'concertation table' has met regularly since the memorandum of understanding was signed. It has been an instrument of local governance, planning coordinated development actions and stimulating numerous joint initiatives.

Initially promoted by the provincial administration in 1997, the Ferrara Pact (Rossetti 2003) involved fourteen municipalities. Its purpose was to address signs of backwardness in the province with respect to the rest of Emilia Romagna, one of the most dynamic and wealthy regions of Italy. After a phase of intense concertation, which involved the main institutional and collective actors, the Pact was approved by the Ministry of the Treasury in 1998. The principal signatories were, besides the provincial administration, the municipalities, the employers' association, the trade unions (CGIL, CISL and UIL again), the crafts and agriculture associations, the tourism board, banks and the underwriting consortium. The regional government did not sign the Pact, although it was urged to do so, and it did not participate in the negotiations. After lengthy deliberations, responsibility for implementing the Pact was given to Sipro, a company founded in 1975, and in which the province and the municipality of Ferrara are the majority shareholders. The Pact had mixed fortunes. From the institutional point of view, it achieved a certain amount of success: communication and cooperation between local government bodies and the interest associations were intense. The Pact was especially influential in the launching of new initiatives for integrated action in provincial development (these included the creation of an economic council with representatives of all the actors in the area, the signing of an agricultural pact, and a provincial development plan). However, despite the efforts of individuals and awareness and consultancy campaigns in the province, the management agency, Sipro, encountered considerable difficulties in administering the Pact. There was no continuity between the start-up and implementation phases; on conclusion of the concertation phase the Pact was treated from a mainly technical financial point of view, and local businesses pronounced it a failure. Only thirty-four out of the fifty-eight projects submitted were accepted, and of these only eighteen were undertaken (following withdrawals, cancellations, use of other incentive schemes like legislation for industrial renewal known as the Legge 488, etc.). To conclude, while the Pact has yielded some significant results at the level of local governance (by institutionalising already widespread collaborative practices), it has not been successful in terms of its original aims: to implement an overall strategy for local development; to generate innovation; and to attract outside investment.

An examination of the factors that may affect the success of territorial pacts is required in order to assess the possible influence of social capital. Some of the factors that penalise the performance of pacts are external in nature. As shown by our cases (Caltanisetta in particular), they may be bureaucratic inefficiency and delays in the payment of funds, which demotivate some of the actors involved; or they may be incentive schemes that are alternatives to pacts (like those established by Legge 488), which induce entrepreneurs to seek other forms of support.

Factors which have instead led to the success of pacts are internal to the local context. The first is the presence of a strong and stable leadership (as in the cases of Canavese and Locride). This must be able to motivate and aggregate social actors and convince them of the advantages of cooperation, and then integrate political and technical administrative functions, coordinate and monitor sectoral initiatives, and above all stimulate and maintain the interest of the subscribers to the pact and promote communication among them. The second factor is the strength of the partnership, or the degree of commitment to it by the actors, the continuity of their participation, and their joint initiatives. Other factors of prime importance are continuity between the start-up and implementation stages of the pact, and interaction and mutual support between political decision-makers and the management company – that is, between political and technical functions (as in the cases of the Locride and Canavese Pacts). A final factor is the willingness of institutional actors to assume direct political responsibility for the process and to include it in a political design, rather than view it mainly from the technical financial point of view and thus deprive it of its distinctive features (as in the cases of Caltanisetta and Ferrara). This distinction is crucial for subsequent development and the generation of cooperative relations in the post-implementation phase.

Although its participation takes various forms, in all four of the cases examined civil society performed a crucial role in putting together the network of cooperation engendered by the pact. In two cases (Locride, Caltanisetta), the pact sprang from the initiative of members of civil society – two trade unionists and an entrepreneur. But when the promoters have been institutional actors, then local associations – trade union and employer organisations especially – have been the mainstays of projects. The pact stimulates latent potential, involves civil society and gives it new ways to participate, and generates new coalitions among local actors.

Which notion of social capital, therefore, is best suited to an interpretation of these new linkages that create cohesion, solidarity, social habits and pride? As the case studies reveal, there is no systematic relation between the performance of a pact and the development of an area: in Putnam's analysis, the latter is directly linked to the degree of social capital. In fact, pacts function just as well in the depressed areas of the south of Italy as they do in the more economically advanced areas of the north, and vice versa. An interpretation *à la* Putnam which identifies social capital with the presence of a healthy and dynamic civil society (measured by the degree of associative activity), and with a propensity for collective action due to a system of values rooted in the local culture (measured by previous experiences of partnership), may indeed be useful. But it does not help us to understand the new forms of participation by civil society in the decision-making process. The case studies have shown that a good initial endowment of social capital is positively associated with the quality of governance and the overall results of the pact (as in the Canavese area); but they have also shown that, from the economic point of view, areas with the lowest endowments of social capital have achieved the best results (as in the Locride case). In areas of the north, with relatively dynamic associative networks and pre-existing cooperative experiences, the pacts have not delivered the results expected (the case of Ferrara), while in the south (where the Locride Pact is emblematic), even in areas where the initial conditions seemed hopeless, a strong and combative leadership has been able to break with the past and achieve significant successes.

This is not to imply that previous social capital does not exert an influence. A scant endowment of social capital upon start-up of a pact (or the presence of its negative or harmful effects) may actually be a factor which hinders the reversal of long-standing negative trends in the development of certain areas. Consequently, an interpretation based on Putnam may be reasonable to consider. But it is necessary to go further. Social capital should be examined from a more dynamic perspective that accounts for the interaction engendered by a pact. It should be considered (*à la* Coleman) as an intentional product by actors pursuing a specific goal. Social capital should therefore be identified as a central objective or even a byproduct of the new forms of interaction produced by pacts within and among organisations and associations. It consists of the new relations and forms of collaboration that have arisen among private actors (entrepreneurs), but also between private and collective ones, and in the horizontal relationships among actors – especially public institutions and interest organisations – which have proved crucial in promoting innovative forms of local development.

Social capital, as Coleman has shown, is often a byproduct of activities undertaken for other purposes. It may be directed towards ends other than those for which it was formed, and prove useful in the achievement of subsequent goals. In cases of success, 'good practices' learnt during implementation of the pact have given rise to concrete actions in subsequent phases, with the production of public goods and the joint development of further projects for local development (e.g. territorial integrated projects, green pacts or pacts for tourism). Nevertheless, it should be borne in mind that the coalitions produced by concertation may weaken, that the initial enthusiasm may wane, and that important social actors may quit the project, so that the pact loses its most distinctive features of interaction and constant collaboration among local actors. In short, as (partly) shown by two of the case studies (Caltanisetta and Ferrara), after an initial phase of great organisational enthusiasm, social capital and trust may dwindle – although they may subsequently revive.

Urban strategic plans

Whereas territorial pacts concern local areas and may involve a variable number of municipalities, strategic planning exclusively concerns cities. With greater international competition and the transfer of powers from the central to local level, cities have acquired a new role, as the motors of development and the proponents of cultural identity. This applies to both global cities (London, Paris, Frankfurt, etc.) – nodes of strategic relations which cross the boundaries of regions and nations

(Perulli 2000; Bagnasco 2003), acting as Europe's interlocutors – and to small and medium-sized cities. Concentrated in cities are the advanced technologies and business services essential to the competitiveness of a knowledge-based economy (Rullani 2004). Strategic plans therefore manifest the new political role of cities and the awareness that development requires joint action by several actors, institutional and otherwise.

Like territorial pacts, strategic plans are not simply instruments of local development to be assessed according to their efficacy and efficiency; they are also a means by which policy is implemented. It is not only economic targets that are important; so too are the means by which those targets are achieved. The aim of strategic plans is to introduce specific decision-making procedures which promote constant interaction between public and private actors and thereby stimulate participation, dialogue and collective action. Strategic plans require a broader coalition of actors than do territorial pacts. This coalition consists of local administrators, civil servants, experts, technicians, representatives of interest organisations and associations, and of the financial and business sectors. They also involve actors usually excluded from, or marginal to, negotiations on local development: representatives of environmental and other social movements, of new economic sectors, cultural institutions, research centres, universities, and so on. These actors carefully examine the features of their city – its resources and sectoral specialisation, its strengths and weaknesses. They assess the competitive advantages of various possible paths of development in order to determine the city's new role in the global economy. These may be paths that harness common resources and revitalise traditional specialisations, or they may require restructuring and a change of course. Whatever the case may be, urban strategic plans seek to promote collective and long-term goods. What matters is that all the actors involved, from a wide variety of institutional and non-institutional settings, must cooperate on a common project and pool their energies and ideas. These ideas are often in competition with each other and must be adjusted and merged into a long-term development plan compatible with the environment and sustainable over time (Bagnasco 2003). It is the drawing up of the strategic plan which demands constant interaction among the actors, as the process is complex and open ended. The subscribers to the plan – who may be many dozens, even hundreds, of people – form an association which holds public sessions for presentation and discussion of the plan, as well as periodic plenary meetings. A technical office is created with the task of monitoring progress, circulating information and linking the various actors together, while concertation tables are set up among working groups. Hence monitoring, discussion and verification are constant.

Like territorial pacts, urban strategic plans are not initiatives imposed from above or from outside, as the exclusive preserve of technicians and bureaucrats. Rather, they are political processes which acknowledge and set value on all the city's individual and collective capabilities and resources. They involve civil society and generate new forms of democratic participation. Strategic plans are thus at odds with urban intervention and planning models in which the public authorities play a key role in promotion of local development, with little space left for private actors and organisations; or in which decisions on land planning are delegated to public or quasi-public agencies consisting of external 'technicians', who have no close involvement with the local context. Finally, unlike territorial pacts – which once they have been defined must be brought to a conclusion in accordance with the initial project – urban strategic plans (which are more complex but also more flexible) can be redefined and improved as they are implemented, and with the contribution of specific actors. They are therefore incremental, negotiated and open to new solutions; they give rise to constant collective learning, which fosters innovation in local governance.

Numerous European cities have adopted these principles. Examples are the strategic plans of Glasgow, the first of which was drawn up in the second half of the 1970s, and those of Lyon, Lille, Manchester, Frankfurt, Bilbao, Lisbon, Barcelona and Munich. These are cities which have organised large-scale events (sporting or cultural) or undertaken major projects, like their radical restructuring from industrial centres to cities of culture or new technologies. The most significant case in Italy is the 'International Turin' Project, drawn up in the spring of 1998 and subscribed to by the mayors of municipalities in the metropolitan area – and by more than 100 representatives of public institutions, the financial and business communities, the trade unions, associations, cultural institutions and universities (Bagnasco 2003: 118). Other Italian cities, even medium-sized and small ones (e.g. Florence, Pesaro, La Spezia and Trento), have recently altered their development paths in a similar manner. The rapidity with which strategic plans have spread is due to their ability to respond effectively to urban problems in an age of globalisation, which offers new opportunities to cities. Whether external constraints and stimuli are converted into opportunities for growth and innovation depends on the socio-institutional context, and on the choices made by political and social actors – and also on the ability of the latter to mobilise and coordinate local resources, whether public, private or associative. Like territorial pacts, strategic plans are innovative experiments in governance. They generate new relations, new practices and new forms of participation by civil society which affect policies and enlarge the bases of the democratic process, to mark out new modes of democratic legitimation.

The case of Barcelona

The main problem for urban planning projects intended to foster a city's growth and competitiveness is reconciling these with social equity and justice. Research has shown that urban restructuring intended to promote local economic development often increases social inequality and exclusion (Bagnasco and Le Galès 2000). Strategic plans, however, are specifically concerned with producing a model of common action which supports a development path that combines economic competitiveness and social cohesion, through appropriate welfare projects. Experience has shown that economic growth and social equity are not incompatible and may even reinforce each other. Emblematic in this regard is the case of Barcelona (Marshall 1996; McNeill 2003; Borja 2004; Guzzo 2004).

The positive outcome of the urban restructuring of the city, which has assumed a role of central importance for its entire metropolitan region, has depended on specific governance measures which have encouraged collective action by local actors. Since the early 1980s, the process has been driven by local governments, especially by mayors heading coalitions on the political left, led by the Catalan Socialist Party. This has been a strategic process which has involved the combined action of all the city's most representative actors, both individual and collective, and channelled their energies and abilities into a shared development project. It is consequently a process which has fostered a participative culture and built a common identity. Its protagonists have been all the city's industrial associations, trade unions, churches, cultural and voluntary associations, banks, professionals and representatives of the arts – in short, all the main components of civil society. Cooperative relations have been established between universities and industries (with the creation of technological parks and a biomedical research park), and between the tourism and culture sectors. Numerous sectoral platforms have been set up to boost various sectors of the local economy with the creation of consortia of firms (for example the Consorcio Turismo Barcelona, which handles increasingly large numbers of visitors). Since the Olympic Games of 1992, the city has become one of the most important tourist destinations in Europe. And, because of its tertiary and advanced technology sector, it has not only achieved notable self-sustained growth but also attracted a substantial number of foreign firms, especially large multinationals.

Besides the objectives of economic growth and competitiveness, those of social equity and cohesion have also been pursued. Economic development policies have been accompanied by social inclusion measures such as: renewal of the city's neighbourhoods, creation of public spaces and civic centres, decentralisation of social and cultural services, upgrading of peripheral areas, and the modernisation of the communication infrastructure. All sectors of civil society have been protagonists in the process. Not only have politicians rediscovered the importance of civil society but the urban strategic planning has constantly stimulated it and politicians have even asked civil society to provide criticism. This has been particularly evident when policies for urban renewal and the building of new residential estates (mainly by foreign firms) have had a number of undesirable effects: inflation and increased living costs, the expulsion of poor residents from upgraded areas, the non-completion of public building projects, and so on. These effects have provoked the immediate response of citizens, intellectuals, professionals and social movements. Neighbourhood committees have been set up, which in turn have established or renewed links with other associations (environmental, consumer, etc.) in pursuit of a common goal. Hence, the participation and consensus of civil society is essential for policies of this kind, which may facilitate and orient the action of public authorities, which must engage in constant dialogue with civil society to gain and nurture a consensus.

Once again, we can ask which version of social capital yields the best interpretation of civil society. Firstly, existing social capital – or an area's social capital endowment before the start-up of a plan – measured (according to Putnam) in terms of 'civicness', cultural capital, the extent of associationism, partnerships and so on – may be an important factor in the success of strategic plans. As in the case of Barcelona, it may significantly influence subsequent interaction. Barcelona started with a healthy endowment of social capital, in fact: the presence of a closely integrated productive system, experiences of cooperation, a strong local identity and relatively widespread associationism. Nevertheless, although a good endowment of previous social capital is a necessary condition – and this assertion itself is open to debate – it is certainly not sufficient. Innovative public policies for local development, such as strategic plans, may greatly encourage cooperative behaviour and the production of organised social capital, even when the initial conditions are unfavourable. Social capital should consequently be analysed in the same experimental context as the plan designed to alter the relationships among the institutions and to promote collective action. It should there-fore be measured in terms of the achievement of those objectives. The analysis must accordingly focus (following Coleman) on the processes of interaction induced during the social-institutional mobilisation phase of the strategic plan. Social capital should be identified in the inter-actions that a strong leadership is able to generate in pursuit of a shared goal, in the coalitions established by individual actors, in the horizontal cooperative networks which arise among local institutions, interest organisations and various types of associations. In short, social capital should be identified in the presence and combination of interactional (among actors) and organisational (among organisations) social capital.

Situational and dynamic patterns

The foregoing discussion has shown that territorial pacts and urban strategic plans reflect many of the arguments adduced in support and explanation of governance. Firstly, as envisaged by many governance arguments, these pacts and plans are types of public policy which structure collective action through cooperation, shared commitment, and reciprocal adaptation between public and private actors. They foreground the role of civil society and non-state actors (Della Sala 2001). Decision-making is no longer the exclusive prerogative of the institutions of formal government; rather, it is the result of a process which involves – on an equal footing – a wide variety of actors external to the formal political institutions.

Secondly, territorial pacts and urban strategic plans are interventions for local development which alter conventional conceptions of the organisation of a territory and its inhabitants. Depending on the projects approved, territorial pacts may involve diverse municipalities, in the same province or in different ones, adjoining and non-adjoining. Urban strategic plans may concern large or small cities, or metropolitan areas, which may be structured in various ways but which are nevertheless unconstrained by territorial limits and traverse the administrative boundaries of numerous municipalities and provinces in search of new identities, and in pursuit of new strategic goals. The territory and its population constantly change, and people are no longer constrained within a single ambit of belonging, thus superseding the notion of a permanent community defined by territorial boundaries.

Thirdly, decision-making authority is exercised in numerous sites: municipalities, provinces, regions, ministries, management companies, nation states and Europe. A new relationship is emerging between centre and periphery with respect to development policy. A large part of regulation can be carried out by a broad array of new actors, and in locations that do not coincide with the organisational hierarchy of political power. Important decision-making structures can certainly be identified, but the emphasis should be on the relations, processes and organisation of collective action (Hooghe and Marks 2001; Della Sala 2001).

In every innovative political process initiated by territorial pacts and urban strategic plans, the features described above combine in different ways according to the variables concerned: context, pre-existing social capital, the nature of the local political system, the strength of leadership, idiosyncratic factors and the cultural environment, for example. Different combinations produce different practices, arrangements, and co-opting and participative mechanisms, and therefore different models of governance (Crouch et al. 2001, 2004; Burroni 2004). There are procedures with fewer or greater degrees of institutionalisation, broad or narrow geographical areas (from the thirteen municipalities covered by the Caltanisetta Pact to the more than 100 by the Canavese Pact) with greater or less contiguity, more compact or more dispersed decision-making levels, and different levels of involvement of civil society. There are different configurations of administrators, associations, individual and collective actors – all of them with their own perceptions and conceptions, and all of them with their particular and not necessarily consistent perspectives. We have seen that, in some cases, the initiative is taken by members of civil society; in others, it is taken by institutional actors. In some cases, the promoter brings together mainly institutional subjects; in others, the promoter mobilises an array of organised interests together with these subjects.

It must be emphasised that, in all cases, these are processes or dynamic patterns that arise and change over time. They are not causal relationships but interactions; not compact structures but discourses and practices; not processes of linear construction but constantly changing outcomes (consider the case of Barcelona) of the interaction and combination of diverse social and administrative logics of action. Moreover, the recent history of urban development policies shows that one model of governance may be replaced by another in the space of a few years. Already activated, in fact, are new projects for local development that differ from those analysed above: territorial integrated projects; green pacts; pacts for tourism; and others.

Different configurations generate different models of governance and different roles for civil society. Each model of governance includes certain forms of government, albeit to different extents. In the most traditional ones, characterised by the predominant role of public and bureaucratic authority, the presence of civil society is weak and lacks influence. Even the two cases analysed here, although they represent the most innovative policy models, display a number of differences. With a territorial pact, the dominant coalition consists of local government and interest organisations. Industrial associations and trade unions are the protagonists, but there is substantial participation by other organised interests (e.g. crafts associations, chambers of commerce and industrial development consortia), including – especially in mixed or agri-tourism pacts – those superintending cultural assets, and environmental associations. The mechanism on which the coalition operates is mainly that of local-level concertation. Strategic plans, in contrast, are more open to the involvement of organisations and civil society actors: neighbourhood associations, cultural and environmental movements, professionals and intellectuals. They pay closer attention to the public dimension and are based less on concertation than on models of 'deliberative democracy', using procedures similar to those of Brazilian 'participative democracy' (de Sousa Santos 2002).

It should be borne in mind, however, that each case has its own dynamic, and it should be investigated with regard to its specific features and within its specific context. Research is indispensable if proper assessment is to be made of the effects of these policies on the long-term development and social wellbeing of the community in question; we need to conduct comparisons and to obtain useful indications on how to improve these experiments in integrated planning. However, all this should not induce facile generalisations.

The new role of the political institutions

As we have seen, a radical change is taking place in the making of public policy. Policies derive not from acts of formal government but from governance processes that involve institutional and private actors, organised interests and associations: in short, all the resources and capabilities of civil society. Does this mean that the functions of political authority are diminishing? Does it mean that political regulation has decreased in importance? Absolutely not, and for several reasons. The competition between cities and regions engendered by globalisation and the decline of state regulation has given renewed vigour and strength to local governments, furnishing them with new modes of intervention and new spheres of action.

Firstly, all recent institutional changes have been in this direction, although patterns and time scales obviously differ between countries. In some European countries, France for example, the devolution of powers from the central bureaucracies to local ones has come about earlier than in others, so that even in the 1970s it was possible to talk of the strong 'administrative activism' of mayors (Tarrow 1979). For instance, in Italy, since the reform law of 1993 which introduced the direct election of mayors, municipal governments have become the political institutions most important for citizens and those closest to them, as they offer resources for cultural identity and political participation, and carry forward local development (Catanzaro et al. 2002).

Secondly, even in areas where the political institutions have been rejected or ignored in the past, they are regaining importance now it has been realised that social capital and civil society are not enough. Cases in point are the industrial districts of north-eastern Italy, whose spread was considered to be largely a spontaneous phenomenon, a bottom-up process (although political action played its part) without a specific territorial development plan promoted by some institutional actor. The social and economic model of the industrial district has been in difficulty for some time and now requires restructuring and innovation. While some forms of social capital, like family- and kin-based relations, work well during the development phase of a district, they may subsequently introduce suffocating rigidities, which require changes to be made. Social capital is a dynamic resource, not a 'natural given', defined and acquired once and for all. Like all forms of capital, it is the product of constant innovation and investment. The small and medium-sized firms that operate in districts, largely based as they are on informal social capital, must embed themselves in broader and more formal networks of cooperation which also include institutional collective actors: that is, organised interests and public institutions. A form of organisation which works well for a certain period of time may not do so subsequently. Necessary as a consequence are new forms of territorial organisation which give the public institutions a central role. In the past, small entrepreneurs wanted to free themselves of the 'straitjacket' of politics; today, as shown by territorial pacts, they are changing their view of local development and the means to achieve it. They realise that they must interact with various levels of governance – municipalities, provinces, regions, Europe – and they are thus rediscovering the role and importance of the public authorities.

Thirdly, in all 'negotiated planning' projects (like territorial pacts and urban strategic plans), the political and administrative institutions undertake explicit and crucial tasks of organisation and integration, which the proponents of governance often undervalue. The political authorities must, in fact, stimulate and coordinate a composite set of infrastructure and entrepreneurial projects – sometimes discordant and in competition – adapt them, and direct them towards shared and sustainable development targets. They must strike a balance between economic efficiency and social justice. Therefore, they must, on the one hand, exploit all the endogenous resources available so that they can produce the collective goods necessary for competitiveness in the new conditions of the global market. On the other hand, they must obstruct deviation from policy, devise policies encompassing the various territorial units subject to innovation (e.g. metropolitan strategic plans involving numerous municipalities must respect the local identities of small cities). And they must also introduce welfare measures to combat hardship, exclusion and new inequalities.

Finally, the public institutions, at various levels, must ensure transparency, integrity and respect for the rules (and apply sanctions when they are breached). They must prevent sectoral interests from gaining privileged access to, or dominance over, administrative decision-making and thus curb particularist pressures applied by the actors involved. They must strike a balance between efficiency and flexibility. On the one hand, they must be able to take decisions and implement them (i.e. convert them into results) and gain legitimacy. On the other, they must guarantee increasing levels of participation and representation in the decision-making process, and therefore ensure that ever broader sectors of civil society have access to that process. In short, local administrations are still identifiable centres of authority and decision-making power, but as the promoters of the 'good practices' that ensure good governance (Della Sala 2001).

Leadership clearly plays a decisive role. In areas with strong institutional leadership – often personified by directly elected mayors (but also by other institutional actors) – it has been easier to create consensus, to promote coherent action to achieve a particular outcome, to involve non-state actors and to ensure forms of participative governance. As we have seen, the differing results of territorial pacts are not significantly conditioned by the local pattern of development, or by an area's previous endowment of social capital. In some instances of particularly weak and fragmented civil society (Locride, for example), incisive institutional leadership has promoted 'cooperative games' among actors: it has, that is to say, created new forms of social capital and thus actualised innovative potential for local development. Moreover, political-institutional authority is particularly important, indeed indispensable, in the case of urban strategic plans.

Politics matter, therefore. Contrary to the contentions of certain more 'radical' proponents of governance, political authority has a strategic role: it orients the forms and practices of interaction between state and non-state actors; it establishes relations with higher-level government authorities; and it creates and utilises linkages that traverse political parties, bureaucracies, organised interests and groups in civil society. It thus builds social capital as the resource with which to start and sustain local development. This is no longer a matter of an interventionist institutional actor which inflexibly imposes its decisions from above. Rather, it concerns acts of governance, flexible discourses and practices which raise public awareness of politics and thus generate democratisation. These are not hierarchical structures but networks of actors rooted in highly diverse social, geographical and institutional spaces, which consequently communicate in different ways and produce different dynamics of democratisation.

Conclusion

As we have seen, territorial pacts and urban strategic plans are innovative public measures intended to promote systematic cooperation between the public and private actors in a particular area so that they undertake projects to improve local conditions. They express a new-found protagonism for local authorities and their ability to pursue development by creating new forms of institutional and social partnership. They express new models of governance based on new intergovernmental relations between centre and periphery, and on new relations between local bodies, which break down their isolation, redefine their identities, generate common strategies of local government, and promote joint initiatives.

Civil society performs a crucial role in these new forms of governance. We have seen a wide variety of situations which, in various ways, signal the presence of public-interest associations (institutionalised or otherwise), businesses and professional bodies. Despite this wide variety, however, it is always the active participation of civil society that gives weight and substance to these new models of governance. In some cases, the promoters and protagonists of every phase of a pact have been members of civil society; in others, they have been institutional actors.

We have investigated which notion of social capital is most productive for an analysis of the role of civil society in these new processes of governance. Putnam's normative and culturalist approach identifies social capital with 'civicness', associative participation and a long-standing propensity to cooperate. It establishes a strict relation between social capital endowment and economic and institutional performance. As we have seen, the approach is useful for the identification of an area's existing social capital, but it does not take account of the various combinations and outcomes of the processes examined. In some cases, the presence of relatively dynamic associationism and of previous cooperative practices has positively influenced the outcomes of pacts. But in other cases territories with low levels of trust and traditional difficulties of spontaneous association (and therefore with few social capital resources at the outset) have seen very positive outcomes with pacts. For instance, in some of the Italian cases, the provisions of the pact (e.g. protocols on legality) have countervailed forms of negative social capital like those characteristic of Mafia criminal organisations, thereby changing behaviour seemingly ingrained in local society.

Social capital should therefore be considered, taking a cue from Coleman, from a strategic and dynamic perspective, as a stock of relations that actors create and deploy in order to achieve their goals in constantly new ways, giving rise to a variety of combinations. Research is required on how the actors make ever-changing use of their relationships, of how these relationships are transformed, and of the emergent effects of the interaction, without neglecting (as Putnam and Fukuyama do) the actions of collective institutional actors. Social capital should therefore be analysed within the experimental context itself of territorial pacts and urban strategic plans, which, as repeatedly stressed, have the specific goal of introducing practices of interaction and cooperation between public and private actors in order to improve local conditions.

How should empirical analysis proceed? There follow some suggestions as to lines of enquiry and criteria with which to verify empirically forms of participation by civil society, and its role in the formation of an area's social capital. The discussion will be limited to territorial pacts, as urban strategic plans are longer and more complex processes, although the points made will largely be applicable to them as well.

Analysis of existing social capital (*à la* Putnam) is a useful starting point. The measures analysed here do not arise in a vacuum but in contexts which may be more or less resistant to them, which may be more or less willing to adapt to them pragmatically, and which may therefore influence their outcomes. Existing social capital should therefore be included, as long as Putnam's deterministic causal approach is discarded; for, as we have seen, trust and cooperative relations may develop within the context of a pact itself. The focus should therefore be on this feature and on its dynamic evolution. At least four time points are relevant: T0, before start-up of the pact, when previous social capital is measured; T1, in the initial phase of the pact (mobilisation and concertation); T2, during the implementation phase of the pact; and T3, in the post-implementation phase.

In each of the three phases, the analyst must identify the social actors involved (individual and collective, institutional and non-institutional), and the cooperative relationships they have established, both horizontal (among local bodies or organisations or firms) and vertical (between firms or members of civil society and the local leadership). Social capital does not consist simply of the number and extent of the associations existing at a particular time, but also of the relations that they deliberately establish between themselves, and all the links and alliances among the various civil society actors (individual and collective) involved in the decision-making process. Social capital also comprises the resources that flow among actors: material resources (monetary and financial), normative resources like trust, cognitive resources like information, and experiential resources acquired through the sharing of experiences, collaboration and constant discussion. In short, social capital consists of all the interactional and organisational relations (between individual actors and organisations) that facilitate communication, the circulation of competencies and economic exchange.

Secondly, the analysis must be conducted from the dynamic perspective as well. It must therefore identify the changes that have taken place in the relational network from one phase to the next: the civil society or institutional actors which have joined the coalition and those which have left it; the relationships that have broken down and those that have strengthened, and the new ones that have arisen. It should be constantly borne in mind that just as social capital and trust may develop through pacts, so they may also diminish and disappear.

Finally, once appropriate indicators and procedures (quantitative and qualitative) for formalising social capital have been selected, its effects on the differing performances of 'negotiated planning' policies can be analysed. This can be done along at least three dimensions: economic performance, social performance, and governance. Hence, the concept of social capital becomes of key importance for the exploration of civil society's role in the configuration of new models of local governance, and therefore for investigation of the various levels, patterns and dynamics of democratic legitimacy and participation.

Notes

1 External economies can be classified as two main types: tangible and intangible. The former comprise infrastructures and services. The latter, which constitute social capital in the strict sense, are cognitive resources – the specialised languages that spring from shared experiences of life and work, communication and cooperation networks among firms and among public and private operators – and the trust relations and reciprocity arrangements which favour the circulation of information and facilitate exchanges (Becattini and Rullani 1993; Trigilia 2001; Crouch et al. 2001).
2 More recently, Putnam (2000) and Fukuyama (2001), too, have considered the possible negative consequences of social capital, respectively examining criminal gangs in cities and self-interest lobbies. However, neither regards the nexus between trust and civil commitment (i.e. social capital) and democracy as having lost its validity (Field 2003).
3 The regulations provide for a long phase of concertation among local public and private actors, followed by a management phase involving the creation of a company which supervises the activities envisaged by the pact and the fulfilment of its objectives. Subscription to the pact entails costs: the various initiatives undertaken are eligible for public funding but they also require the actors to co-participate in expenditure.

Conclusion: linking governance and civil society

Carlo Ruzza

Finding the threads that link new forms of governing (that is, governance) with newly (re)found political subjects and objects (such as civil society) constitutes a challenge for political and policy studies. While more direct forms of popular participation and involvement in policy-making have acquired strong prescriptive tones – as have the participation and involvement of different kinds of non-state actor – the concrete modalities through which the exertion of influence and inclusion in policy networks are accomplished matter a great deal for policy outcomes. Thus, the policy network dynamics that characterise different sectors, and the arrangements that filter processes of inclusion and influence, matter significantly. Governance, with its multiplicity of institutional forms, its variety of network arrangements and changing distribution of powers, affects the institutional dynamics and outcomes of the inclusion of civil society actors, often in unanticipated ways.

A large body of literature suggests that high levels of associationism are inherently a positive factor that contributes to the quality of institutional performance. However, the chapters suggest a number of variables that may shape policy outcomes. These range from the role of concrete institutional arrangements, to the strategic considerations of specific policy-making actors and to their political cultures acting as filters; the contributors to this volume therefore stress the need for further study of the policy processes that open up policy decision-making, at different stages, to certain sectors of civil society, while excluding others. Evidence from the studies reported in this volume suggests that inclusion and exclusion mechanisms vary across several dimensions, which pertain to network factors, institutionalised operating traditions, and coalitions of political actors who define and redefine friends and allies in civil society; there are also broader, cultural dimensions and related issues of political legitimacy.

All the chapters consider the relationship between governance and civil society in Europe, with specific attention to local, national or European contexts and, in some cases, the interaction between territorial levels. Overall, they document the high hopes that private and public actors will increasingly involve civil society in governance roles, but they also point to the problems, uncertainties and disappointments that both government actors and civil society representatives frequently experience. At all territorial levels, expectations connected to the inclusion of civil society often feature an improvement in the quality of decision-making, better adherence to the needs and desires of citizens and, more generally, higher standards in democratic life. But a positive outcome, either for democracy or for effective policy-making, cannot be taken for granted.

This concluding chapter will constitute an analysis of why civil society has acquired relevance in different contexts. More specifically, in the context of a perceived crisis of electoral politics and the emergence of models of 'participatory democracy', it will identify the distinctive impact of the political structure of the European Union (EU), with its unique operating procedures and participatory ethos, and of the interaction between county-specific traditions and the multi-level structure of the EU.

Civil society and governance

Our concern with linking 'governance' and 'civil society' reflects the fact that these two terms refer to interrelated issues that became prominent at the same time because they share several causes. However, the relationship remains under-researched, both in terms of normative basis and with respect to policy-making. Notably, both views of 'governance' – that is, as an emphasis on decentralised and changeable decision-making structures and as a more participatory style of policy-making which is more inclusive of civil society – are reactions to a perceived dissatisfaction with state-centred, top-down, unchangeable decision-making structures. These structures have become dysfunctional in economic terms; moreover, they lack cultural legitimacy and are politically incompatible with processes of regional aggregation such as the EU. The lack of cultural legitimacy is, in turn, connected to a wider process, often referred to as the 'crisis of politics' or the 'crisis of democracy', that is, the inability of some of the dominant arrangements of political representation and decision-making to retain diffused cultural acceptability. Although the extent and nature of this crisis is contested by some scholars, its thematisation is a recurrent element in media discourse and recurs formulated as a grievance in the programmes of populist parties (Norris 2000). A search for decentralised political solutions to replace the Westphalian concept of the nation state has ensued – resulting in a set of models often referred to as governance structures; these structures are intended to replace the more hierarchical and fixed governing arrangements, and to allow for the inclusion of civil society or, more broadly, non-state actors in policy-making or quasi-policy-making capacities.

While experimentation with different forms of governance is widespread throughout a range of social, geographic, political and cultural contexts, it is the EU which provides the most interesting laboratory. The attention to the inclusion of civil society in the EU parallels a growing general interest, both theoretical and empirical, in the role of public intermediary organisations (Cohen and Rogers 1995; Keane 1999; Edwards et al. 2001; Warren 2001). It is in Europe, with the presence of an integrated institutional framework and long-standing, largely successful efforts to institute the single market, that experiments with new governance structures are most advanced. Moreover, the frequently argued recent decline in several member states of legitimacy of political classes and structures (Meny and Surel 2002) has accelerated the search for more participatory solutions for the conduct of political activities.

There is a wide-ranging literature spanning several decades on all aspects of the 'crisis of politics' and its changing features but it is useful here to point to a few salient aspects. While extreme versions of the thesis of a collapse of trust in governments are easily challenged, there is no doubt that some processes of erosion of conventional political interfaces between states and societies have occurred in recent decades. A general indicator of disaffection with politics lies in the decline in electoral participation, which has been related to processes of generational change and youth disengagement with electoral politics, to a measurable erosion of trust in government and to declining attachment to political parties (Dalton 2005: 39). Each of these factors is historically linked to others, in a self-reinforcing constellation.

Taking a 'Europeanisation from below' perspective help us to understand how the activities and advocacy functions of grassroots civil society organisations develop in member states and are then referred upwards to Brussels as a response, in part, to the disenchantment with existing systems of representation, as well as outwards towards an expanded and transnational space of political communication.

All the different European party systems tend to engender complaints about conventional electoral politics, as illustrated by the chapters in this volume. For instance, in Italy and to an extent in France, governmental instability and citizen alienation from politics are connected to a highly conflictual multiparty system which is so internally divisive as to be in a frequent state of impasse. In Italy, but also in some other EU member states, the institutionalisation of political parties within the state and their consequent isolation from society mean that, overall, the party system is a poor mechanism of interest aggregation. Disengagement from political parties reflects their increasing closeness to the machinery of the state, but this does leave space open for alternative channels of popular participation (Deth 1997).

Episodes of political corruption have emerged in several member states, casting doubt on how the political process selects people for office, its incentive structures and the efficacy of any monitoring. This again has encouraged many citizens to advocate the presence of external controls on the political system – a monitoring role that the media have also come to play more thoroughly, and which has further undermined the legitimacy of elected institutions. Anti-politics sentiments have emerged in several member states. They have spurred a search for solutions, which have included populist formations in which a charismatic leader short-circuits the electoral process to establish a sort of apparently unmediated relation with the electorate – a relation that is maintained through political discourse that further undermines the legitimacy of electoral politics (Taggart 2000).

If a crisis of majoritarian politics has concerned several EU member states, this is even more the case for transnational institutions, which have had a relatively short time to acquire political relevance and credibility and which now suffer pervasive legitimacy problems (these will be examined in more detail below).

However, a growing emphasis on governance and the role of civil society is not simply related to changing political cultures and to strategies to increase economic adaptability. It has also been related to the increasing social relevance of actors that wish to bridge the gap between private and public roles (Pizzorno 1993). This is a desire that has multifarious aspects. It can be linked to the ideal interests of conscience constituencies wishing for a more participatory role in communities, or to other kinds of interest (e.g. professional). Suffice to say here that an emphasis on civil society is particularly relevant at the EU level, for reasons of bureaucratic politics. As Justin Greenwood and Anthony Zito point out in their chapters, the desire of parts of the Commission to strengthen their power can lead them to finance civil society groups. Thus, for a variety of reasons, civil society actors are acquiring new relevance both at EU level and in member states, and membership and support for civil society organisations are growing.

Efforts at political advocacy are also apparent outside of the conventional political space in a set of expanding and increasingly differentiating public spheres, as Klaus Eder points out in chapter 1. This contributes to redefinition and expansion of the political space (see Maier 1987) in which civil society organisations take a prominent role, of links between citizens, of the sphere of political communication and an expanded repertoire of political activism.

A sharp increase in alternative forms of political activity often off-sets the decline in voting and other conventional forms of political participation. New opportunities include the availability enjoyed by the postwar generations of an enlarged repertoire of collective action, which emerged with the social movements of the 1980s, and more forms of political participation, ranging from petitions to referenda, demonstrations and grassroots mobilisation, but also involvement in advocacy coalitions and single-issue political campaigning. This has, for instance, been documented in some large EU member states and in the United States. As the World Values Survey points out, civil associations, environmental groups, peace groups and women's groups have been on the rise since the 1980s, even in countries with a limited tradition of associationism, like France (Dalton 2005: 48–9).

New issues have emerged which the European political system finds difficult to address, as it is still mainly sensitive to cleavages along the right–left axis. The result is that they are then often left to organised civil society, such as single-issue movements or groups concerned with delivering social policy to marginalised sectors of the population, such as migrants, and fighting discrimination. Civil society in the policy arena contributes to a reopening of policy options that the party system had prematurely closed, or just not processed (Maier 1987). In societies where the political system is unable to cope effectively, new forms of participation become especially relevant. Electoral politics is displaced by social movements and the civil society sector, which has grown rapidly in size and function in recent years. As the chapters show, a distinct configuration of operating procedures *vis-à-vis* civil society organisations has emerged at EU level, which includes criteria for selecting groups to be consulted, for supporting them and for articulating their demands and their discourse to justify their role. All these factors are reactions to the needs and specific features of the overall EU system of governance with its crises – more specifically, as chapter 3 argues, the policy output crisis (particularly difficulties of implementation and the horizontal diffusion of policies) and the legitimacy crisis.

The problems that emerge at the local community or at the national levels are somewhat different to those at the EU level; the differences relate, as Fortunata Piselli points out for the Italian case in chapter 6, to the degree of social capital and trust between actors engaged in governance structures. Thus, the question to be addressed is not simply whether hierarchical state-centred systems are better or worse than decentralised multi-actor structures. Rather, there is a need to identify the concrete and changing political opportunities which, in some contexts, have created inclusive mechanisms and opened avenues to address political themes through civil society formations, and which, in others, have produced ineffective, ritualistic or insufficient attempts at including civil society organisations.

At EU level we can identify several interconnected advocacy coalitions, in fields such as social and environmental policy, which can play a useful linking role between EU institutions, and between EU institutions and other levels of government. There is, for instance, an advocacy coalition that joins green parties and other concerned actors in the European Parliament, sections of the Commission and environmental groups, and that links these actors in a practice of governance that enriches the work of institutions. As Anthony Zito points out with reference to environmental policy, they do so even while highlighting well known resource and access problems. Thus, the specific features of EU environmental policy shape the interests and strategies of different types of actor within this coalition, which are different from the participatory logics that will develop in other contexts. Contexts shape the institutional arena but also the civil society sector. As chapter 3 points out, inclusion and exclusion mechanisms and strategic considerations orient both the demands and the tactics of civil society.

At the member state level, the formation of civil society organisations is equally oriented by the political opportunities afforded to the sector. We can note, then, that whether environmental concerns find a voice in green parties or in citizens' groups depends upon variables such as national political cultures, electoral laws, the presence of elite alliances, the amount of repression and the host of variables examined by the political opportunity approach in social movement research (Rootes 2003). These include the modalities of inclusion of citizens' groups at different levels of governance – and specifically of environmental groups – which several states have accomplished in the broader framework of the so-called transition from government to governance. Thus, there is a direct link between governance and civil society, but it is one that needs to be examined as an evolving relationship between actors and which is oriented by path dependencies, strategic and ideal interests, and changing political opportunities. In all these considerations, organised civil society is increasingly important. If governance structures are necessary to respond to the globalisation-driven need for economic effectiveness, to react in a timely fashion to new information, and to include stakeholders in order to facilitate compliance with regulatory change, then the stakeholders must, in addition to business groups, also increasingly include citizens as consumers and in the many other guises of public interests that are represented by citizens' organisations. Their exclusion would deprive policy-making of channels of representation that could enhance both input and output legitimacy.

To the extent that it is possible to be included in quasi-decision-making roles without paying some of the costs of electoral competition, many single-issue movements, but also other social concerns, will find that advocacy outside electoral politics is an increasingly appealing alternative. Advocacy then becomes a strong channel to inject policy-making with sensibilities that are developing in society but that are not, or not yet, reflected in conventional politics. The result may be that a triangulation between the media, regular politics and public interest groups comes to characterise governance activities in several contexts.

The relevance of the EU to civil society

Even a cursory examination of websites or other information materials produced by EU institutions shows the importance attributed to civil society. As previously noted, this is no surprise – 'civil society' emerges in a variety of shapes and almost everywhere as the basis for a new ideology. We find generally positive references to civil society in all EU member states, in the electoral programmes of many parties of all types, in political communication and policy documents of different sorts. As the chapters in this volume show, at the EU level, calls for the involvement of civil society appear frequently. We need to ask why references to civil society have multiplied in EU discourse and what the implications are of involving non-state actors in activities that used to be the reserve of branches of the state, such as decision-making activities and policy formation. Chapters 1–3 examine the reasons for the recent attention to the role of organised civil society in EU-level governance. They argue that it is explained by the flexibility of the input of civil society into policy-making activities, its adaptability to address a number of related topical problems and, therefore, the fact that it can be utilised by different constituencies, which come together in policy networks. In particular, chapters 2 and 3 in this volume and chapter 6 in volume 1 stress that the EU faces overwhelming problems of political legitimacy, which have resulted in the acceleration of a broad and multifaceted strategy adopted by political elites to widen forms of participation.

Civil society can help address problems of legitimacy and policy output and it can do so in different and even incompatible ways. Several contributions to this volume argue that the specific manner in which civil society can be involved in EU policy-making is contested, and depends upon different visions of the European project, which can vary across different actors and normative positions. The chapters seek to clarify and systematise them by considering some of the different contexts in which the construct of 'civil society' has been utilised. Taken in its entirety, the volume attempts to identify common elements and investigates whether the EU system of governance takes a distinctive approach to civil society. In the inclusive aspiration of the EU, the chapters identify what has sometimes been called the 'European social model'. They also identify: an attempt to redress the dominance of business interests; a concern on the part of the European left for redistributive justice and the inclusion of marginalised constituencies; and normative compliance with the emphasis on civil society that has emerged in other transnational institutions. Above all, they stress concern with the legitimacy of the European project, which needs to be framed here with some reference to its historical context.

The process of European construction is a complex and long-term project, which for most of its history has been characterised by an integrationist agenda pursued through a variety of means, at a stop/start pace and with unanticipated outcomes. It is a process that scholars have described as typically relying on a permissive consensus and benign neglect by European publics. When the basis of this neglect has been called into question, notably during and after the process of ratifying the 1992 Maastricht Treaty, the political discourse of many of its elite proponents has shifted to include new political concepts, such as 'subsidiarity', 'Europe of the regions', 'the open method of coordination' and, perhaps the one used most broadly and frequently, 'civil society'. However, as with all new concepts, its precise meaning and applicability are still somewhat undefined and contested.

The emphasis on civil society together with the sometimes confusing and contradictory strategies of civil society organisations have, therefore, played a fundamental but ambiguous role in recent years. Calls for deeper involvement of civil society in government can be identified in the discourse of a range of political and administrative actors, as well as in the discourse emerging in a range of institutions and organisations and in a number of policy areas. For instance, it emerges in the debates that accompanied the publication of the Commission's white paper on governance (Commission of the European Communities 2001b) and the Treaty Establishing a Constitution for Europe (TCE, signed in 2004). A deeper involvement of civil society has been frequently advocated to address concerns with the legitimacy of the European system of governance. But, even more frequently, an input of civil society has been advocated as a way to improve the quality of policies, whose formation, implementation and monitoring can benefit from the competence and the time and energy of a multifarious set of actors. It is in specific relation to these two issues – legitimacy and policy improvement – that the role of civil society has been examined by the authors of this volume.

The EU as a form of defensive regional integration initially resulted from ideals of peace and prosperity in Europe. More recently, it has grown, in an attempt both to address the perception of a loss of national sovereignty engendered by economic globalisation and to react to historical events that have accelerated the reduction of the centrality of EU states on the world stage. The transformation and adaptation to changed European deep-rooted national identities, which is necessary to accommodate the progression of integration, has not taken place easily. As the relevant literature points out, the process of European construction started and remained a relatively unproblematic elite project for much of the latter part of the last century, when it therefore required only minimal adaptation on the part of society. Civil society was included from the beginning, but only in the form of economic interest groups, which, in the expectations of neo-functionalists, were supposed to spearhead calls for common policies across an ever-increasing number of fields. But political legitimacy was not a concern and neither was the inclusion of other sectors of civil society in the European institutional framework. In continental Europe, concern for political legitimacy did not appear prominently in public opinion until the debate over the ratification of the Maastricht Treaty brought European integration issues to the attention of the media. In the span of a few years, support for integration declined throughout the Union and ambivalence about the ultimate goals of the project put supranational institutions on a defensive footing. Within European publics, Euroscepticism mounted and took a variety of forms (Tiersky 2001). This spurred both a search for new solutions to the legitimacy issue among political elites and, paradoxically, governments' and political parties' attempts to obtain advantage by realigning their political discourse to ride the wave of resurgent nationalism. In other words, the same political elites who at times lament the negative consequences of mounting anti-European sentiments at other times attempt to take advantage of this mounting Euroscepticism by reproducing it in their political discourse.

Thus, as several observers have pointed out, in addition to being connected to a perception of intractable problems of input legitimacy related to strong national identities, Eurosceptic attitudes have been in part generated by governments that have blamed 'Europe' for difficult policy problems they had exported to supranational level to take them off the domestic agenda. Thus, mounting perceptions of dissatisfaction with EU policies – or, in other words, problems of output legitimacy – also emerged. Nonetheless, while multiple factors contributed to undermining EU-level politics, the supranational arena increasingly constituted a needed domain to respond in a coherent fashion to issues that could not be solved at member state level, such as coordinated responses to globalisation. It has allowed the adoption of unpopular but necessary policies that would have been too controversial at the domestic level. But the continuation of this approach is now in doubt. The inclusion of civil society together with the pervasive inclusion of economic groups is, then, a way of continuing market and social integration outside the formal political process. The argument of the neo-functionalists has, in a way, been reversed: groups' involvement in EU policy-making is no longer a precondition of political integration, but is self-referential and part of a vision of an at least partly self-regulating society which no longer needs the same levels of political steering. Civil society can be recruited to deal with some of the debris left over by the difficult history of integration.

European integration has, over the years, produced a set of incoherent policies in need of systematisation. The process of enlargement has further undermined the ability of the EU to respond to emerging challenges, as the institutional machinery developed for a much smaller Europe is now visibly strained. It is in this context that we have to frame the recent attempt to streamline and systematise the European project. For a still relevant part of the elites of funding member states, at least, Europe clearly needs an institutional overhaul. To many, this also suggests that it requires a stronger political and social counterpart to its economic policies, and that the needed institutional renewal has to be addressed by some kind of constitutionalisation process, in which a new, simplified but also clarified and integrated system of rules emerges. It is in this context that calls have been made for a change in the operating rules of policy-making, in a more participative direction. It is in response to this need that we can read many policy attempts at institutional change; while these attempts have been gradual and diffused, they have accelerated in recent years.

To be clear, the integrationist agenda pursued by European elites amounted to a multifaceted but undeclared constitutionalising project, which has been increasingly characterised by an overarching problem of political legitimacy. We can trace the impact of the emerging legitimacy discourse in a number of arenas. In recent years, the debate on the involvement of civil society has to a large extent been oriented by this discourse, for several reasons. At a general level, civil society can provide alternative forms of legitimacy, which can be seen as a substitute for the type of legitimacy which in member states is provided by representative government and which many observers think is not sufficiently present at EU level.

The concept of 'constitutionalisation' indicates a few related processes.[1] In the EU context, it often refers to the transformation of the EU, away from a structure akin to that of an international organisation and towards a constitutional legal order (Craig 2001). In the history of the EU, 'constitutionalisation' also refers to a diffused and long-lasting process in which various European elites have exerted their influence over time. In this sense, the TCE was only the last of a related set of initiatives, which therefore, as Shaw, among others, argues, does not represent a break with the history of constitutionalism in the EU (Shaw 2005). It is a process that has seen the active involvement of several actors, notably the European Court of Justice, which has interpreted the EU's founding treaties in constitutional terms (Szyszczak 1995). Moreover, key events have significantly contributed to the process of constitutionalisation, such as intergovernmental conferences (Shaw 2000), and the debate which developed in connection with the white paper on governance. Clearly, with so many actors involved over an extended period, different visions have emerged of what should be an ideal constitutional structure for the EU.

In the blueprints for Europe, organised civil society has represented a crucial tool from the beginning. It was initially not necessarily connected to legitimacy issues. Rather, it came to be employed in support of the typical problems that emerged at specific points in time. And, as Stijn Smismans points out in chapter 4 of volume 1, over the years its institutional framing was shaped by the evolving styles of institution building (see also Smismans 2004). In recent years, calls have multiplied for a stronger input of civil society but, as Justin Greenwood points out in chapter 2, increasingly the legitimacy issue has come to the fore (see also Greenwood 1997). Expansion has also taken place of the role of civil society in decision-making processes through a set of new policy instruments, such as the formation of 'compacts' with civil society organisations in the UK[2] and at EU level, the open method of coordination and formalised consultations in the context of the 'civic dialogue'. The role of civil society has, then, generally expanded and current definitions include a growing number of public interest groups, churches, promotional groups and social movements; some authors even include economic groups, although others keep them distinct (Cohen and Arato 1992). An inclusive definition of civil society is utilised by EU institutions.[3] However, as the chapter by Fortunata Piselli reminds us, when discussing the role of civil society we have to bear in mind that civil society includes a variety of organisations and individuals who have widely different objectives, resources and effects when they approach decision-making institutions. They also have roots, often very strong, in member states, and this highlights the importance of the functional and territorial dimensions when European civil society is examined.

Given the breadth of the concept, calls have been made for stricter criteria to evaluate the contributions of organised civil society. For example, EU policy documents set out criteria relating to whether civil society associations operate on the basis of openness, transparency, representation and internal democracy. These criteria and the related new policy instruments mark a fundamental shift in the EU philosophy of policy-making in a more decentralised, participatory and voluntary direction, and have appropriately received sustained academic attention (Armstrong 2003). However, as argued in chapter 3, these criteria are often used in ways that are internally inconsistent and even contradictory. A useful clarification of criteria emerges in the contribution of Dawid Friedrich and Patrizia Nanz to volume 1. In the context of EU migration policy, they focus on four key criteria: access to political deliberative processes; transparency and access to information; inclusion of all concerns; and responsiveness to stakeholders' concerns. Along with other chapters, their contribution emphasises two main legitimacy-acquiring strategies in this respect. One is to embrace globalisation and to justify integration in terms of a necessary adaptation to a broader political environment, one that recognises interests and identities beyond the state. This implies, for instance, borrowing legitimacy from other international institutions, and giving the EU legitimacy by using the language of rights, or emphasising the need to face transborder threats to the environment, or the need to react efficiently and in a coordinated manner to an internationalised business environment. Anthony Zito points out that policy ideas and supranational institutions are piggy-backing on each other and that the EU has staked its claims to legitimacy in relation to the legitimacy claims of the United Nations and other international institutions. However, the main thrust in the search for legitimacy has been on improving output legitimacy. In this effort, civil society has been recruited by different institutions in multiple capacities.

Civil society and output legitimacy

As pointed out in several chapters, EU institutions use civil society to address policy-makers' information deficit. Such concerns are similar to those voiced in member states to justify the inclusion of civil society, as these are framed in terms of improving the quality of policies as a result of better information, monitoring of outcomes, crisis management, policy innovation and aggregation of interests. The involvement of civil society to enrich decision-making with new policy ideas and to spur collective processes of policy learning is particularly valuable in policy sectors where there is a perception, on the part of both member states and the EU, that change is needed. At the EU level, however, the emphasis is not only on consultation but also on participation, at least more expressly than in member states. In several member states we would not find a webpage with 'interactive policy-making' listed as a 'service'[4] and 'civil society' in the page that lists policy sectors,[5] whereas both appear on the Commission's website.

One reason why civil society is crucial for the EU is that, in some respects, it can join input and output legitimacy considerations. Its involvement can be shown to improve not only policies but also the representation process, by giving voice at the EU level to marginalised or isolated constituencies. As Anthony Zito in this volume points out, emphasising the territorial bases of civil society in member states can be an important opportunity for EU institutions to improve their policies, as knowledge of events taking place at national and subnational levels is often important and difficult to achieve without the contribution of civil society. The networked aspect of civil society not only provides informational resources but also confers legitimacy.

Along the same lines, the Commission's strong emphasis on civil society reflects an awareness that frequent use of the strategy of justifying the EU in merely economic terms has, in some respects, backfired. The involvement of private interest groups and the taken-for-granted neo-liberal ethos that has traditionally dominated the EU have produced a perception of an uneven playing field, in which general societal interests come second to private business concerns. Stronger civil society involvement can improve the representational process and may come to be seen as a strategy for acquiring legitimacy, and consequently justifies the EU's willingness to finance public interest groups. However, several chapters note that resource problems continue to plague the sector. It is interesting to note that lack of resources also plagues institutions, which can in fact strengthen their relations with civil society actors. As Anthony Zito points out with reference to the European Parliament, its lack of resources makes it more dependent on information from civil society and therefore more receptive to some of those organisations.

Civil society and its difficulties at the EU level

In examining different types of involvement of civil society, the chapters differentiate the outcomes of citizens' participation at the individual level from the impact of organised advocacy groups. In both cases, outcomes are far from satisfactory for many civil society actors. They complain about limitations of access, about poor feedback on their lobbying efforts and lack of resources.

Emanuela Bozzini shows that organisational and individual citizens' opinions submitted through a website were aggregated in a manner which was haphazard; moreover, the individuals involved received no feedback and exercised no control over the aggregation of their preferences. Institutional filters, unsurprisingly, tend to frame outcomes in terms that are acceptable to institutions. Anthony Zito points to the difficulties faced by environmental groups in dealing with the EU's institutional complexity, their limited access to particular arenas, and limitations due to lack of resources. This results in the frequent inability of civil society organisations to address all the stages of the policy process and all institutions. He also argues that European organised civil society seems to lack the ability to lobby national delegations and the Council secretariat; groups find it difficult to maintain issues on the agenda, and are unable to control the long chain of bargains characteristic of supranational policy processes.

Another problem that civil society faces is the fact that its inclusion is often ritualistic. As pointed out in chapter 3, there is often a large discrepancy between the lively discourse about the participation of civil society and the empirical reality of modest and often inconsequential involvement.

Europeanisation from below

The relevance of interconnections of civil society actors with their member state base has been documented in these chapters as well as more broadly in the literature in a number of policy domains, such as migration policy and environmental policy. The processes of Europeanisation of civil society have been observed both from the viewpoint of dynamics in specific member states and by studying relations between EU-level organisations and member states (Ruzza 2004; Gray and Statham 2005). In general, a picture emerges of slowly advancing processes of Europeanisation among civil society organisations, which create a counterpart to the integration of state institutions in multi-level governance structures. On the one hand, among environmental organisations Anthony Zito identifies strategies of forum shopping across levels of government. On the other hand, other authors report a substantial inability of national organisations to access EU institutions. Indeed, they have pointed to significant difficulties of civil society in their advocacy efforts, which are rooted in the fact that many groups in member states see advocacy as secondary to other functions, such as service delivery.

It appears that multi-level relations are easier for established organisations and in larger policy areas, such as the environment, while the general picture is one of substantial difficulties in the relations between levels of government. Some authors have pointed to the different challenges and opportunities that emerge at different levels of governance – differentiating, for instance, the benefits of community involvement at the local level from the benefits of the Europeanisation of civil society through EU-level non-governmental networks.

Conclusion

All the contributors to the volume see the role of civil society as potentially promising but also identify many obstacles. They stress the role of civil society organisations as providing alternative channels of representation, as contributors to the formation and expression of a European demos, as channels of interest aggregation, and as a source of help in monitoring and facilitating the implementation and transposition of EU legislation. They emphasise the role of civil society in helping to develop a better, more integrated, more active citizenship and to connect multiple territorial identities.

Given appropriate rules of inclusion, civil society formations might work in effective cooperation with political parties and governments, or form broad advocacy coalitions that are transversal to any one institution or public pressure group but which enrich democratic life. However, all the contributors emphasise that ambiguity continues to plague the concept of civil society. They also warn that civil society could easily become a justification for the retrenchment of states from society, that it could see intractable policy problems being thrown on voluntary organisations, and that its involvement in policy-making may be tolerated for merely ritualistic reasons. To avoid these risks it is necessary that a continuing process of clarification of the rules of involvement takes place, that rules are given sufficient publicity and organisations are given political relevance, and thus that in Europe the 'civic dialogue' grows alongside the more developed social dialogue.

Notes

1 It can refer to the preparation of a 'constitution' or can indicate a constitutive, stable, superior law, which is justiciable, but also refers to an entrenched, common ideology, with contestable features. Connected to this, 'constitutionalism' can relate to the legitimacy and applicability of a constitution; it can also refer to an enquiry into whether a legal system possesses the characteristics of a constitution and, if not, how it can move towards their attainment. It can refer to the juridical shifts seen since 1945, when state institutions were established that derive their authority from a written constitution. More broadly, it can refer to the institutional embedding of important principles – such as accountability of government, mainstreaming of human rights and precepts of good governance – or to the extent to which norms applying to the relation between citizens and the state apply among private citizens (i.e. societal application of the Convention on Human Rights).

2 See www.thecompact.org.uk (accessed October 2006).

3 For instance, a key Commission document states that, although problematic, the concept of civil society: 'can nevertheless be used as shorthand

to refer to a range of organisations which include: the labour-market players (i.e. trade unions and employers' federations – the 'social part-ners'); organisations representing social and economic players, which are not social partners in the strict sense of the term (for instance, consumer organisations); NGOs (non-governmental organisations), which bring people together in a common cause, such as environmental organisa-tions, human rights organisations, charitable organisations, educational and training organisations, etc.; CBOs (community-based organisations), i.e. organisations set up within society at grassroots level which pursue member-oriented objectives, e.g. youth organisations, family associa-tions and all organisations through which citizens participate in local and municipal life; and religious communities' (Commission of the European Communities 2002).

4 See http://europa.eu/index_en.htm (accessed October 2006).

5 See http://ec.europa.eu/policies/index_en.htm (accessed October 2006).

Bibliography

Alexander, J. C. (1995). 'I paradossi della società civile', *Rassegna Italiana di Sociologia*, 36(3): 319–39.

Alhadeff, G., Wilson, S. and Forwood, G. (2002). *European Civil Society Coming of Age*, Brussels: Social Platform.

Alink, F., Boin, A. and T'Hart, P. (2001). 'Institutional Crises and Reforms in Policy Sectors: The Case of Asylum Policy in Europe', *Journal of European Public Policy*, 8(2): 286–306.

Amoore, L. and Langley, P. (2004). 'Ambiguities of Civil Society', *Review of International Studies*, 30: 89–110.

Anheier, H., Glasius, M. and Kaldor, M. (eds) (2001). *Global Civil Society*, Oxford: Oxford University Press.

Armstrong, K. A. (2001). 'Civil Society and the White Paper – Bridging or Jumping the Gaps?', in C. Joerges, Y. Mény and J. H. H. Weiler (eds), *Mountain or Molehill? A Critical Appraisal of the Commission White Paper on Governance*, Jean Monnet Working Paper No. 6/01, New York: Jean Monnet Center for International and Regional Economic Law and Justice, available at www.jeanmonnetprogram.org/papers/01/011601.html (accessed October 2006).

Armstrong, K. A. (2002). 'Rediscovering Civil Society: The European Union and the White Paper on Governance', *European Law Journal*, 8(1): 102–32.

Armstrong, K. A. (2003). 'Tackling Social Exclusion Through OMC: Reshaping the Boundaries of EU Governance', in R. Cichowski (ed.), *The State of the Union: Law, Politics and Society*, Oxford: Oxford University Press.

Arrighi, G. and Piselli, F. (1987). 'Capitalist Development in Hostile Environments: Feuds, Class Struggles, and Migrations in a Peripheral Region of Southern Italy', *Review: A Journal of the Fernand Braudel Center*, 10(4): 649–751.

Aspinwall, M. and Schneider, G. (2001). 'Institutional Research on the European Union: Mapping the Field', in M. Aspinwall and G. Schneider (eds),

The Rules of Integration: Institutionalist Approaches to the Study of Europe, Manchester: Manchester University Press.

Bagnasco, A. (2001). 'Teoria del capitale sociale e *political economy* comparata', in A. Bagnasco, F. Piselli, A. Pizzorno and C. Trigilia, *Il capitale sociale: istruzioni per l'uso*, Bologna: Il Mulino.

Bagnasco, A. (2003). *Società fuori squadra*, Bologna: Il Mulino.

Bagnasco, A. and Le Galès, P. (eds) (2000). *Cities in Contemporary Europe*, Cambridge: Cambridge University Press.

Baker, M. (1992). 'Voluntary Group Lobbying in the EC – A Case Study in Animal Testing of Cosmetics', *European Access*, 4: 8–9.

Banfield, E. C. (1958). *The Moral Basis of a Backward Society*, Glencoe: Free Press.

Barbera, F. (2001). 'Le politiche della fiducia. Incentivi e risorse sociali nei patti territoriali', *Stato e mercato*, 63(3): 413–49.

Barbera, F. (2003). 'Il Patto Territoriale del Canavese', in *La lezione dei Patti territoriali*, Rome: Ministero dell'Economia e delle Finanze.

Bates, S. (1998). 'EU Lifts Blocks on Aid Funds', *Guardian*, 18 July, p. 15.

Becattini, G. (2000). *Dal distretto industriale allo sviluppo locale*, Torino: Bollati Boringhieri.

Becattini, G. and Rullani, E. (1993). 'Sistema locale e mercato globale', *Economia e politica industriale*, 80: 25–48.

Beck, U. (1997). *Was ist Globalisierung? Irrtumer des Globalismus – Antworten auf Globalisierung*, Frankfurt: Suhrkamp.

Benhabib, S. (1996). 'Toward a Deliberative Model of Democratic Legitimacy', in S. Benhabib (ed.), *Democracy and Difference. Contesting the Boundaries of the Political*, Princeton: Princeton University Press.

Birmingham Race Action Partnership (2004). 'Response to the Communication from the Commission, COM(2004) 693 final', available at http://ec.europa.eu/justice_home/news/consulting_public/fundamental_rights_agency/doc/contribution_brap_en.pdf (accessed October 2006).

Blondel, J., Sinnott, R. and Svensson, P. (1998). *People and Parliament in the European Union: Participation, Democracy, and Legitimacy*, Oxford: Oxford University Press.

Boli, J. and Thomas, G. M. (1997). 'World Culture in the World Polity. A Century of International Non-governmental Organization', *American Sociological Review*, 62(2): 171–90.

Boli, J. and Thomas, G. M. (eds) (1999). *Constructing World Culture: International Nongovernmental Organizations Since 1875*, Stanford: Stanford University Press.

Bomberg, E. (2003). 'Environmental NGOs, NEPIs and EU Enlargement', paper presented to the ECPR Conference, Marburg, September.

Bomberg, E. and Burns, C. (1999). 'The Environment Committee of the European Parliament: New Powers, Old Problems', *Environmental Politics*, 8(4): 174–9.

Borja, J. (2004). 'Barcelona y su urbanismo. Exitos pasados, desafios presentes, oportunidades futuras', in J. Borja and Z. Muxi (eds), *Urbanismo en el siglo XXI*, Barcelona: UPC.

Bourdieu, P. (1980). 'Le capital social: notes provisoires', *Actes de la Recherche en Sciences Sociales*, 3: 3–5.

Brechon, P. (ed.) (1998). *Les enquêtes eurobaromètres: analyse comparée des données socio-politiques*, Paris: Harmattan.

Breuilly, J. (1996). 'Civil Society and the Public Sphere in Hamburg, Lyon and Manchester, 1815–1850', in H. Koopman and M. Lausler (eds), *Vormärz-literatur in europäischer Perspektive I: Öffentlichkeit und nationale Identität*, Bielefeld: Aisthesis Verlag.

Brunkhorst, H. (2003). *A Polity Without a State? European Constitutionalism Between Evolution and Revolution*, ARENA Working Paper No. 14/03, Oslo: Centre for European Studies, University of Oslo, available at www.arena. uio.no/publications/working-papers2003/papers/wp03_14.pdf (accessed October 2006).

Budge, I. (2000). 'Deliberative Democracy Versus Direct Democracy – Plus Political Parties!', in M. Saward (ed.), *Democratic Innovation*, London: Routledge.

Burroni, L. (2001). *Allontanarsi crescendo*, Torino: Rosenberg and Sellier.

Burroni, L. (2004). 'Modelli di governance nelle città europee', in M. Carbognin, E. Turri and G. M. Varanini (eds), *Una rete di città*, Verona: Cierre Edizioni.

Butt Philip, A. (1998). 'The European Union: Environmental Policy and the Prospects for Sustainable Development', in K. Hanf and A.-I. Jansen (eds), *Governance and Environment in Western Europe: Politics, Policy and Administration*, Harlow: Longman.

Catanzaro, R. F., Piselli, F., Ramella, F. and Trigilia, C. (2002). *Comuni nuovi: Il cambiamento nei governi locali*, Bologna: Il Mulino.

Cerase, F. P. (ed.) (2005). *Azione pubblica e imprenditorialità. L'esperienza dei Patti Territoriali in Campania*, Milan: Franco Angeli.

Cersosimo, D. (2000). 'I patti territoriali', in D. Cersosimo and C. Donzelli, *Mezzo Giorno*, Rome: Donzelli.

Cersosimo, D. and Wolleb, G. (2001). 'Politiche pubbliche e contesti istituzionali. Una ricerca sui patti territoriali', *Stato e mercato*, 63: 369–412.

Chalmers, D. and Lodge, M. (2003). *The Open Method of Co-ordination and the European Welfare State*, London: Centre for Analysis of Risk and Regulation.

Cohen, J. (1996). 'Procedure and Substance in Deliberative Democracy', in S. Benhabib (ed.), *Democracy and Difference: Contesting the Boundaries of the Political*, Princeton: Princeton University Press.

Cohen, J. and Arato, A. (1992). *Civil Society and Political Theory*, Cambridge: MIT Press.

Cohen, J. and Rogers, J. (1995). *Associations and Democracy*, Real Utopias Project Series, London: Verso.

Cohen, J. and Sabel, C. (1997). 'Directly-Deliberative Polyarchy', *European Law Journal*, 3(4): 313–42.

Coleman, J. S. (1990). *Foundation of Social Theory*, Cambridge: Belknap Press of Harvard University Press.

Commission of the European Communities (1992). *An Open and Structured Dialogue Between the Commission and Special Interest Groups*, SEC(92) 2272 final.

Commission of the European Communities (1993). *Towards Sustainability. A European Community Programme of Policy and Action in Relation to the*

Environment and Sustainable Development, available at http://ec.europa.eu/environment/env-act5/5eap.pdf (accessed October 2006).

Commission of the European Communities (2000a). *The Commission and Non-governmental Organisations: Building a Stronger Partnership*, Commission Discussion Paper COM(2000) 11, available at http://ec.europa.eu/civil_society/ngo/docs/communication_en.pdf (accessed October 2006).

Commission of the European Communities (2000b). *Developing New Modes of Governance*, John Paterson Working Paper, Brussels: Forward Studies Unit, Notis Lebessis.

Commission of the European Communities (2001a). 'Directive 2000/60/EC/ of the European Parliament and of the Council of 23 October 2000, Establishing a Framework for Community Action in the Field of Water Policy', *Official Journal of the European Communities*, L327.

Commission of the European Communities (2001b). *European Governance: A White Paper*, COM(2001) 428 final, available at http://eur-lex.europa.eu/LexUriServ/site/en/com/2001/com2001_0428en01.pdf (accessed October 2006).

Commission of the European Communities (2001c). *Report of the Working Group 'Networking People for a Good Governance in Europe' (Group 4b)*, available at http://ec.europa.eu/governance/areas/group9/report_en.pdf (accessed October 2006).

Commission of the European Communities (2001d). *Report of the Working Group 'Consultation and Participation of Civil Society' (Group 2a)*, available at http://ec.europa.eu/governance/areas/group3/report_en.pdf (accessed October 2006).

Commission of the European Communities (2002). *Towards a Reinforced Culture of Consultation and Dialogue – General Principles and Minimum Standards for Consultation of Interested Parties by the Commission*, COM(2002) 704 final, available at http://europa.eu.int/eur-lex/en/com/cnc/2002/com2002_0704en01.pdf (accessed October 2006).

Commission of the European Communities (2003). *Proposal for a Directive on Access to Justice in the Field of the Environment*.

Commission of the European Communities (2005a). 'The Aarhus Convention', available at http://ec.europa.eu/environment/aarhus/index.htm (accessed October 2006).

Commission of the European Communities (2005b). *EU Forum Science in Society: Report of the Specific Session 'Civil Society and Science: An Increased Role for NGOs?'*, RTD-C2/VWM, available at http://ec.europa.eu/research/conferences/2005/forum2005/docs/library_report_ong_en.pdf (accessed October 2006).

Commission of the European Communities (2005c). *Proposal for a Decision of the European Parliament and of the Council Establishing for the Period 2007–2013 the Programme 'Citizens for Europe' to Promote Active European Citizenship*, COM(2005) 116 final.

Commission of the European Communities (2005d). *Proposal for a Council Regulation Establishing a European Union Agency for Fundamental Rights*, COM(2005) 280 final.

Cooke, B. and Kothari, U. (eds) (2001). *Participation: The New Tyranny?*, London: Zed Books.

Corrie, H. (1997). 'Experiences and Realities of Participation in Regional Development', in U. Collier, J. Golub and A. Kreher (eds), *Subsidiarity and Shared Responsibility: New Challenges for EU Environmental Policy*, Baden-Baden: Nomos Verlagsgesellschaft.

Craig, P. (2001). 'Constitutions, Constitutionalism, and the European Union', *European Law Journal*, 7(2): 125–50.

Cram, L. (1997). *Policy-Making in the European Union: Conceptual Lenses and European Integration*, London: Routledge.

Crook, A. (2000). *Listening to Civil Society: What Relationship Between the European Commission and NGOs?*, Brussels, European Citizen Action Service, available at www.globalpolicy.org/ngos/role/globalact/int-inst/2001/0601ecas.htm (accessed October 2006).

Crouch, C., Le Galès, P., Trigilia, C. and Voelzkow, H. (2001). *Local Production Systems in Europe: Rise or Demise?*, Oxford: Oxford University Press.

Crouch, C., Le Galès, P., Trigilia, C. and Voelzkow, H. (2004). *Changing Governance of Local Economies: Responses of European Local Production Systems*, Oxford: Oxford University Press.

Dahl, R. (1969). *Who Governs? Democracy and Power in the American City*, New Haven: Yale University Press.

Dalton, R. J. (2005). *Citizen Politics: Public Opinion and Political Parties in Advanced Democracies*, Washington, DC: CQ Press.

de la Porte, C. E. and Pochet, P. E. (2002). *Building Social Europe Through the Open Method of Co-ordination*, Brussels: Peter Lang.

de Schutter, O. (2002). 'Europe in Search of Its Civil Society', *European Law Journal*, 8(2): 198–217.

de Sousa Santos, B. (ed.) (2002). *Democratizar a Democracia: Os caminhos da democracia participativa*, Rio de Janeiro: Civilizaçao Brasileira.

de Vivo, P. (2004). *Pratiche di concertazione e sviluppo locale*, Milan: Franco Angeli.

Della Sala, V. (2001). 'Constitutionalising Governance: Democratic Dead End or Dead on Democracy?', Constitutionalism Web-Paper, ConWEB, No. 6/2001, Belfast: Queen's University of Belfast.

Dervin, B. (1989). 'Audience as Listener and Learner, Teacher and Confidante. The Sense-Making Approach', in R. E. Rice and C. K. Atkin (eds), *Public Communication Campaigns* (2nd edn). Newbury Park: Sage.

Deth, J. V. (1997). *Private Groups and Public Life: Social Participation, Voluntary Associations and Political Involvement in Representative Democracies*, London: Routledge.

Di Gioacchino, R. (2001). *Patti a rapporto*, Rome: Ediesse.

Dryzek, J. S. (1999). 'Transnational Democracy', *Journal of Political Philosophy*, 7(1): 30–51.

Dryzek, J. S. (2000). *Deliberative Democracy and Beyond: Liberals, Critics, Contestations*, Oxford: Oxford University Press.

Dudley, G. and Richardson, J. (1998). 'Arenas Without Rules and the Policy Change Process: Outsider Groups and British Roads Policy', *Political Studies*, 46(4): 727–47.

Economic and Social Committee (ESC) (1999). 'Opinion of the Economic and Social Committee on Transparency and the Participation of Civil Society

Organisations in the WTO Millennium Round', *Official Journal of the European Communities*, 368: 43–6.

Economic and Social Committee (ESC) (2000a). *Concise Report of the Debates of the First Convention of Civil Society Organised at European Level*, available at http://ec.europa.eu/governance/areas/group3/contribution_concisereport_en.pdf (accessed October 2006).

Economic and Social Committee (ESC) (2000b). *Opinion of the Economic and Social Committee on the Commission Discussion Paper 'The Commission and Non-governmental Organisations: Building a Stronger Partnership'*, COM(2000) 11 final.

Economic and Social Committee (ESC) (2001). *Opinion of the Economic and Social Committee on Organised Civil Society and European Governance: The Committee's Contribution to the Drafting of the White Paper*, available at http://ec.europa.eu/governance/areas/group3/esc_opinion_en.pdf (accessed October 2006).

Economic and Social Committee (ESC) (2002). *Opinion of the Economic and Social Committee on European Governance – a White Paper (COM(2001) 428 final)*, available at http://ec.europa.eu/governance/contrib_esc_en.pdf (accessed October 2006).

Eder, K. and Trenz, H.-J. (2003). 'The Making of a European Public Space. The Case of Justice and Home Affairs', in B. Kohler-Koch (ed.), *Linking EU and National Governance*, Oxford: Oxford University Press.

Edwards, B., Foley, M. W. and Diani, M. (eds) (2001). *Beyond Tocqueville: Civil Society and the Social Capital Debate in Comparative Perspective*, Hanover: University Press of New England.

Eisenstadt, S. N. (2002). 'Concluding Remarks: Public Sphere, Civil Society, and Political Dynamics in Islamic Societies', in M. Hoexter, S. N. Eisenstadt and N. Levtzion (eds), *The Public Sphere in Muslim Societies*, Albany: SUNY Press.

ENDS Environment Daily (2005). 'EU Governments Square the Circle on REACH', *ENDS Environment Daily*, issue 2002, 13 December.

Eriksen, E. O. and Fossum, J. E. (2000). *The EU and Post-national Legitimacy*, ARENA Working Paper No. 00/26, Oslo: Centre for European Studies, University of Oslo, available at http://www.arena.uio.no/publications/wp00_26.htm (accessed October 2006).

Eriksen, E. O. and Fossum, J. E. (2001). *Democracy Through Strong Publics in the European Union?*, ARENA Working Paper No. 01/16, Oslo: Centre for European Studies, University of Oslo, available at www.arena.uio.no/publications/wp01_16.htm (accessed October 2006).

European Citizen Action Service (ECAS) (2003). 'ECAS Comments on the New EU Constitution', Brussels: ECAS.

European Citizen Action Service (ECAS) (2004). *The European Commission and Consultation of NGOs*, Brussels: ECAS.

European Environmental Bureau (EEB) (2003). *EEB Annual Report 2002 and Plans for 2003*, Brussels: EEB.

European Environmental Bureau (EEB) (2004). *EEB Briefings: The Aarhus Convention*, Brussels: EEB.

European Environmental Bureau (EEB) (2005). 'EU Aarhus Regulation Second

Reading: Call for Strong Response from European Parliament', Briefing from the European Environmental Bureau to the European Parliament Environment Committee on Proposal for a Regulation on the Application of the Aarhus Convention to EC Institutions and Bodies, COM(2003) 622, Brussels: EEB.

European Parliament Directorate-General for Research (2003). *Lobbying in the European Union: Current Rules and Practices*, Working Paper No. AFCO 104 EN, Constitutional Affairs Series, Luxembourg: European Parliament, available at www.eu-oplysningen.dk/upload/application/pdf/a0071587/104_en.pdf (accessed October 2006).

European Policy Evaluation Consortium (EPEC) (2005). *Evaluation of the Activities of the European Migration Network*, Final Report to the European Commission DG Justice, Freedom and Security, Brussels: EPEC.

Ferguson, J. (2003). *Improving Citizens' Access to Documents: ECAS Recommendations to the European Commission and Other Institutions*, Brussels: European Citizen Action Service (ECAS).

Ferree, M. M., Gamson, W. A., Gerhards, J. and Rucht, D. (2002). 'Four Models of the Public Sphere in Modern Democracies', *Theory and Society*, 31(3): 289–324.

Field, J. (2003). *Social Capital*, London: Routledge.

Fischer, F. (2003). *Reframing Public Policy*, Oxford: Oxford University Press.

Fischer, F. and Forester, J. (eds) (1993). *The Argumentative Turn in Policy Analysis and Planning*, Durham: Duke University Press.

Fisher, C. (1994). 'The Lobby to Stop Testing Cosmetics on Animals', in R. H. Pedler and M. P. C. M. van Schendelen (eds), *Lobbying the European Union: Companies, Trade Associations and Issue Groups*, Aldershot: Dartmouth.

Fishkin, J. S. and Luskin, R. C. (2000). 'The quest for deliberative democracy', in M. Saward (ed.), *Democratic Innovation*, London: Routledge.

Flynn, B. (2003). *Subsidiarity and the Evolution of EU Environmental Policy*, PhD thesis, University of Essex.

Forester, J. (1999). *The Deliberative Practitioner: Encouraging Participatory Planning Processes*, Cambridge: MIT Press.

Fukuyama, F. (1995). *Trust: Social Virtues and the Creation of Prosperity*, New York: Free Press.

Fukuyama, F. (2001). 'Social Capital, Civil Society and Development', *Third World Quarterly*, 22(1): 7–20.

Gamson, W. A. (1999). 'Policy Discourse and the Language of the Life-World', in J. Gerhards and R. Hitzler (eds), *Eigenwilligkeit und Rationalität sozialer Prozesse. Festschrift zum 65. Geburtstag von Friedhelm Neidhardt*, Opladen: Westdeutscher Verlag.

Geddes, A. (2000). 'Lobbying for Migrant Inclusion in the European Union: New Opportunities for Transnational Advocacy?', *Journal of European Public Policy*, 7(4): 632–49.

Geddes, A. (2003). *The Politics of Migration and Immigration in Europe*, London: Sage.

Gellner, E. (1994). *Conditions of Liberty: Civil Society and Its Rivals*, London: Hamish Hamilton.

Gerhards, J. (2001). 'Missing a European Public Sphere', in M. Kohli and M. Novak (eds), *Will Europe Work? Integration, Employment and the Social Order*, London: Routledge.

Geyer, R. (2001).'Can EU Social NGOs Co-operate to Promote EU Social Policy?', *Journal of Social Policy*, 30(3): 477–94.

Giner, S. (2000). 'La società civile: prospettive storiche e sociologiche', *Sociologia e politiche sociali*, 3(1): 9–34.

Glynn, C. J., Herbst, S., O'Keefe, G. J. and Shapiro, R. Y. (1999). *Public Opinion*, Boulder: Westview Press.

Goehring, R. (2002). 'Interest Representation and Legitimacy in the European Union: The New Quest for Civil Society Formation', in A. Warleigh and J. Fairbrass (eds), *Influence and Interests in the EU: The New Politics of Persuasion and Advocacy*, London: Europa.

Goldstein, J. (1993). *Ideas, Interests, and American Trade Policy*, Ithaca: Cornell University Press.

Goldstein, J. and Keohane, R. (1993). 'Ideas and Foreign Policy: An Analytical Framework', in J. Goldstein and R. Keohane (eds), *Ideas and Foreign Policy: Beliefs, Institutions and Political Change*, Ithaca: Cornell University Press.

Gould, C. C. (1996). 'Diversity and Democracy: Representing Differences', in S. Benhabib (ed.), *Democracy and Difference. Contesting the Boundaries of the Political*, Princeton, Princeton University Press.

Grande, E. (1996). 'The State and Interest Groups in a Framework of Multilevel Decision Making: The Case of the European Union', *Journal of European Public Policy*, 3(3): 318–38.

Grant, W., Matthews, D. and Newell, P. (2000). *The Effectiveness of European Union Environmental Policy*, Basingstoke: Macmillan.

Gray, E. and Statham, P. (2005). 'Becoming European? The Transformation of the British Pro-migrant NGO Sector in Response to Europeanization', *Journal of Common Market Studies*, 43(4): 877–98.

Greenwood, J. (1997). *Representing Interests in the European Union*, Basingstoke: Macmillan.

Greenwood, J. (2003). *Interest Representation in the European Union*, Basingstoke: Palgrave Macmillan.

Greenwood, J. and Aspinwall, M. (eds) (1998). *Collective Action in the European Union*, London: Routledge.

Guidry, J. A., Kennedy, M. D. and Zald, M. N. (eds) (2001). *Globalizations and Social Movements: Culture, Power and the Transnational Public Sphere*, Ann Arbor: University of Michigan Press.

Guiraudon, V. (2000). 'European Integration and Migration Policy: Vertical Policy-Making as Venue Shopping', *Journal of Common Market Studies*, 38(2): 251–71.

Guiraudon, V. (2003). 'The Constitution of a European Immigration Policy Domain: A Political Sociology Approach', *Journal of European Public Policy*, 10(2): 263–82.

Gunn, J. A. W. (1995). '"Public Opinion" in Modern Political Science', in J. Farr, J. S. Dryzek and S. T. Leonard (eds), *Political Science in History. Research Programs and Political Traditions*, Cambridge: Cambridge University Press.

Guzzo, F. (2004). 'Governance urbana tra competitività, equità e coesione sociale: il caso di Barcellona', paper presented to the Conference 'Governo delle città e trasformazioni urbane', Università della Calabria, Arcavacata di Rende, 27–28 October.

Haas, P. M. (1992). 'Introduction: Epistemic Communities and International Policy Coordination', *International Organization*, 46(1): 1–35.

Habermas, J. (1962). *Strukturwandel der Öffentlichkeit. Untersuchungen zu einer Kategorie der bürgerlichen Gesellschaft*, Neuwied: Luchterhand. Translated (1989) as *The Structural Transformation of the Public Sphere. An Inquiry into a Category of Bourgeois Society*, Cambridge: MIT Press.

Habermas, J. (1987). *The Theory of Communicative Action. Lifeworld and System. A Critique of Functionalist Reason. Volume II*, Boston: Beacon Press.

Habermas, J. (1996). *Between Facts and Norms: Contributions to a Discourse Theory of Law and Democracy*, Cambridge: MIT Press.

Habermas, J. (2001). *The Postnational Constellation: Political Essays* (translated, edited and with an introduction by M. Pensky), Cambridge: MIT Press.

Hajer, M. and Wagenaar, H. (eds) (2003). *Deliberative Policy Analysis: Understanding Governance in the Network Society*, Cambridge: Cambridge University Press.

Hall, P. (1993). 'Policy Paradigms, Social Learning and the State', *Comparative Politics*, 25(3): 275–96.

Hallo, R. (2003). 'Assessing the Results of the Convention', *Metamorphosis*, 30: 1–12.

Halpin, D. (2001). 'Integrating Conceptions of Interest Groups: Towards a Conceptual Framework of Sectional Interest Group Imperatives', paper presented to the European Consortium for Political Research General Conference, University of Kent, 6–8 September.

Helfferich, B. and Kolb, F. (2001). 'Multilevel Action Coordination in European Contentious Politics: The Case of the European Women's Lobby', in D. Imig and S. Tarrow (eds), *Contentious Europeans: Protest and Politics in an Integrating Europe*, Lanham: Rowman and Littlefield.

Héritier, A. (1997). 'Policy-Making by Subterfuge: Interest Accommodation, Innovation and Substitute Democratic Legitimation in Europe – Perspectives from Distinct Policy Areas', *Journal of European Public Policy*, 4(2): 171–89.

Héritier, A. (1999a). 'Elements of Democratic Legitimation in Europe: An Alternative Perspective', *Journal of European Public Policy*, 6(2): 269–82.

Héritier, A. (1999b). *Policy-Making and Diversity in Europe: Escape from Deadlock*, Cambridge: Cambridge University Press.

Hirst, P. (1997). *From Statism to Pluralism: Democracy, Civil Society and Global Politics*, London: UCL Press.

Hirst, P. (2000). 'Democracy and Governance', in J. Pierre (ed.), *Debating Governance*, Oxford: Oxford University Press.

Hirst, P. and Khilnani, S. (1996). *Reinventing Democracy*, Cambridge: Blackwell.

Hix, S. (1999). *The Political System of the European Union*, Basingstoke: Macmillan.

Hollingsworth, J. R., Schmitter, P. and Streeck, W. (1994). *Governing Capitalist*

Economies: Performance and Control of Economic Sectors, Oxford: Oxford University Press.

Hooghe, L. (1997). 'Serving "Europe": Political Orientations of Senior Commission Officials', *European Integration Online Papers (EIoP)*, 1(8), available at http://eiop.or.at/eiop/texte/1997-008a.htm (accessed October 2006).

Hooghe, L. and Marks, G. (2001). *Multi-level Governance and European Integration*, Boston: Rowman and Littlefield.

Hull, R. (1993). 'Lobbying the European Community: A View from Within', in S. Mazey and J. Richardson (eds), *Lobbying in the European Community*, Oxford: Oxford University Press.

Immergut, E. (1992). 'The Rules of the Game: The Logic of Health Policy-Making in France, Switzerland, and Sweden', in S. Steinmo, K. Thelen and F. Longstreth (eds), *Structuring Politics: Historical Institutionalism in Comparative Analysis*, Cambridge: Cambridge University Press.

Jeffery, C. (2002). 'Social and Regional Interests: ESC and Committee of the Regions', in J. Peterson and M. Shackleton (eds), *The Institutions of the European Union*, Oxford: Oxford University Press.

Joerges, C. and Neyer, J. (1997). 'From Intergovernmental Bargaining to Deliberative Political Processes: The Constitutionalisation of Comitology', *European Law Journal*, 3(3): 273–99.

Jordan, A. (1999a). 'Editorial Introduction: The Construction of a Multilevel Environmental Governance System', *Environment and Planning C*, 17(1): 1–27.

Jordan, A. (1999b). 'The Implementation of EU Environmental Policy: A Policy Problem Without a Political Solution?', *Environment and Planning C*, 17(1): 69–90.

Jordan, A., Wurzel, R., Zito, A. and Brückner, L. (2003). 'European Governance and the Transfer of "New" Environmental Policy Instruments', *Public Administration*, 81(3): 555–74.

Judge, D. (1993). '"Predestined to Save the Earth": The Environment Committee of the European Parliament', in D. Judge (ed.), *A Green Dimension for the European Community: Political Issues and Processes*, London: Frank Cass.

Juhem, P. (2001). 'Entreprendre en politique. De l'extrême gauche au PS: la professionnalisation politique des fondateurs de SOS-Racisme', *Revue française de science politique*, 51(1–2): 131–54.

Kastoryano, R. (2003). 'Transnational Networks and Political Participation. The Place of Immigration in the European Union', in M. Berezin and M. Schain (eds), *Europe Without Borders: Remapping Territory, Citizenship and Identity in a Transnational Age*, Baltimore: Johns Hopkins University Press.

Keane, J. (1999). *Civil Society*, Stanford: Stanford University Press.

Keane, J. (2003). *Global Civil Society*, London: Cambridge University Press.

Keck, M. and Sikkink, K. (1998). *Activists Beyond Borders: Advocacy Networks in International Politics*, Ithaca: Cornell University Press.

Kellow, A. (1999). *International Toxic Risk Management: Ideals, Interests and Implementation*, Cambridge: Cambridge University Press.

Kellow, A. and Zito, A. (2002). 'Steering Through Complexity: EU Environmental Regulation in the International Context', *Political Studies*, 50(1): 43–60.

Keohane, R. and Nye, J. (1989). *Power and Interdependence* (2nd edn), Glenview: Scott, Foresman.

Kickert, W. (1993). 'Complexity, Governance and Dynamics: Conceptual Explorations of Public Network Management', in J. Kooiman (ed.), *Modern Governance: New Government–Society Interactions*, London: Sage.

Kitschelt, H. (1986). 'Political Opportunity Structures and Political Protest: Anti-nuclear Movements in Four Democracies', *British Journal of Political Science*, 16(1): 57–85.

Kleinsteuber, H. J. (2001). 'Habermas and the Public Sphere: From a German to a European Perspective', *The Public*, 8(1): 95–108.

Kohler-Koch, B. (2000). *Network Governance Within and Beyond an Enlarged European Union*, Quebec: Canadian European Studies Association.

Kooiman, J. (1993). 'Findings, Speculations and Recommendations', in J. Kooiman (ed.), *Modern Governance: New Government–Society Interactions*, London: Sage.

Kriesi, H. (1995). *New Social Movements in Western Europe: A Comparative Analysis*, London: UCL Press.

Lahusen, C. (2004). 'Joining the Cocktail Circuit: Social Movement Organizations at the European Union', *Mobilization*, 9(1): 55–71.

Lenschow, A. (1999). 'Transformation in European Environmental Governance', in B. Kohler-Koch and R. Eising (eds), *The Transformation of Governance in the European Union*, London: Routledge.

Lenschow, A. and Zito, A. (1998). 'Blurring or Shifting of Policy Frames? Institutionalization of the Economic–Environmental Policy Linkage in the European Community', *Governance*, 11(4): 415–41.

Linz, J. and Stepan, A. (1996). *Problems of Democratic Transition and Consolidation*, Baltimore: Johns Hopkins University Press.

Long, T. (1998). 'The Environmental Lobby', in P. Lowe and S. Ward (eds), *British Environmental Policy and Europe*, London: Routledge.

Long, T. (2003). 'This is My Life: Tony Long', *E!Sharp*, April, 64–6.

Magnatti, P., Ramella, F., Trigilia, C. and Viesti, G. (2005). *Patti territoriali: Lezioni per lo sviluppo*, Bologna: Il Mulino.

Maier, C. S. (ed.) (1987). *Changing Boundaries of the Political*, Cambridge: Cambridge University Press.

Majone, G. (ed.) (1996). *Regulating Europe*, London: Routledge.

Majone, G. (1997). 'From the Positive to the Regulatory State: Causes and Consequences of Changes in the Mode of Governance', *Journal of Public Policy*, 17(2): 139–67.

Majone, G. (1999). 'The Regulatory State and Its Legitimacy Problems', *West European Politics*, 22(1): 1–24.

March, J. and Olsen, J. (1989). *Rediscovering Institutions: The Organizational Basis of Politics*, New York: Free Press.

Marks, G. and McAdam, D. (1996). 'Social Movements and the Changing Structure of Political Opportunity in the European Union', in G. Marks, F. W. Scharpf, P. C. Schmitter and Streeck, W. (eds), *Governance in the European Union*, London: Sage.

Marshall, T. (1996). 'Barcelona – Fast Forward? City Entrepreneurialism in the 1980s and 1990s', *European Planning Studies*, 4(2): 147–65.

Martin, A. and Ross, G. (2001). 'Trade Union Organizing at the European Level', in D. Imig and S. Tarrow (eds), *Contentious Europeans*, Lanham: Rowman and Littlefield.

Mazey, S. (2000). 'Introduction: Integrating Gender–Intellectual and "Real World" Mainstreaming', *Journal of European Public Policy*, 7(3): 333–45.

Mazey, S. and Richardson, J. (1992). 'Environmental Groups and the EC: Challenges and Opportunities', *Environmental Politics*, 1(4): 109–28.

McCombs, M. E. (2001). *Setting the Agenda: The News Media and Public Opinion*, Cambridge: Polity Press.

McCormick, J. (2001). *Environmental Policy in the European Union*, Basingstoke: Palgrave.

McNeill, D. (2003). 'Mapping the European Urban Left: The Barcelona Experience', *Antipode*, 35(1): 74–94.

Meny, Y. and Surel, Y. (2002). *Democracies and the Populist Challenge*, Basingstoke: Palgrave.

Meyer, J. W., Boli, J., Thomas, G. M. and Ramirez, F. (1997). 'World Society and the Nation-State', *American Journal of Sociology*, 103(1): 144–81.

Michelmann, H. J. (1978). *Organizational Effectiveness in a Multinational Bureaucracy*, Farnborough: Saxon House.

Moore, B. (1978). *Injustice: The Social Bases of Obedience and Revolt*, White Plains: M. E. Sharpe.

Mutti, A. (1994). 'Il particolarismo come risorsa. Politica ed economia nello sviluppo abruzzese', *Rassegna Italiana di Sociologia*, 35(4): 451–518.

Mutti, A. (1998). *Capitale sociale e sviluppo: La fiducia come risorsa*, Bologna: Il Mulino.

Neidhardt, F. (1994). 'Öffentlichkeit, öffentliche Meinung, soziale Bewegungen', in F. Neidhardt (ed.), *Öffentlichkeit, öffentliche Meinung, soziale Bewegungen*, Kölner Zeitschrift für Soziologie und Sozialpsychologie, Sonderheft 34, Opladen: Westdeutscher Verlag.

Nentwich, M. (1998). 'Opportunity Structures for Citizens' Participation: The Case of the European Union', in A. Weale and M. Nentwich (eds), *Political Theory and the European Union: Legitimacy, Constitutional Choice and Citizenship*, London: Routledge.

Niedermayer, O. and Sinnott, R. (eds) (1998). *Public Opinion and Internationalized Governance*, Oxford: Oxford University Press.

Norris, P. (2000). *A Virtuous Circle: Political Communications in Postindustrial Societies*, Cambridge: Cambridge University Press.

Offerle, M. (ed.) (2003). *La Société civile en question, problèmes politiques et sociaux*, Paris: La documentation française.

Organisation for Economic Co-operation and Development (OECD) (2001). *The Well-being of Nations. The Role of Human and Social Capital*, Paris: OECD.

Page, B. I., Shapiro, R. Y. and Dempsey, G. R. (1987). 'What Moves Public Opinion?', *American Political Science Review*, 81: 23–44.

Pérez-Díaz, V. M. (1998). 'The Public Sphere and a European Civil Society', in J. C. Alexander (ed.), *Real Civil Societies: Dilemmas of Institutionalization*, London: Sage.

Perri, A. (2003). 'Il Patto Territoriale della Locride', in *La lezione dei Patti territoriali*, Rome: Ministero dell'Economia e delle Finanze.

Perulli, P. (2000). *La città delle reti: Forme di governo nel postfordismo*, Turin: Bollati Boringhieri editore.

Peters, B. G. (1997). 'Globalization and Governance', paper presented to the conference 'Political Impacts of Globalization', University of Birmingham.

Pharr, S. J. and Putnam, R. D. (eds) (2000). *Disaffected Democracies: What's Troubling the Trilateral Countries?*, Princeton: Princeton University Press.

Piattoni, S. (1999). 'Politica locale e sviluppo economico nel Mezzogiorno', *Stato e mercato*, 55: 117–49.

Pierre, J. and Peters, B. G. (2000). *Governance, Politics and the State*, New York: St Martin's Press.

Pizzorno, A. (1993). *Le Radici della Politica Assoluta*, Milan: Feltrinelli.

Porter, M. (1998). *On Competition*, Boston: Harvard Business School Press.

Portes, A. (1998). 'Social Capital: Its Origins and Applications in Modern Sociology', *Annual Review of Sociology*, 24: 1–24.

Portes, A. and Landolt, P. (1996). 'The Downside of Social Capital', *American Prospect*, 26: 18–21.

Price, V. and Roberts, D. F. (1987). 'Public Opinion Processes', in C. R. Berger and S. H. Chaffee (eds), *Handbook of Communication Science*, Newbury Park: Sage.

Putnam, R. D. (1993). *Making Democracy Work: Civic Tradition in Modern Italy*, Princeton: Princeton University Press.

Putnam, R. D. (2000). *Bowling Alone: The Collapse and Revival of American Community*, New York: Simon and Schuster.

Radaelli, C. (2000). 'Whither Europeanization? Concept Stretching and Substantive Change', *European Integration Online Papers (EIoP)*, 4(8), available at http://eiop.or.at/eiop/texte/2000-008.htm (accessed October 2006).

Radaelli, C. (2002). *The Code of Conduct Against Harmful Tax Competition: Open Method of Coordination in Disguise*, Florence: European University Institute.

Radaelli, C. (2003). 'The Europeanization of Public Policy', in K. Featherstone and C. Radaelli (eds), *The Politics of Europeanization*, Oxford: Oxford University Press.

Radaelli, C. and Featherstone, K. (eds) (2003). *The Politics of Europeanization*, Oxford: Oxford University Press.

Reif, K.-H. and Inglehart, R. (eds) (1991). *Eurobarometer: The Dynamics of European Public Opinion*, London: Macmillan.

Rein, M. and Schon, D. (1994). *Frame Reflections*, New York: Basic Books.

Rhodes, R. A. W. (1996). 'The New Governance: Governing Without Government', *Political Studies*, 44(4): 652–67.

Riker, W. (1980). 'Implications from the Disequilibrium of Majority Rule for the Study of Institutions', *American Political Science Review*, 74(2): 432–46.

Rootes, C. (ed.) (2003). *Environmental Protest in Western Europe*, Oxford: Oxford University Press.

Rossetti, P. E. (2003). 'Il Patto territoriale di ferrara', in *La lezione dei Patti territoriali*, Rome: Ministero dell'economia e delle Finanze.

Rucht, D. (1993). '"Think Globally, Act Locally"? Needs, Forms and Problems of Cross-national Cooperation Among Environmental Groups', in

J. D. Liefferink, P. D. Lowe and A. P. J. Mol (eds), *European Integration and Environmental Policy*, London: Belhaven Press.

Rullani, E. (2004). *Economia della conoscenza: creatività e valore nel capitalismo delle reti*, Rome: Carocci.

Ruzza, C. (1996). 'Inter-organizational Negotiation in Political Decision-Making: EC Bureaucrats and the Environment', in N. South and C. Samson (eds), *Policy Processes and Outcomes*, London: Macmillan.

Ruzza, C. (2000). 'The Europeanization of Environmental and Tourism Policy and Southern Europe', *Innovations*, 13(3).

Ruzza, C. (2002). '"Frame Bridging", and the New Politics of Persuasion, Advocacy and Influence', in A. Warleigh and J. Fairbrass (eds), *Influence and Interests in the European Union: The New Politics of Persuasion and Advocacy*, London: Europa Press.

Ruzza, C. (2004). *Europe and Civil Society: Movement Coalitions and European Governance*, Manchester: Manchester University Press.

Ruzza, C. (2006a). 'European Institutions and the Policy Discourse of Organised Civil Society', in S. Smismans (ed.), *Civil Society and Legitimate European Governance*, London: Elgar.

Ruzza, C. (2006b). 'Frame Analysis', in K. Brown (ed.), *Encyclopedia of Language and Linguistics*, Oxford: Elsevier.

Salvatore, A. (2007). *The Public Sphere: Liberal Modernity, Catholicism, Islam*, New York: Palgrave Macmillan.

Sandholtz, W. and Zysman, J. (1989). '1992: Recasting the European Bargain', *World Politics*, 42(1): 95–128.

Saward, M. (ed.) (2000). *Democratic Innovation: Deliberation, Representation and Association*, London: Routledge.

Sbragia, A. (1993). 'The European Community: A Balancing Act', *Publius: The Journal of Federalism*, 23(3): 23–38.

Scharpf, F. W. (1999). *Governing in Europe: Effective and Democratic?*, Oxford: Oxford University Press.

Schattschneider, E. (1960). *The Semisovereign People*, Hinsdale: Dryden Press.

Schlesinger, P. and Kevin, D. (2000). 'Can the European Union Become a Sphere of Publics?', in E. O. Eriksen and J. E. Fossum (eds), *Democracy in the European Union: Integration Through Deliberation*, London: Routledge.

Schmitter, P. (2000). *How to Democratize the European Union and Why Bother*, Lanham: Rowman and Littlefield.

Schout, A. and Jordan, A. (2003). 'Coordinated European Governance Environmental Policy: Self-organizing or Centrally Steered?', *Public Administration*, 83(1): 201–20.

Sciulli, D. (1992). *Theory of Societal Constitutionalism*, Cambridge: Cambridge University Press.

Sennett, R. (1977). *The Fall of Public Man*, New York: Knopf.

Shaw, J. (2000). 'Process and Constitutional Discourse in the European Union', in C. Harvey, J. Morrison and J. Shaw (eds), *Voices, Spaces and Processes in Constitutionalism*, Oxford: Blackwell.

Shaw, J. (2005). 'Europe's Constitutional Future', *Public Law*, spring: 132–51.

Sikkink, K. (1993). 'The Power of Principled Ideas: Human Rights Policies in the United States and Western Europe', in J. Goldstein and R. Keohane (eds), *Ideas and Foreign Policy: Beliefs, Institutions, and Political Change*, Ithaca: Cornell University Press.

Smismans, S. (2002). '"Civil Society" in European Institutional Discourses', *Cahiers Européens de Sciences Po*, 4, available at www.portedeurope.org/IMG/pdf/cahier_4_2002.pdf (accessed October 2006).

Smismans, S. (2004). *Law, Legitimacy, and European Governance: Functional Participation in Social Regulation*, Oxford: Oxford University Press.

Snow, D. A., Zurcher, L. A. J. and Ekland-Olson, S. (1980). 'Social Networks and Social Movements: A Microstructural Approach to Differential Recruitment', *American Sociological Review*, 45(5): 787–801.

Social Platform (2000). *Response of the Platform of European Social NGOs to 'The Commission and Non-governmental Organisations: Building a Stronger Partnership'*, Brussels: Social Platform.

Social Platform (2001). *Democracy, Governance and European NGOs: Building a Stronger Structured Civil Dialogue*, Brussels: Social Platform, available at www.socialplatform.org/module/FileLib/democracy_governance_and_european_ngos.doc (accessed October 2006).

Somers, M. R. (1993). 'Citizenship and the Place of the Public Sphere. Law, Community, and Political Culture in the Transition to Democracy', *American Sociological Review*, 58(5): 587–620.

Somers, M. R. (1995a). 'Narrating and Naturalizing Civil Society and Citizenship Theory', *Sociological Theory*, 13(3): 221–65.

Somers, M. R. (1995b). 'What's Political or Cultural About Political Culture and the Public Sphere? Toward an Historical Sociology of Concept Formation', *Sociological Theory*, 13(2): 113–44.

Somers, M. R. (2001). 'Romancing the Market, Reviling the State: Historizing Liberalism, Privatization, and the Competing Claims to Civil Society', in C. Crouch, K. Eder and D. Tambini (eds), *Citizenship, Markets, and the State*, Oxford: Oxford University Press.

Stoker, G. (1998). 'Governance as Theory: Five Propositions', *International Social Science Journal*, 50(1): 17–28.

Streeck, W. (2000). 'L'internazionalizzazione delle relazioni industriali', *Quaderni di Rassegna Sindacale*, 2(2): 19–53.

Streeck, W. and Schmitter, P. (1985). 'Community, Market, State – and Associations? The Prospective Contribution of Interest Governance to Social Order', *European Sociological Review*, 2(2): 119–38.

Sudbery, I. (2003). 'Bridging the Legitimacy Gap in the EU: Can Civil Society Help to Bring the Union Closer to Its Citizens?', *Collegium*, 26: 75–95.

Sviluppo Italia (2000). *Caratteristiche e potenzialità dei patti territoriali*, Rome: Sviluppo Italia.

Swanson, D. L. (1981). 'A Constructivist Approach', in D. D. Nimmo and K. R. Sanders (eds), *Handbook of Political Communication*, Beverly Hills: Sage.

Szyszczak, E. (1995). 'Social Rights as General Principles of Community Law', in N. Neuwhal and A. Rosas (eds), *The European Union and Human Rights*, The Hague: Kluwer.

Taggart, P. (2000). *Populism*, London: Open University Press.

Tarrow, S. (1979). *Tra centro e periferia: Il ruolo degli amministratori locali in Italia e in Francia*, Bologna: Il Mulino.

Tiersky, R. (2001). *Euro-skepticism: A Reader*, Lanham: Rowman and Littlefield.

Tilly, C. (1985). 'Models and Realities of Popular Collective Action', *Social Research*, 52(4): 717–48.

Tilly, C. (1986). 'European Violence and Collective Action Since 1700', *Social Research*, 53(1): 158–84.

Tilly, C., Tilly, L. A. and Tilly, R. (1975). *The Rebellious Century*, Cambridge: Harvard University Press.

Trenz, H.-J. (2004a). *Europäische Integration und Öffentlichkeit. Institutionelle Selbstdarstellung und mediale Repräsentation der politischen Gesellschaft Europas*, Berlin: Habilitationsschrift, Humboldt Universität zu Berlin.

Trenz, H.-J. (2004b). 'Media Coverage on European Governance. Testing the Performance of National Newspapers', *European Journal of Communication*, 19(3): 291–319.

Trenz, H.-J. and Eder, K. (2004). 'The Democratising Dynamics of a European Public Sphere. Towards a Theory of Democratic Functionalism', *European Journal of Social Theory*, 7(1): 5–25.

Trigilia, C. (1998). *Sociologia economica*, Bologna: Il Mulino.

Trigilia, C. (2001). 'Capitale sociale e sviluppo locale', in A.Bagnasco, F. Piselli, A. Pizzorno and C. Trigilia, *Il capitale sociale. Istruzioni per l'uso*, Bologna: Il Mulino.

Trigilia, C. (2005). *Sviluppo locale: Un progetto per l'Italia*, Rome: Laterza.

United Nations (2001). 'Reference Document on the Participation of Civil Society in United Nations Conferences and Special Sessions of the General Assembly During the 1990s', 55th Session of the United Nations General Assembly, New York: Office of the President of the Millennium Assembly.

Vertovec, S. (1999). 'Minority Associations, Networks and Public Policies: Re-assessing Relationships', *Journal of Ethnic and Migration Studies*, 25(1): 21–42.

Vignon, J. (2003). 'The White Paper on Governance – Challenges and Opportunities for EU Business Associations', in J. Greenwood (ed.), *The Challenge of Change in EU Business Associations*, Basingstoke: Palgrave Macmillan.

Wapner, P. (1995). 'Politics Beyond the State: Environmental Activism and World Civic Politics', *World Politics*, 47: 311–40.

Warleigh, A. (2000). 'The Hustle: Citizenship Practice, NGOs and "Policy Coalitions" in the European Union – The Cases of Auto Oil, Drinking Water and Unit Pricing', *Journal of European Public Policy*, 7(2): 229–43.

Warleigh, A. (2001). 'Europeanizing Civil Society: NGOs as Agents of Political Socialization', *Journal of Common Market Studies*, 39(4): 619–39.

Warleigh, A. (2003). *Democracy in the European Union: Theory, Practice and Reform*, London: Sage.

Warren, M. (2001). *Democracy and Association*, Princeton: Princeton University Press.

Weale, A. (1996). 'Environmental Rules and Rule-Making in the European Union', *Journal of European Public Policy*, 3(4): 594–611.

Weale, A., Pridham, G., Cini, M., et al. (2000). *Environmental Governance in Europe*, Oxford: Oxford University Press.

Weiler, J. (1995). 'Fundamental Rights and Fundamental Boundaries: On Standards and Values in the Protection of Human Rights', in N. Neuwhal and A. Rosas (eds), *The European Union and Human Rights*, The Hague: Kluwer.

Wilson, J. Q. (1995). *Political Organizations*, Princeton: Princeton University Press.

Wincott, D. (2002). 'The Governance White Paper, the Commission and the Search for Legitimacy', in A. Arnull and D. Wincott (eds), *Accountability and Legitimacy in the European Union*, Oxford: Oxford University Press.

Wolleb, G. (2003). 'Il Patto Territoriale di Caltanisetta', in *La lezione dei Patti territoriali*, Rome: Ministero dell'Economia e delle Finanze.

Young, O. (1994). *International Governance: Protecting the Environment in a Stateless Society*, Ithaca: Cornell University Press.

Zito, A. (2000). *Creating Environmental Policy in the European Union*, New York: Macmillan/St Martin's Press/Palgrave.

Zito, A. (2001). 'Epistemic Communities, Collective Entrepreneurship and European Integration', *Journal of European Public Policy*, 8(4): 585–603.

Zito, A. (2005). 'The European Union as an Environmental Leader in a Global Environment', *Globalizations*, 2(3): 1–13.

Index

Note: 'n' after a page reference indicates the number of a note on that page.